EL MAESTRO

Folio. II.

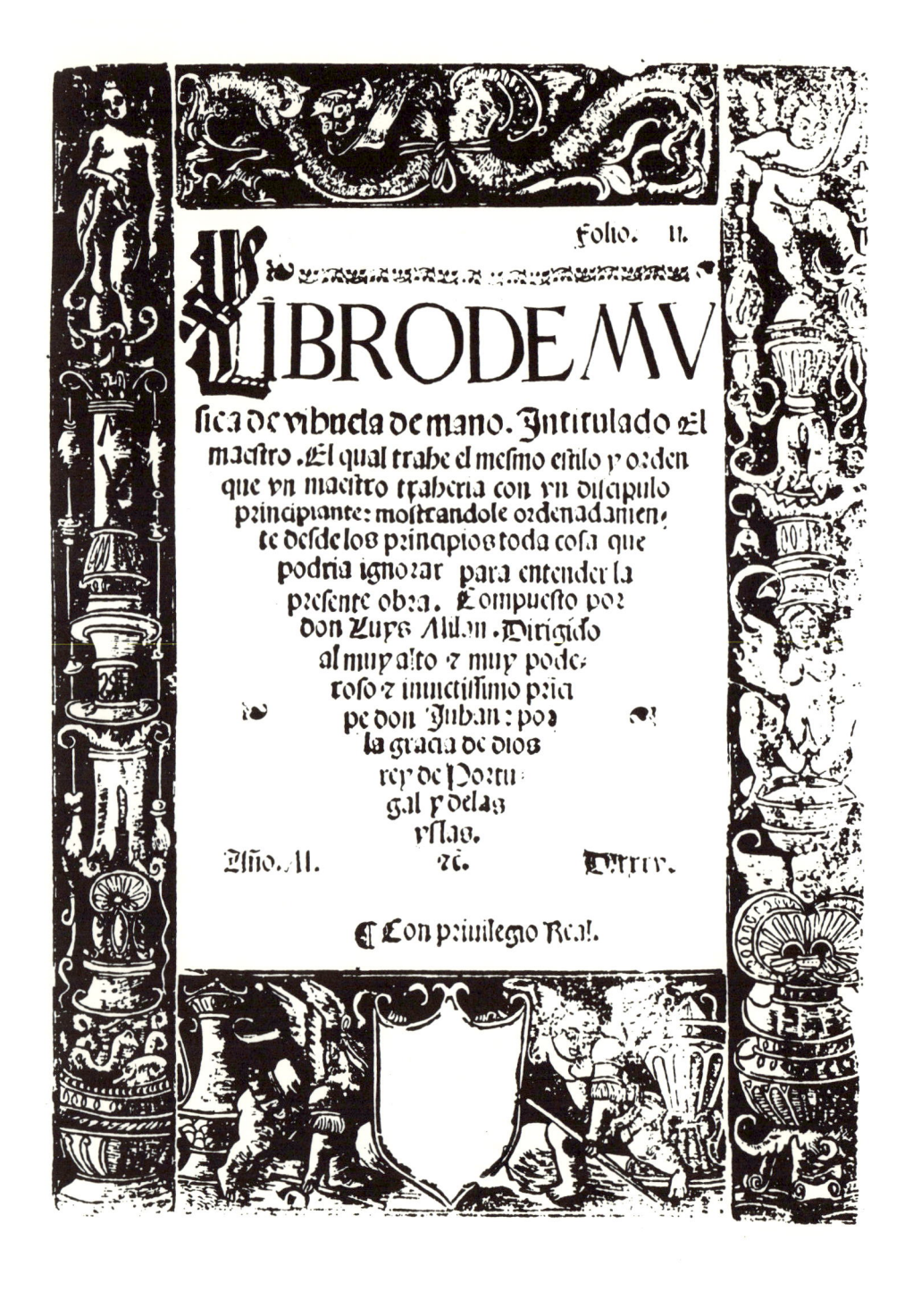

Libro de Mu

sica de vihuela de mano. Intitulado El
maestro. El qual trahe el mesmo estilo y orden
que vn maestro traheria con vn discipulo
principiante: mostrandole ordenadamen
te desde los principios toda cosa que
podria ignorar para entender la
presente obra. Compuesto por
don Luys Milan. Dirigido
al muy alto y muy pode
roso y inuictissimo prin
cipe don Juban: por
la gracia de dios
rey de Portu
gal y delas
yslas.

Año. M.   zc.   D.xxxv.

¶ Con priuilegio Real.

Luis de Milán

EL MAESTRO

Edited, Translated, and Transcribed
by Charles Jacobs

The Pennsylvania State University Press

University Park and London

Standard Book Number 271-00091-0
Library of Congress Catalogue Card Number 70-78939

Copyright © 1971 by The Pennsylvania State University
All Rights Reserved
Printed in the United States of America

Designed by Glenn Ruby

The Pennsylvania State University Press
University Park, Pennsylvania

The Pennsylvania State University Press Ltd.
London, England

Dedication

For

D. José Miguel Ruiz Morales

    Plenipotentiary Minister

    Ambassador of Spain to the Republic of Colombia

    President and founder, in conjunction with
        Maestro Andrés Segovia, of *Música en Compostela*, institute
        for advanced studies in Spanish music

    Patron of the arts and my esteemed friend.

Contents

Preface   1

El Maestro

Textual Matter   7
   A. Milán's Introduction   11
   B. Milán's Discussion of the Modes   25

The Music   29

   1. Fantasia No. 1 in Tone I   33
   2. Fantasia No. 2 in Tone I   35
   3. Fantasia No. 3 in Tone I   38
   4. Fantasia No. 4 in Tone II   41
   5. Fantasia No. 5 in Tone II   42
   6. Fantasia No. 6 in Tones I and II   45
   7. Fantasia No. 7 in Tone III   49
   8. Fantasia No. 8 in Tone IV   51
   9. Fantasia No. 9 in Tones III and IV   54
   10. Fantasia No. 10 in Tones I and II   57
   11. Fantasia No. 11 in Tones I and II   59
   12. Fantasia No. 12 in Tones III and IV   62
   13. Fantasia No. 13 in Tone I   65
   14. Fantasia No. 14 in Tones III and IV   68
   15. Fantasia No. 15 in Tones V and VI   69
   16. Fantasia No. 16 in Tones V and VI   73
   17. Fantasia No. 17 in Tones V and VI   76
   18. Fantasia No. 18 in Tones VII and VIII   78
   19. Fantasia No. 19 in Tone V   82
   20. Fantasia No. 20 in Tone VI   87
   21. Fantasia No. 21 in Tone VII   93
   22. Fantasia No. 22 in Tone VIII   96

   23. Pavan No. 1 in Tones I and II   101
   24. Pavan No. 2 in Tones III and IV   102
   25. Pavan No. 3 in Tones V and VI   104
   26. Pavan No. 4 in Tones VII and VIII   105
   27. Pavan No. 5 in Tone VIII, *"La bella franceschina"*   107
   28. Pavan No. 6 in Tone VIII   108

   29. Villancico No. 1, *"Toda mi vida hos amé"*   109
   30. Villancico No. 2, *"Sospiró una señora que yo vî"*   112
   31. Villancico No. 3, *"Agora viniesse un viento"*   115
   32. Villancico No. 4, *"Quien amores ten"*   116
   33. Villancico No. 5, *"Falai miña amor"*   120
   34. Villancico No. 6, *"Poys dezeys que me quereys ben"*   122

   35. Romance No. 1, *"Durandarte, Durandarte"*   124
   36. Romance No. 2, *"Sospirastes Baldovinos"*   128

37. Sonnet No. 1, "*Amor che nel mio pensier vive*" [Petrarch]   133
38. Sonnet No. 2, "*Porta chiascun nela fronte signato*"   139
39. Sonnet No. 3, "*Nova angeleta*" [Petrarch]   144

40. Fantasia No. 23 in Tone I   147
41. Fantasia No. 24 in Tone II   151
42. Fantasia No. 25 in Tones I and II   156
43. Fantasia No. 26 in Tones III and IV   161
44. Fantasia No. 27 in Tone III   165
45. Fantasia No. 28 in Tone IV   170
46. Fantasia No. 29 in Tones III and IV   176
47. Fantasia No. 30 in Tones III and IV   181
48. Fantasia No. 31 in Tone VI   185
49. Fantasia No. 32 in Tone VI   191
50. Fantasia No. 33 in Tone VI   195

51. Tento No. 1 in Tones I and II   201
52. Tento No. 2 in Tones III and IV   207
53. Tento No. 3 in Tones V and VI   212
54. Tento No. 4 in Tones VII and VIII   217

55. Fantasia No. 34 in Tone VII   222
56. Fantasia No. 35 in Tone VIII   227
57. Fantasia No. 36 in Tones VII and VIII   231
58. Fantasia No. 37 in Tones VII and VIII   236
59. Fantasia No. 38 in Tone VI   238
60. Fantasia No. 39 in Tones VII and VIII   243
61. Fantasia No. 40 in Tones VII and VIII   248

62. Villancico No. 7, "*Al amor quiero vencer*"   254
63. Villancico No. 8, "*Aquel cavallero*"   257
64. Villancico No. 9, "*Amor que tan bien sirviendo*"   261
65. Villancico No. 10, "*Levayme amor da questa terra*"   265
66. Villancico No. 11, "*Un cuydado que mia vida ten*"   268
67. Villancico No. 12, "*Perdida teñyo la color*"   270

68. Romance No. 3, "*Con pavor recordo el moro*"   273
69. Romance No. 4, "*Triste estava, muy quexosa, la triste reyna troyana*"   277

70. Sonnet No. 4, "*O gelosia d'amanti*" [Sannazaro]   280
71. Sonnet No. 5, "*Madonna per voi ardo*"   285
72. Sonnet No. 6, "*Gentil mia donna*" [Petrarch]   289

Postface: Critical Notes   293

Preface

Little is known about the life of Luis de Milán, author of *El Maestro*. Born ca. 1500, he seems to have spent most or all of his life in Valencia, dying ca. 1562. Valencia was, for over two decades, scene of the culturally and socially brilliant court of Germaine de Foix, niece of Louis XII and, earlier, second wife of Ferdinand V, "the Catholic." Upon the death of the latter in 1516, Germaine married John of Brandenburg, governor of Valencia, and so became vicereine of Valencia. Her third marriage, to Ferdinand of Aragón, Duke of Calabria, took place in 1525 and lasted until her death thirteen years later. Luis de Milán was among the most accomplished noblemen of Germaine's court, which is portrayed in his *El Cortesano*, an adaptation of Castiglione's *Il Cortegiano*. *El Cortesano*, published in Valencia in 1561, forms a kind of epitaph to the illustrious court in which Milán had spent many happy years of his life. His first book, written in the heyday of that court, is a wholly unpretentious manual of directions to an amorous party game entitled *Libro de motes de damas y cavalleros: Intitulado el juego de mandar* (1525). *El Maestro*, published, like Milán's other books in Valencia, in 1536, on the other hand, contains one of the most significant repertories of Renaissance music.[1]

El Maestro, written for the *vihuela de mano*, is the earliest of a number of volumes published for that instrument in Spain during the sixteenth century.[2] The *vihuela*, favored over the lute in Spanish court circles, was in reality a guitar. *El Maestro* is thus the earliest extant collection of guitar music.

The sole surviving exemplar of a vihuela forms part of the holdings of the Musée Jacquemart-André in Paris.[3] Like the lute, the vihuela was strung with six courses (double strings). In contradistinction to the former instrument, however, the strings of each of the vihuela's courses were tuned at the unison (certain courses of the lute comprised strings tuned in octaves). Otherwise, the tuning—that is, the

---

1. An attractive sketch of the ambiance of Germaine de Foix's Valencian court and of Milán's rôle in it may be found in J.B. Trend's *Luis de Milán and the Vihuelists* (series *Hispanic Notes and Monographs*, XI, 1925). There is a portrait of Germaine de Foix by Maura (reproduced in the Espasa-Calpe *Enciclopedia Universal Ilustrada* [1924], under "Germana de Foix").
2. The definitive study of the vihuela and its literature is J. Ward's "The Vihuela de Mano and its Music (1536–1576)," (unpubl. diss., New York University, 1953). For additional information on Milán and *El Maestro*, see H. Brown, *Instrumental Music Printed Before 1600* (Cambridge, 1965), 47–50. See also E. Pujol (ed.), *Alonso Mudarra: Tres Libros de Música en Cifra para Vihuela, 1546* (series *Monumentos de la Música Española*, VII, 1949), 1–15.
3. *Musée Jacquemart-André: Catalogue Itinéraire* (7th ed., Paris, 1933), 131. The description of Item 931 reads as follows: "Guitare espagnole, décorée de marqueterie de travail *mudejar*. Estampille au fer du monastère de *Guadalupe* (Estremadure), vers 1500." See also Ward, "Vihuela de Mano," 19–21; Pujol, *Alonso Mudarra*, 6 and fn. 4.

intervallic relationship between adjacent courses—of both instruments was identical.[4]

There was no fixed pitch for the courses of the vihuela. Actual pitch depended on the specific size of each individual instrument and the material and strength of the strings with which it was strung.[4] For transcription of the music of *El Maestro*, the "A-tuning" seems to produce a most satisfactory result; that is, one that conforms, from the viewpoint of notation, to the modes to which Milán assigns various compositions and which provides a vocabulary of accidentals reasonable for sixteenth-century Spanish music. No alternative tunings are called for in *El Maestro*. Utilizing Milán's designations for the courses of the vihuela, the A-tuning reads as follows:

Course 1: a′
2: e′
3: b
4: g
5: d
6: A

The tablature employed in *El Maestro* has been amply discussed.[5] Relative pitches, in semitones, on each course are indicated by the numbers one through ten, which represent frets. Although the performer is provided with the rhythmic placement of the pitches in the measures both by rhythmic symbols above the graph of the notation (that is, the six parallel horizontal lines which represent the fingerboard of the vihuela) and by the placement of the numerals in the measures, the actual *duration* of individual pitches is almost always not shown. This peculiarity, characteristic of vihuela and lute notation in general, has led to a nonpolyphonic transcription of the music in many editions.

There is no reason to assume that the sonorities of lutes or vihuelas, or of any other plucked stringed instrument, decay more quickly than those of the average clavichord.[6] This reason, if no other, calls for the so-called polyphonic method of transcription. More pertinent support for polyphonic transcription, however, comes from *El Maestro* itself, for Milán often has indicated, by means of ties *over the barline*, that he wishes certain notes to be understood as having a specific duration.[7] This is not to say that the texture of all the music contained in *El Maestro* is polyphonic; rather, the polyphonic approach to transcription reveals the true *voice-leading* of the music, whatever its texture.

Flats and sharps have been used to form signatures in a number of compositions.

---

4. Ward, "Vihuela de Mano," 37–53; G. Reese, *Music in the Renaissance* (rev. ed., New York, 1959), 619–20.
5. W. Apel, *The Notation of Polyphonic Music 900–1600* (4th ed., rev., Cambridge, 1953), 56–62; J. Wolf, *Handbuch der Notationskunde* (series *Kleine Handbücher der Musikgeschichte*, VIII, Leipzig, 1913 and 1919), II (1919), 106–108.
6. Ward, "Vihuela de Mano," 127–129.
7. *El Maestro*, fols. [A v^v], B iii^v, [B iv^r], [B iv^v], [H v^r], J^r, J^v, etc. Proof positive for polyphonic transcription is also found on fols. [F v^r] and [F vi^r]; cf. L. Schrade, *Luys Milán: Musikalische Werke* (series *Publikationen Älterer Musik . . . der Deutschen Musikgesellschaft*, II.1, 1927), 112–13, 116–17.

Preface

These signatures should not be interpreted to imply major or minor keys; they only represent a notational convenience. In certain works, Milán has transposed the modes; signatures obviously are called for in these instances. In other works, a preponderance of, for example, B-flat over B-natural or F-sharp over F-natural, made use of a signature highly desirable for increasing the legibility of the music.

El Maestro occupies a very special position in the history and literature of music. It is not only the earliest source of guitar music: it contains the earliest verbal indications of tempo.

These tempo indications were discussed in my study, *Tempo Notation in Renaissance Spain*,[8] where it is shown that "reduction of rhythmic symbols" in transcription of the music is often necessary. The entire corpus of music in *El Maestro* makes it evident that the minim indeed is the "motor unit" therein, rather than the semiminim.[9] It should be noted that, except in compositions employing *tempo rubato*, the quarter note, or any other rhythmic value, has more or less the same duration within any given tempo, regardless of changes in meter (time) signature, except as otherwise indicated (e.g., at the introduction into the music of a section in triple meter, when an equation like that used in Fantasia No. 19, measures 71–72, has been employed to indicate the temporal relationship between preceding and subsequent note values).

Terms and expressions Milán uses to indicate the tempi called for in his book are provided in the CRITICAL NOTES (Postface) to this edition. The tempi, "reduction" utilized, and the number of compostions in each tempo follow:

Tempo	*Reduction*	*Number of Compositions*
Molto Lento	2:1	8
Lento	2:1	7
Andante	2:1	1
Moderato	2:1	15
Moderato e Rubato	2:1	14
Allegro Moderato	2:1	14[10]
	4:1	10
Allegro	4:1	9
Molto Allegro	4:1	4

Interpretation of the tempo of Fantasias Nos. 10–18 and the four Tentos, as well as Romance No. 3, in *El Maestro* as "*Moderato e Rubato*" is borne out by remarks at the head of each of these works, but the specific *moderato* aspect of the tempo is

8. C. Jacobs, *Tempo Notation in Renaissance Spain* (New York, 1964), 15–18, 53–69.
9. Jacobs, *Tempo Notation*, 12–15.
10. Includes a single composition bearing the indication *Piuttosto Giocoso*.

El Maestro

particularized in the introductory remark to Tento No. 3 (refer to CRITICAL NOTES). The style of playing called for in these works was known as *"tañer de gala"* in Renaissance Spain. Transcription of the compositions in *allegro moderato* was more problematical; wholesale reduction by 4:1 would have led, in many instances, to lengthy passages of thirty-second notes, certainly inconsistent with Milán's tempo indication. Reduction by 2:1 in fourteen works and by 4:1 in the other ten seemed reasonable; perhaps the former compositions are supposed to tend more toward the *moderato* aspect of *Allegro Moderato*, the latter toward the *allegro* aspect of the tempo.

Reduction often mandated rebarring the music. This is especially evident in music reduced by 4:1; it would be curious to have a signature of $\frac{1}{4}$ and a succession of single quarter-note measures comprising an entire composition. (Milán's *compáses*, "measures," almost invariably contain the rhythmic value of a semibreve.[11]) The vocal music presented a special problem, since accented places in the music should carry the natural accents of the language (Spanish, Portuguese, or Italian) of the lyrics. Sometimes this necessitated rebarring music so that conflicting accents of two or three lines of lyrics, intended for the same phrase of music, could be accommodated.

I was sorely tempted to apply *musica ficta* to the music but refrained from doing so, in accordance with the principle that the tablature notation employed in *El Maestro* indicates the exact finger position and hence the exact pitch desired by the composer.

Most of *El Maestro* is taken up by the forty fantasias contained in the volume. These are, in the main, either lightly-textured polyphonic or homophonic works, characterized by abundant use of sequence and by occasional imitation.

The fantasias bearing the tempo indication *Moderato e Rubato*, are more homophonic in texture than the other fantasias and are marked by elaborate figuration and passagework. Indeed, these fantasias might well be called "tentos," since they share their form and style with the four tentos in *El Maestro*. Milán himself, in fact, relates the two groups of compositions.[12]

To some extent, Milán's use of the term "fantasia" is a generic one; that is, he uses it to indicate *solo instrumental music*. This is particularly evident in his initial reference to *El Maestro*'s six pavans.[13]

Milán implies an Italian origin for the pavan.[14] In *El Maestro* the pavans are in duple *or* triple meter, and all, in this source, are in *allegro moderato*. Milán states that the first four pavans were newly created ("invented") by him. The remaining

---

11. Jacobs, *Tempo Notation*, 16–17; Ward, "Vihuela de Mano," 118–29. The reader is reminded that the term *compás* had a double meaning in sixteenth-century Spain; depending on the context, it may be translated as "measure" or as *"tactus"* (i.e., beat, pulse).
12. Cf. fols. [M iv^v] and N^r (see CRITICAL NOTES).
13. Cf. fol. G iii^v, where Milán first speaks of the pavans as "fantasias."
14. Milán, *El Maestro*, fol. G. iii^v.

Preface

two, on the other hand, he says, bear his *compostura* (elaboration) on their *sonada* (sound), which originated in Italy. We have here an early (the earliest?) use of the term "sonata."

Milán states that the *sonada* of his fifth pavan is sung in Italy with the lyrics "*qua la bella franceschina*." This and the sixth pavan are based on the *passamezzo moderno* bass formula.[15]

The performance practice of the *villancicos*, *romances*, and *sonetos* in *El Maestro* is provided by Milán for formal disposition of the lyrics and, as already noted, tempo. However, he does not provide examples of the vocal ornamentation (referred to by the expressions *hacer garganta*, *quiebro*, and *glosa*) called for in performance.[16] Nor does he clearly state whether the vihuela should or should not perform the vocal line.[17] The implied polyphony of the vihuela part often demands incorporation of notes sung by the vocalist. Specific designation by Milán that vocal notes be performed simultaneously on two courses of the vihuela—as in measures 16-17 of the *romance*, "Con pavor recordo el moro"—would seem to imply that the vihuela did in fact play the vocal line.

Milán is of little help in connection with textual underlay; that is, the setting of specific syllables and words of the lyrics to specific notes or melodic fragments of the vocal line. In underlaying the text of the lyrics, I have attempted always to promote the natural accentuation of the specific language used.[18]

My thanks are due to Professor Gustave Reese of the Graduate School of Arts and Science of New York University and to Professor Barry Brook, Executive Officer of the Ph.D. Program in Music of the City University of New York, for the valuable advice they were always willing to provide.

I would like also to express my sincere gratitude to Professor Denis Stevens of Columbia University, General Editor of the Penn State Music Series, for helpful suggestions and for his sustained interest in this edition.

Realization of the edition was made possible by a generous grant from the American Philosophical Society, whose Executive Officer, Dr. George W. Corner, has shown an extremely kind interest in my work.

Montréal, Québec, Canada   C.J.
January 1970

15. Reese, *Renaissance*, 524. Valuable musical and bibliographical information on these two pavans may be found in Ward, "Vihuela de Mano," 185-88; on the origin of the pavan, 349-55.
16. See CRITICAL NOTES. The vocal ornamentation will form the subject of a future article.
17. J. Bal, "Fuenllana and the Transcription of Spanish Lute Music," *Acta Musicologica*, XI (1939), 16-27, with whom I concur in believing that the vocal part—notated in red ciphers in the vihuela score in *El Maestro*—should be played on the vihuela. The same opinion is held by Ward, "Vihuela de Mano," 95-100.
18. The spelling found in *El Maestro* has been retained—which occasionally raises questions concerning pronunciation; for example, "*oxalla*," today spelled "*ojalá*"; etc. Syllabification is modern.

EL MAESTRO

Textual Matter

REX

Inuictissimus *Lusitanorum.*

Prologo. folio. iij.

Libro de musica de vihuela de mano. Intitulado El maestro. El qual trahe el mismo estilo y horden que vn maestro trahería con vn discipulo principiante: mostrandole hordenadamente dende los principios toda cosa que podria ignorar: para entender la presente obra: dandole en cada disposicion que se hallara: la musica: conforme a sus manos. Compuesto por don Luys Milan. Dirigido al muy alto y muy poderoso z inuictissimo principe don Juã: por la gracia de dios rey de Portugal: y delos Algarues: desta parte y dela otra del mar: z Affrica: z señor de Guinea: z dela conquista z nauegacion. zc.

Muy alto, catholico z poderoso principe rey z señor: el muy famoso Frãcisco Petrarcha dize en sus sonetos y triumphos: que cada vno de nosotros sigue su estrella: cõ estas palabras. Ogniun seque sua stella. Affirmando que nascemos debaxo de vna estrella/ala qual somos sometidos por inclinaciõ. Muy bien considerauan esto los Romanos en tiempo passado/enel nascimiẽto dellos: que hazian mirar por natural filosophia/en que estrella nascian: para saber a que eran sometidos: y sabido esto/hazian exercitar a sus hijos en aquello que eran inclinados: y por esta sabia ocasiõ/auia entre ellos muy excellentes hõbres/o en letras/o en armas/o en musica: y otras virtudes. Agora en nuestros tiempos/aunque los padres no tengan esta diligencia en los hijos: natura como a madre de todos la tiene: pues trahe a muchos que se exerciten en aquello que son naturales. Y que esto sea verdad/en muchos se vee: y en mi lo he conoscido: que siempre he sido tan inclinado ala musica/que puedo affirmar y dezir: que nunca tuue otro maestro sino a ella misma. La qual ha tuuido tanta fuerça comigo/para que fuesse suyo: como yo he tenido grado della/ para que fuesse mia. Y siguiendo mi inclinacion/heme hallado vn libro hecho de muchas obras: que dela vihuela tenia sacadas y escritas: y teniendolo entre las manos/pensando lo que del haria: vinome ala memoria lo que vn filosopho griego hizo de vna muy estimada piedra preciosa que se hallo: ala qual teniendo entre sus manos/dixo estas palabras. Si yo te tuuiesse perderias tu valor. Y si tu me tuuiesses/perderia yo el mio. Y dicho esto la echo en la mar. Siguiose despues que de alli a poco tiempo fue hallada vna balena muerta ala orilla de la mar: y abriendola/le hallaron la sobredicha piedra. La qual vino en poder de vn rey: y fue tenida en tanto por el/que siempre la traya consigo. Y offresciẽndose despues oportunidad/vio el dicho filosopho en poder de aquel rey aquella

A iij

Textual Matter

Milán's Introduction

[Fol. A iiiʳ:] Music Book for vihuela de mano. Entitled *El Maestro* [The Teacher]. Which follows the same manner and order a teacher would follow with a beginning student, showing him, in an orderly way from the beginning, everything he may be ignorant of so as to understand this work, [and] providing him music suitable for his hands at each stage [of development] in which he finds himself. Composed by Don Luys Milán. Dedicated to the most high and powerful and invincible prince Don Juan,[1] by the grace of God, King of Portugal and of the Algarve,[2] and of this part and of the other of the sea, and [of] Africa, and lord of Guinea, and of the conquest and navigation, etc.

Very high, Catholic, and powerful prince, king, and lord: the very famous Francisco Petrarcha [sic] says in his Sonnets and Triumphs that each one of us follows his star, with these words: *Ogniun* [sic] *seque sua stella*. Affirming that we are born beneath a star to which, by inclination, we are subject, the Romans in times past studied this closely in [conjunction with] their birth; so that they regarded through natural philosophy under which star they were born, in order to know to which they were subject. And this known, they encouraged their sons in that to which they were [by nature] inclined. And thanks to this wise practice, there were among them very excellent men in letters or in arms or in music, and [in] other virtues. Now in these times, although parents are not diligent with their children, nature, as mother of all, is [diligent]; thus in many she brings about an interest in what is natural [for them]. And that this is true is seen in many; and I have recognized it in my [case]: I have always been so inclined to music that I can assert and say that I never had another teacher but [music] itself. Which[3] has had such force in my [life] that I might be its [own]; [and so much] have I tended toward it that it might be [called] mine. And, following my inclination, I have

---

1. João III of Portugal (r. 1521–57). According to J.B. Trend (*Luis de Milán and the Vihuelists*; series *Hispanic Notes and Monographs*, XI, 1925, 17), João, in appreciation for the dedication of *El Maestro*, awarded Milán a pension of 7000 *cruzados*. João III was notable as a protector of arts and letters; he was largely responsible for the establishment of the University at Coimbra in 1536–37. Refer to F. de Almeida, *História de Portugal* (Coimbra, 1922–29), III, 651–56; J. Ameal, *História de Portugal* (Pôrto 1940, 287–316).
2. The preceding text is substantially that of the Title Page, fol. [A] iiʳ. The Title Page, rather than "the Algarve," reads "the islands."

    The Algarve (whose capital is Faro) is the southernmost province of Portugal; the most Moorish part of that country, the Algarve was formerly an independent kingdom, established by Affonso III (also "Afonso") of Portugal (r. 1248–79) in 1253. See Almeida, *História*, I, 215–19; Ameal, *História*, 88–99.
3. I.e., Music.

El Maestro

created a book made of many things which were derived from the vihuela and written down. And having it on my hands, wondering what I should do with it, there came to my mind what a Greek philosopher did with a very valuable precious stone he found.[4] Having it in his hands, he said to it these words: "If I keep you, you will lose your value; and if you remained with me, I should lose mine." And, this said, he threw it into the sea. Shortly thereafter, a dead whale was found nearby on the seashore. Opening it, they found the above-mentioned stone. The latter came into possession of the king and was held in such [esteem] by him that he carried it with him always. And an opportunity arose afterward [in which] the said philosopher saw in possession of that king that [fol. A iii^v:] valuable stone that he had thrown into the sea; at which, with great wonder, he said these words: "You now belong to your [own]," showing that the stone was in its [proper] place. Truly, I believe that I am this philosopher, [inasmuch] as I have created this book, about which I have said the same words as the philosopher said to his stone. And I can say them with reason, because if I alone should have this book, it would lose its value; thus it would fail to bring about the profit of which it is capable. And if I kept it so that no one could benefit from it, I should lose [what] is mine; it would surely be ungrateful to whomever gave me the knowledge to create it. The sea into which I have thrown this book is fittingly the kingdom of Portugal, which is the sea of music—since [there] they esteem and also understand it so much. I would not wish that some whale—which the envious truly are—should swallow it, because I believe he would [then] find himself dead and confused on the seashore of his envy, when he saw this book before your royal highness, whose grace will defend it against any enemy. And for this and many other reasons, I present and direct it [i.e., *El Maestro*] to your royal highness, saying those words that the philosopher said when he saw his precious stone in the possession of that king, as I have described above: "You now belong to your [own]." Which means that the book is now in its [proper] place, since it could not be better understood or esteemed.

Explanation [*declaración*] of the book, instructing and showing him who is a beginner all that is necessary to know at the beginning and further on.

The intention of this book is to show music for vihuela de mano to a beginner who never has played and to follow the order with him that a teacher [would follow] with a student. For this, it is very necessary that he who wants to learn to play the vihuela learn first *canto de órgano*,[5] until he knows how, [while] singing, to understand how one carries the measure and beat [*compás y mesura*[6]]. After

---

4. The story following has points in common with a series of events in the life of Polycrates, Tyrant of Samos (r. ca. 532–522 B.C.). See Herodotus, *The Persian Wars*, Book III, Ch. 40–43.
5. I.e., mensural notation, in which pitch is notated on the staff and clefs are used.
6. Actually, both *compás* and *mesura* mean "measure" in Spanish. The term *compás* may refer either to the written measure of music or to the tactus. *Mesura* has no specific meaning and

Ste libro como ya aueys oydo: es su intencion formar y hazer vn musico de vihuela de mano: daquella mistma manera que vn maestro haria en vn discipulo que nunca hu uiesse tañido: y por esta razon la presente musica q̃ agora ha de principiar es algo facil: porq̃ da principios al princi piante. Mas facil pudiera ser: pero no tuuiera ser. y por que esta musica para dar principios aya de parecer bien: no sufre ser mas facil deloque es. La qual musica esta figurada por fanta sias como a baxo vereys: desta manera: q̃ qualquiera obra deste libro o qual quier tono que sea: se intitula fantasia: a respecto que sole procede dela fanta sia y industria del auctor que la hizo. El qual muy affectadamente ruega a to dos los que por su libro passaran que no juzgen sus obras hasta que sean ta ñidas como cada vno querria que sus obras lo fuessen: y tañidas en su perfi cion: sino seran tan perfectas sean lo ellos en virtud y bondad que suple a to das faltas.

Inuocando dei auxiliũ: et gloriose virginis Marie matris sue: cuius immaculate conceptionis firmiter credendo inci pit ad predictorum laudem primus liber presentis musice. ¶ Esta primera fantasia que aqui debaxo esta figurada es del primero tono: y quanto mas se tañera cõ el cõpas apres surado mejor parecera el q̃ tañera enla vihuela por los ter minos q̃ esta fantasia anda: tañese por el primero tono. Mi ren bien la dicha fantasia que clausulas haze: y que terminos tiene: y donde fe nece: porque enella veran todo lo que justamente el primero tono puede ha zer. Y es cosas se hã de cõsiderar enlas siguientes fantasias del presente li bro la vna: que se hã de tañer con el cõpas apressurado o espacioso como el au ctor quiere. La otra mirar bien los tonos que siguen porque ellas muestran como se han de tañer los tonos por la vihuela: y para mas pfecto conocimiẽ to delos dichos tonos ala fin deste libro mas largamente se tractara delles.

B

```
    ↓↓↓  ↓↓↓  ↓↓↓   ↓↓↓    ↓↓↓↓↓    ↓↓
────0──────────────────────────────0────
──0───1────3──2──0──────────2──3──2─────
────2──3──2──0─────0─2─3──3─2─0─2─3──3──
──────2────2─0────────2─────────────2───
────0─────────────────────────0─────1───
──────────1─2─0───────────────────────0─
```

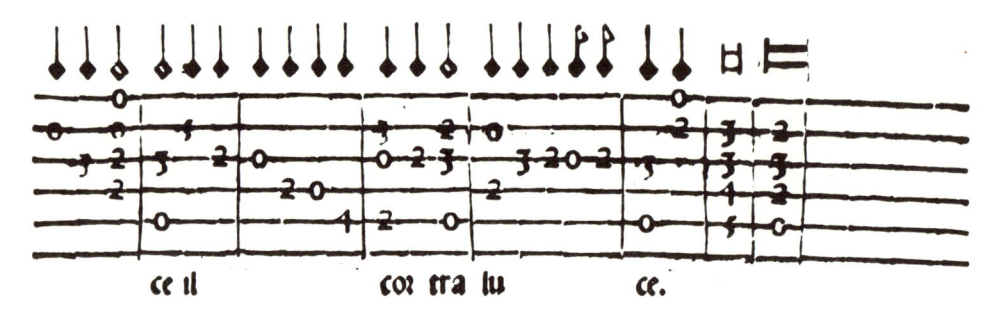

ce ll   cō tra lu   ce.

¶ Intelligencia y declaracion delos tonos que en la musica de canto figurado se vsan.

En el presente libro propuse de dar intelligencia y declaracion delos ocho tonos que en la musica d canto figurado se vsan: porque en las reglas o declaraciones enlos principios delas fantasias que enel libro se contiene no hos di tata intelligēcia delos tonos quāta se requiere para entēderlos. la resolucion delos dichos ocho tonos para que en breue mas se comprehendan es esta. Los tonos se han de conoscer en tres cosas. Primeramente enel termino. Secūdariamēte en las clausulas. Terceramēte en la clausula final q es donde fenecen: y quanto alo primero q es conoscer el tono enel termino: es de saber que el tono se ha de conocer en solo en tiple en las cōposturas de musica: al qual los inuētores delos tonos dierō diez puntos de termino: de manera q el tiple dōde se ha de conoscer el tono ha de tener diez puntos de termino contido q ha de subir nueue pūtos encima d su clausula final y abaxar vno debaxo de su clausula final q son diez. Esto se entiende en los quatro tonos maestros: que son el primero y el tercero y el quinto y el septimo tonos porq los otros quatro tonos discipulos q son el segūdo y el quarto y el sexto y el octauo, tiene el dicho termino de diez puntos: la meytad por arriba q cōtareys seys puntos encima de su clausula final: y la meytad por abaxo q contareys cinco pūtos debaxo la clausula final. ¶ Quanto alo segūdo q es conoscer el tono por las clausulas sabreys que el primero tono clausula en principio de su diapente que es en dlasolre. y quita encima en alamire. y quarta mas ecima en fin d su diathesaron en dlasol ¶ Enel dicho diapente se forma vn diathesaron q es d dlasolre a gsolreut. y enel mesmo. gsolreut. clausula. Estas son las generales clausulas que se dan a cada tono. Otra clausula se da en medio del diapente que es en. ffaut. esta es voluntaria: mas se dize parte o punto para descāçar que clausula. Algunos quierē y se vsa q solo el primero tono pueda clausular vn pūto mas baxo d su clausula final q es en clolfaut. ¶ Esta regla que hos he dicho se ha de tener en todos los ocho tonos comēçando a clausular dl principio de su diapēte q comiença alli donde el tono fenesce prosiguiendo esta orden ya dicha quinta mas arriba. y quarta mas arriba: y enel diathesaron que se forma enel diapēte. y la que se da voluntaria en medio dl diapente.

¶ Los tonos discipulos por tener como hos he dicho el termino la meytad por arriba y la otra meytad por abaxo tiene su diathesaron quatro puntos mas abaxo d donde ellos fenecen. y enel mesmo diathesaron clausulan.

¶ Quanto alo tercero, que es conoscer el tono por la clausula final donde el fenece: sabreys que el primero y segūdo tonos hazē su clausula final en dlasolre: el tercero y quarto en clami. el quinto y sexto en. ffaut. el septimo y octauo en gsolreut.

¶ Los q se intitulā tonos mixtos q en las fantasias passadas del libro haueys visto

Milán's Introduction

this is understood, it is necessary to know how to tune the vihuela very well. And for a vihuela to be well tuned, three things are required. First, to give it its true intonation. Second, to string it with strings that are not false. Third, to tune it by [the] notes of *canto* [*de órgano*].

In regard to the first, which is to give to the vihuela its true intonation, so that it may be well tuned, [this] is to be [effected] in the following way. If the vihuela is large, take [as] the first [*prima*] [string[7] to be tuned, one] more thick than thin; and if it is small, take [as] the first [string, one] more thin than thick. And, this done, raise the first [string] as high as it can be; and afterward, you will tune the other strings to the note [i.e., pitch] of the first [string], as will be told you further on. And tuned in this way, [the vihuela] will be fine and at its true intonation. Because if the vihuela is tuned excessively high, it always becomes untuned in order to descend to its [true] intonation. And if it is tuned very low, it always becomes untuned in order to ascend to its [true] intonation.[8]

Second, [the vihuela] must be strung with strings that are good and not false. And in order to recognize a string that is not false, you will proceed in this way. Stretch with two fingers of each hand the vihuela string, which has to be of a length from one small bridge [*pontezica*] to the other exactly.[9] And thus stretched, pluck it [i.e., the string] as who [ever] wishes to play it; and if the said string seems to produce two strings, [fol. A iiii[r]:] it is good; and if it appears to produce more than two strings, it is bad and should not be placed on the vihuela.[10]

Third, the vihuela is to be tuned in this way by notes of *canto*. After having raised the first [string] of the vihuela as high as I have stated above, tune the second [string], which is four notes below the first. Afterward, tune the third [string], which is four notes below the second. And the fourth [string], which is three notes below the third; and the fifth, which is four notes below the fourth; and the sixth, which is four notes below the fifth. And for a better understanding of the strings of the vihuela presented [in diagram below], you will find the intonation[11] that each one of the strings has to have.

La-mi from the first [string] to the second, [which] means that the [pitch of the] second [string] is four notes below [that of] the first.

La-mi from the second [string] to the third, [which] means that the [pitch of the] third [string] is four notes below [that of] the second.

Mi-ut from the third [string] to the fourth, [which] means that the [pitch of the] fourth [string] is three notes below [that of] the third.

---

apparently is used by Milán to mean only "measure" in the sense of some kind of regular rhythmic organization. Refer to my *Tempo Notation in Renaissance Spain* (New York, 1964), 3–7, 11–15.

7. I.e., the highest string. Refer to J. Ward, "The Vihuela de Mano and its Music (1536–1576)" (unpubl. diss., New York University, 1953), 40–41.
8. It is difficult to imagine a string too loosely strung becoming sharp. Variation in string length may, of course, influence the string gauge necessary to provide proper string tension. Particularly noteworthy in Milán's commentary is that no specific degree of tension and, therefore, no specific pitch is suggested for the "first" string.
9. The "small bridges" are formed by the fingers of each hand.
10. Ward, "Vihuela de Mano," 29.
11. Here Milán means "solmization," not "intonation."

El Maestro

Sol-re from the fourth [string] to the fifth, [which] means that the [pitch of the] fifth [string] is four notes below [that of] the fourth.

Sol-re from the fifth [string] to the sixth, [which] means that [the pitch of] the sixth [string] is four notes below [that of] the fifth.

When the vihuela is tuned [*templada*] by means of these above-mentioned notes of *canto*, you are to fine-tune [*affinar*] it in this way. Place your finger on the fifth fret of the second [string], and play it [i.e., the string]; and if the said second [string] is not so high [in pitch] as the first, tune it, raising or lowering somewhat the second [string] or the said fret.

[Fol. A iiii^v:] Similarly, place your finger on the same fifth fret of the third [string]; and the third [string] has to be as high [in pitch] as the second; and if not, tune it as I have already stated.

Similarly, place your finger on the same fifth fret of the fifth [string]; and the fifth [string] has to be as high [in pitch] as the fourth; and if not, tune it, as I have said.

Similarly, place your finger on the same fifth fret of the sixth [string]; and the sixth [string] has to be as high [in pitch] as the fifth; and if not, tune it as the others.

> There is another way to fine-tune, so as to see if
> the vihuela is well tuned; and it is as follows.

Place your finger on the third fret of the second [string]; and then, play the fourth [string] open; and the fourth [string] has to be an octave below the second.

And placing your finger on the third fret of the third [string], the open fifth [string] has to be an octave below the third.

And placing your finger on the second fret of the fourth [string], the open sixth [string] has to be an octave below the fourth.

Declaracion

Assi mesmo porneys el dedo sobre la tercera/enel mesmo cinqueno traste: y ha de estar la tercera tā alta como la segūda: y sino affinalda como ya he dicho.

Assi mesmo porneys el dedo sobre la quinta: enel mesmo cinqueno traste: y ha de estar la quinta tan alta como la quarta: y sino afinalda como he dicho.

Assi mesmo porneys el dedo sobre la sesta: enel mesmo cinquen traste: y ha de estar la sesta tan alta como la quinta: y sino afinalda como las otras.

Otra manera de afinar ay para ver si la vibuela
esta bien templada: y es desta manera.

Mete el dedo sobre la segūda enel tercer traste: y luego tras esta tañe la quarta en vazio: y ha de estar la quarta octaua baxo dela segunda.

Y metiendo el dedo sobre la tercera: enel tercer traste: ha de estar la quinta en vazio/octaua baxo dela tercera.

Y metiendo el dedo sobre la quarta: enel segūdo traste: ha de estar la sesta en vazio/octaua baxo dela quarta.

En fin que cada vno que se quiera dar a tañer por este libro: primeramēte tiene necessidad de saber algun tanto de canto: y templar vna vibuela: y sabido esto: muy facilmente entendera lo que se sigue.

Declaracion particular de todo lo que el
principiante enel presente libro podria ignorar.

Las seys rayas siguientes que debaxo estan figuradas: son las seys cuerdas dela vibuela: tomando la mas alta raya por prima: y la otra despues della por segunda: discurriendo assi como las que veys estan figuradas.

Prima. ─────────────
Segunda. ─────────────
Tercera. ─────────────
Quarta. ─────────────
Quinta. ─────────────
Sexta. ─────────────

Sobre estas seys cuerdas: vereys enel presente libro figuradas las siguientes cifras: y debaxo dellas escrito lo que cada vna vale.

   1.   2.   3.   4.   5.   6.   7.   8.   9.   X.
vno. dos. tres. quatro. cinco. seys. siete. ocho. nueue. diez.

Dela obra.	folio.	F.

¶ Quādo vereys q̄lq̄era delas dichas cifras sobre las seys cuerdas dela vibuela q̄ arriba he figuradas: aueys de mirar de q̄ valor es la cifra: si vale vno como esta. 1. tañereys la cuerda dela vibuela dōde ella estara enl p̄mero traste. y si vale dos como esta. 2. tañereys la cuerda dōde ella estara enl segūdo traste. y assi os regireys cō todas las otras cifras. De manera q̄ las presentes cifras hā de seruir pa amostraros en q̄ trastes aueys de poner los dedos enla vibuela: como aq̄ debaxo esta figurado.

Prima enel primero traste. ———————1———————
Segunda enel tercero traste. ———————3———————
Tercera enel quarto traste. ————————4————————
Quarta enel tercero traste. ————————3————————
Quinta enel cinqueno traste. ————————5————————
Sexta enel sexto traste. —————————6—————————

¶ Quādo las cifras estā vna despues de otra/tañereys las cuerdas dla vibuela vna despues de otra: como agora arriba vos las he figuradas. y si vienē dos o tres/o quatro cifras jūtas/tañereys las cuerdas dla vibuela jūtas/como ellas vienē: assi como aq̄ debaxo esta figurado.

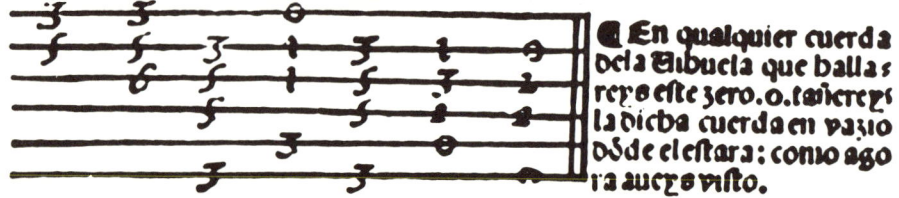

¶ En qualquier cuerda dela vibuela que hallareys este zero. o. tañereys la dicha cuerda en vazio dōde el estara: como agora aueys visto.

¶ Pues auemos tratado delas seys cuerdas dela vibuela: como arriba hos he figurado: por seys rayas: y del valor delas cifras: y para lo q̄ sirue. Es menester q̄ sepays q̄ mesura y ayre se ha de dar ala musica: q̄ por las dichas cifras esta puntada enel presente libro: porq̄ podria dezir alguno/q̄ avnq̄ las cifras puestas sobre las rayas le muestrē q̄ cuerdas ha de tañer dla vibuela: y en q̄ trastes: no por esso se podria entēder q̄ ayre y cōpas se ha de dar ala dicha musica.

¶ El cōpas enla musica no es otra cosa porq̄ sepays/sino vn alçar y abaxar la mano/o pie por vn ygual tiempo.

¶ Pues sabemos q̄ cosa es compas/vengamos a saber quantas delas sobredichas cifras entran en vn compas: pues por esto se ha de saber el ayre y mesura para bien tañer la presente musica.

¶ Es de saber como aq̄ baxo esta figurado/q̄ las cifras q̄ vereys encerradas entre las dos lineas/q̄ trauiessan de alto abaxo: es a saber dela prima ala sexta: aq̄llas tales cifras encerradas/valē vn cōpas: porq̄ las notas del canto q̄ encima dellas esta/vos dizē lo q̄ ellas valē: como aq̄ debaxo vereys.

Milan's Introduction

Thus, anyone who wishes to play through this book first must know something about *canto* and [about] tuning a vihuela; and this known, he will understand easily what follows.

Special explanation of all that the beginner
of this book may be ignorant of.

The six lines following, which are drawn below, represent the six strings of the vihuela, taking the highest line as the first [string], and the next after it as the second [string], continuing as you see they are drawn.

```
First   ─────────────────
Second  ─────────────────
Third   ─────────────────
Fourth  ─────────────────
Fifth   ─────────────────
Sixth   ─────────────────
```

You will see the following ciphers [*çifras*] [printed] on these six strings in this book; and below them [is] written [here] what each one is worth [*vale*] [i.e., means]:[12]

1	2	3	4	5	6	7	8	9	X
one	two	three	four	five	six	seven	eight	nine	ten

[fol. [A] v^r:] When you see any of the said ciphers on the six strings of the vihuela that I have drawn above, you have to observe what the value of the cipher is; if it is worth one, like this "1," play the string of the vihuela where it [the cipher] is, [that is,] on the first fret. And if it is worth two, like this "2," play the string where it [the cipher] is, [that is,] on the second fret. And thus you will manage with all the other ciphers. So that the present ciphers serve to show you on which frets [of] the vihuela you are to place your fingers, as is shown below:

```
First [string], first fret:   ──────1──────────
Second [string], third fret:  ────────3────────
Third [string], fourth fret:  ──────────4──────
Fourth [string], third fret:  ────────3────────
Fifth [string], fifth fret:   ──────────5──────
Sixth [string], sixth fret:   ────────────6────
```

When the ciphers are [printed] one after the other, you will play the strings of the vihuela one after the other, as I now have shown you above. And if two, or three, or four ciphers come [printed] together, you will play the strings of the vihuela together [simultaneously] as they [i.e., the ciphers] come, as is shown here below.[13]

12. Apparently ciphers, that is, Arabic numerals, were not universally employed.
13. In the transcription of all musical examples of Milán's Introduction, rhythmic values and barring of the source have been retained. Neither rhythmic values nor barring, however, is provided for the initial example. The implied polyphony has been reconstructed in all cases.

El Maestro

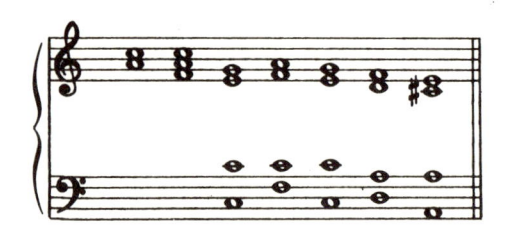

On any string of the vihuela on which you find this zero, "0," play the said string open where it is, as you have now seen [in the above example].

Thus we have considered the vihuela's six strings—six lines, as I have drawn [them] for you above, and the value of the ciphers and for what they serve. It is [also] necessary that you know what measure and spirit [*mesura y ayre*] must be given to the music represented by the said ciphers in this book, because one could say that although the ciphers placed on the lines show on what strings of the vihuela you are to play and on which frets, through this [alone], you will not understand what spirit and measure [*ayre y compás*] should be given to the said music.

Measure [*compás*] in music, so that you [may readily] understand, is nothing but a raising and lowering [of] the hand or foot at an equal speed [*tiempo*].

Thus, knowing what the measure [*compás*] is, we will know how many of the above-mentioned ciphers may enter into á measure [*compás*]; and for this [reason] one has to know the spirit and measure, in order to play this music well.

Observe, as is noted here below, that the ciphers you see contained between the two lines that cross from high to low, that is, from the first [of the six lines representing the strings] to the sixth, those ciphers contained [therein] are [together] worth a measure, as the notes of *canto* placed above them tell you they are worth, as you will see here below.

In measure 13 of these twenty measures of music that I have presented, you will find a semibreve that crosses the [bar]line; this means that half the said semibreve belongs to the thirteenth measure and the other half to the fourteenth measure.

Milan's Introduction

In the seventeenth measure, there is a dot by the hindermost minim. The said dot belongs to the eighteenth measure, and for that [reason], it takes a line ["curve" is meant] and passes [over] to the other measure.

So that you understand them when you find them in the book, I want to show [*pintar*] here below two kinds of proportions. One is of three semibreves to the measure.[14]

14. The reading of the second note of the lowest voice in measure 4 of the following example is ambiguous.

The other [is] of three minims to the measure.
[Fol. [A] vi[r]:]

Milan's Introduction

There is nothing more to tell you now to help you understand all in the book that you may be ignorant of. And in order to understand well all I have said to you, it is necessary for you to know *canto*; because, in knowing how necessary *canto* is, you will know how difficult what I have said to you is.[15]

15. The text remaining of fol [A] vi^r, as well as that on the following folio, pertains specifically to the initial portion of the music of *El Maestro*. Accordingly, the translation of that text has been incorporated into the Critical Notes of this edition, wherein are also included translations of the introductory paragraphs to individual compositions. The list of errata given by Milán at the close of his volume, similarly, has been incorporated into the Critical Notes.

On fol. [A] vi^v, there is a woodcut of Orpheus playing the vihuela; the following text is printed in the margins on four sides of the picture: "Great Orpheus, thanks to whom the vihuela appears in the world. If he was first, he was not unrivaled, since God is of all, of everything, the creator."

El grande Orpheo primero inuentor

Si el fue primero, no fue sin segundo

Pues dios es de todos, de todo hazedor

parece cual huen la vihuela

Milán's Discussion of the Modes

[Fol. [R v^v]:] Information [on] and explanation of the tones which are used in figured music of *canto*.

In this book, I proposed to give information [on] and [an] explanation of the eight tones which are used in figured music of *canto*. Because, in the rules or explanations at the beginnings of the fantasias contained in this book, I was unable to give as much information on the tones as is required to understand them, this is the summary of the said eight tones, so that they may be understood quickly. Tones are recognized in three things. First, in the ending. Second, in the cadences [*clausulas*]. Third, in the final cadence [*clausula final*], which is where they finish.

And with regard to the first, which is to recognize the tone by its ending, note that the tone is to be recognized alone in [the] treble in musical compositions to which the inventors of the tones gave ten terminal notes. So that the treble, where the tone is to be ascertained, must have ten terminal notes, counting that it must rise nine notes above its final cadence and descend one below its final cadence, that is, ten. This is understood in [regard to] the four master [i.e., authentic] tones, which are the first and the third and the fifth and the seventh tones, because [each of] the other four disciple [plagal] tones, which are the second and the fourth and the sixth and the eighth, has the said ten-note terminus half above, so that you count six notes above, its final cadence and half below, so that you count five notes below, the final cadence.

With regard to the second [thing], which is to recognize the tone by its cadences, you will note that the first tone cadences, in principle, on its fifth [*diapente*], which is on D-la-sol-re [*dlasolre*] and a fifth [*quinta*] above on A-la-mi-re and a fourth still higher, in short, its diatessaron, on D-la-sol.

On the said fifth, a diatessaron is formed, which is from D-la-sol-re to G-sol-re-ut, and on the same G-sol-re-ut, [the tone] may cadence. These are the general cadences used in each tone. Another cadence, midway in the fifth, which is F-fa-ut, is used; this is voluntary, but it is called a place or point for resting [rather] than a cadence. Some like and use the first tone only [in a] cadence a note below its final cadence, which is C-sol-fa-ut.

This rule, that I have told you, is to be held in all the eight tones, [each of which, in] beginning to cadence from the beginning of its fifth, which begins where the tone finishes, following this order, thus, a fifth higher, and a fourth higher, and on the diatessaron that is formed on the fifth [*diapente*], and that [cadence] which is used voluntarily midway in the fifth.

The disciple tones, through having, as I have told you, the terminus [i.e., finalis] half above and the other half below, have their diatessaron four notes below where they finish, and on the same diatessaron they cadence.

El Maestro

With regard to the third [thing], which is to recognize the tone by the final cadence, where it [the tone] finishes, note that the first and second tones form their final cadence on D-la-sol-re; the third and fourth [tones] on E-la-mi; the fifth and sixth on F-fa-ut; the seventh and eighth on G-sol-re-ut.

[Regarding] what are entitled "mixed tones," which you have seen[16] in the fantasias contained in the book, [fol. [R vi^r]:] you are to understand that there are only eight tones in music, because the use of the title "mixed [tone]" is [solely] understood in this way: that when the tones do not follow the order that I have indicated for them, they are irregular. And their irregularity is this: if the treble ascends nine notes above its final cadence and descends three or four notes below the said final cadence, then it [i.e., the mixed tone] uses the terminus of the master tone and [that] of the disciple, and mixes them, and for this [reason] it is called "mixed."

I have already told you that you are only to understand this order and explanation in [connection with] figured *canto*, commonly called [*canto*] "*de órgano*," because in plainchant, according to the intonations of the psalms of the church, the tones display liberties in ending and in cadencing, as you will see where they are written about.

In order to understand this information on the tones that I have explained to you in [relation to] the fantasias contained in the book, you have to guide yourself in this way. Look at the explanation given each fantasia, and [when you have] seen from it [i.e., the explanatory paragraph] in which tone it [the fantasia] is, look for the final cadence [*clausula*] that it forms at its end, although not all the fantasias finish on a final cadence, because some finish on a [simple] cadence [*cadencia*] or consonance. And when they finish in such a way, do not take the said [simple] cadence as the final cadence, but instead [take] the hindermost cadence [*clausula*] that the fantasia forms before the [aforementioned simple] cadence [*cadencia*], and the final cadence [will be] found in this way. If the fantasia is in the first or second tones, where its final cadence is, [the latter] will be [on] D-la-sol-re. And if the fantasia is in the third or fourth tones, it forms its final cadence on E-la-mi. And if it is in the fifth or sixth tones, it forms its final cadence on F-fa-ut. And if it is in the seventh and [*sic*] eighth tones, it forms its final cadence on G-sol-re-ut. And with this said final cadence, observe where the treble of the fantasia begins, and what terminus it has, and what cadences it forms, and if it is [in a] mixed tone or not, as I have told you above. And in this way, you will know perfectly, through practice, in which tone each fantasia or work of the book is.

---

16. Milán's discussion of the modes follows the music of *El Maestro* in the original edition.

Milan's Discussion of the Modes

To the honor and glory of God all powerful and of the most holy virgin Mary, His mother and our advocate. This book of music for vihuela de mano, entitled El Maestro, was printed by Francisco Díaz Romano. In the metropolitan and crown city of Valencia. It was finished on the fourth day of the month of December [in the] year of our atonement, 1536.

EL MAESTRO

The Music

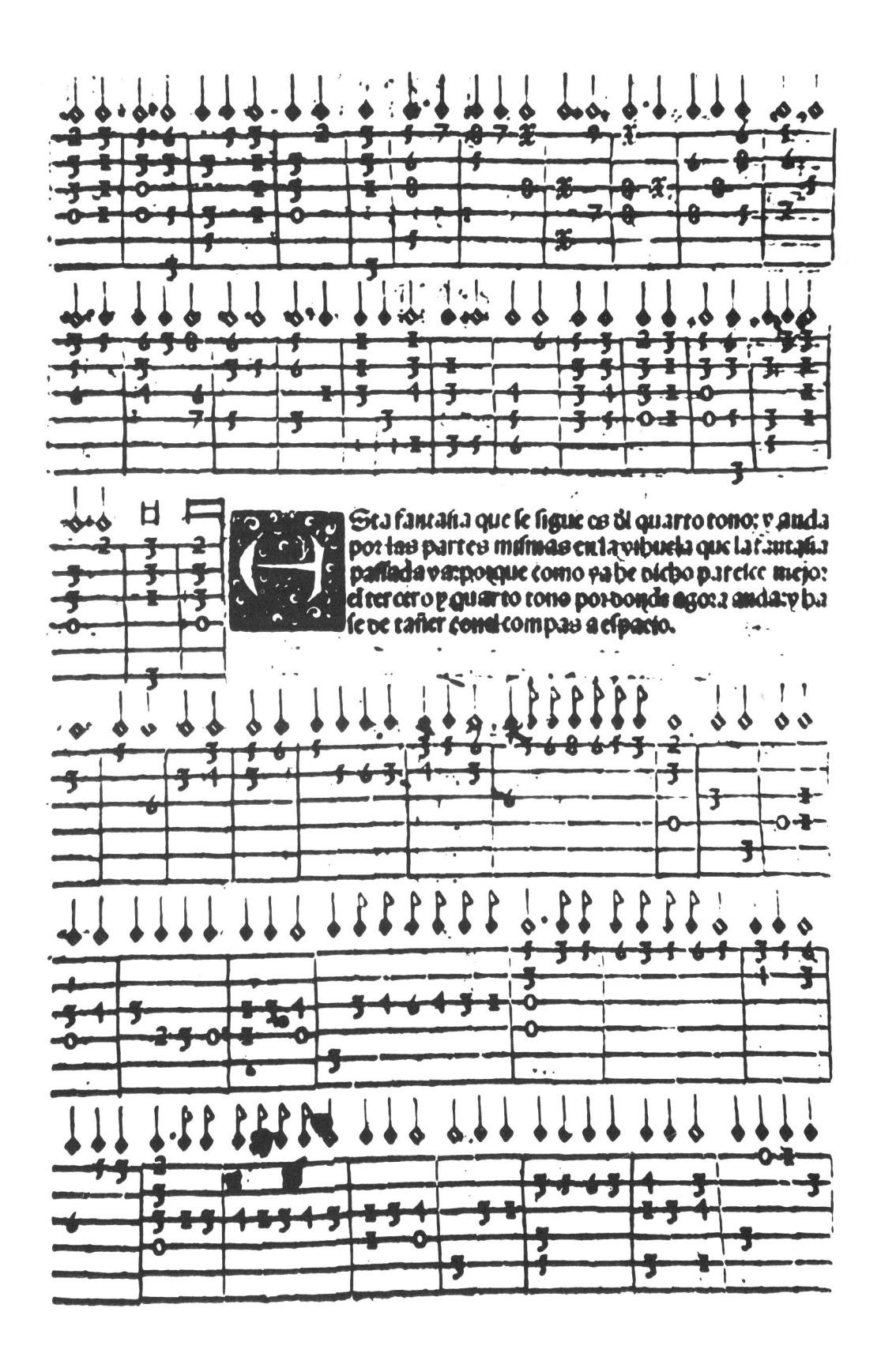

Esta fantasia que se sigue es del quarto tono: y anda por las partes mismas en la vihuela que la fantasia passada va: porque como ya he dicho pareçe mejor el tercero y quarto tono por donde agora anda: y hase de tañer con el compas a espacio.

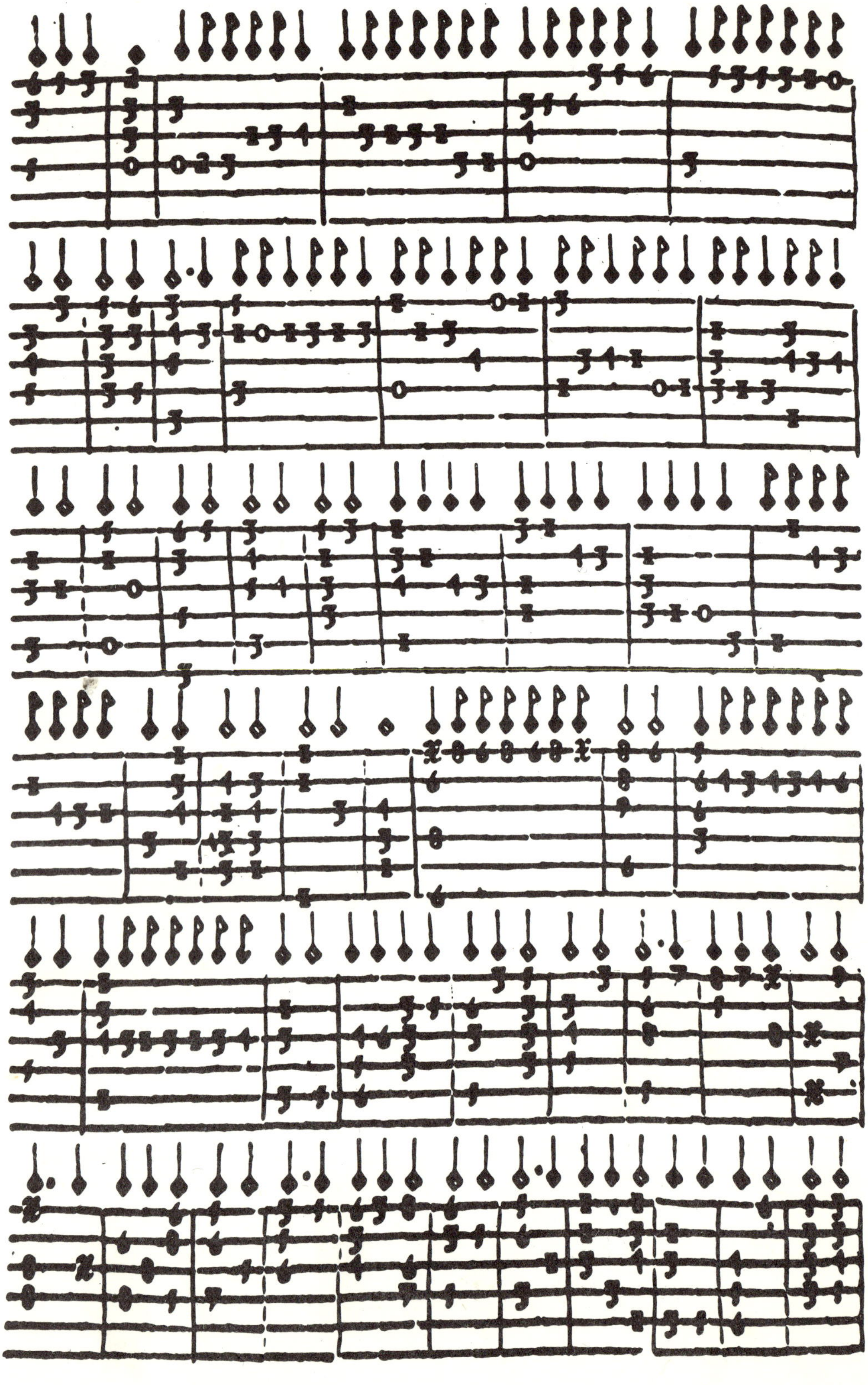

1. FANTASIA NO. 1 in Tone I (Fol. B^v)

Molto Allegro

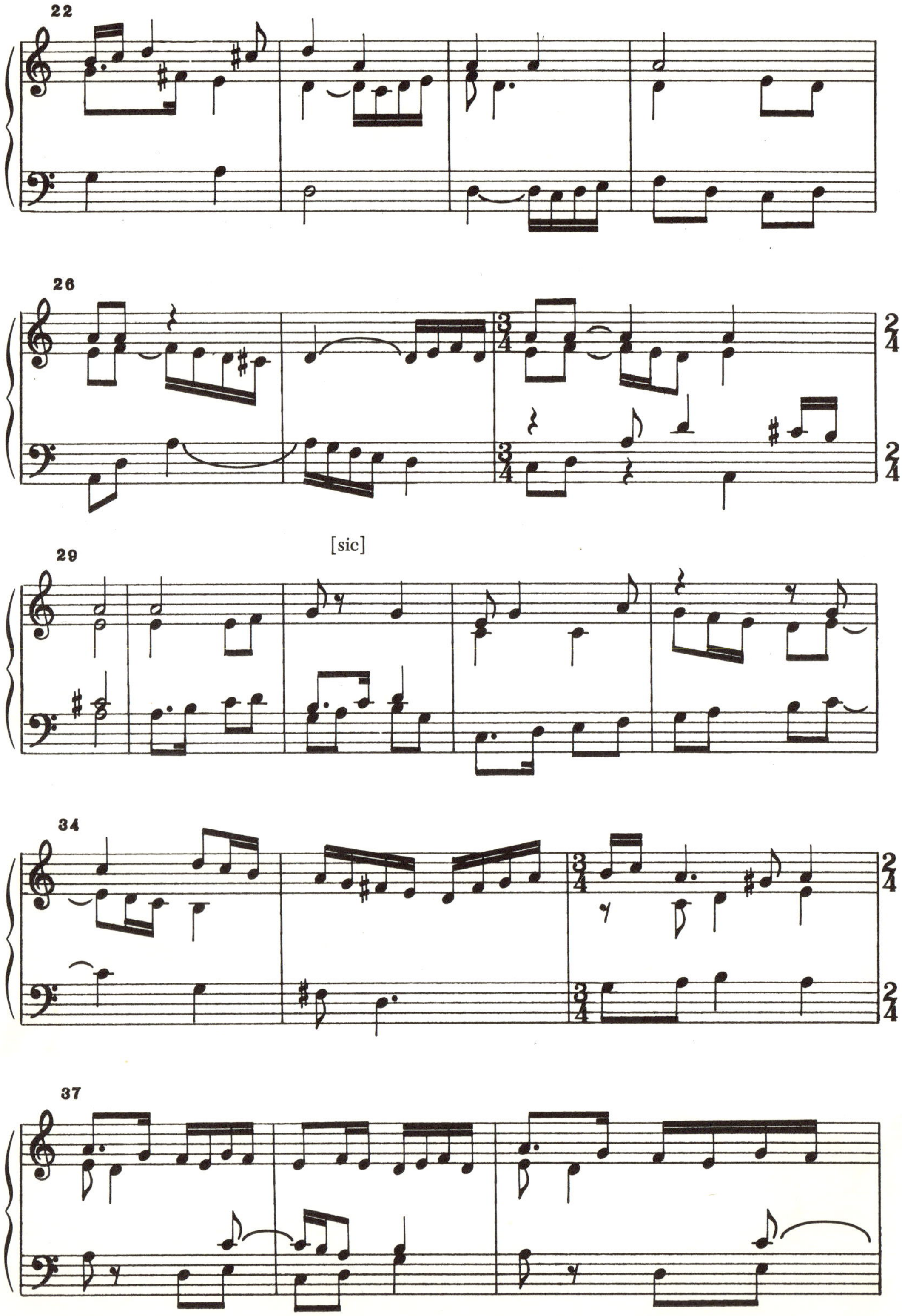
22
26
29
[sic]
34
37

2. FANTASIA NO. 2 in Tone I (Fol. B ii^v)

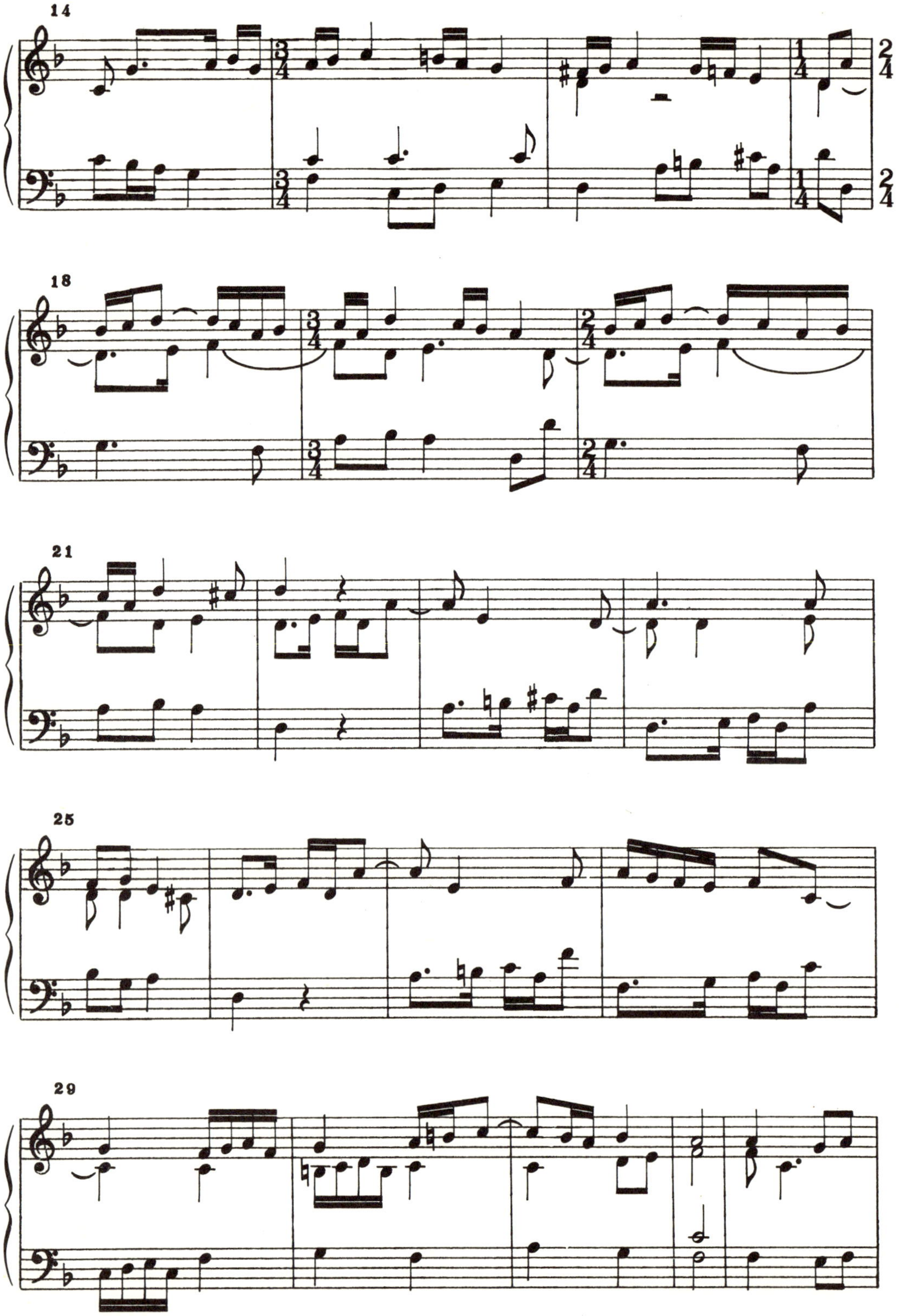
14
18
21
25
29

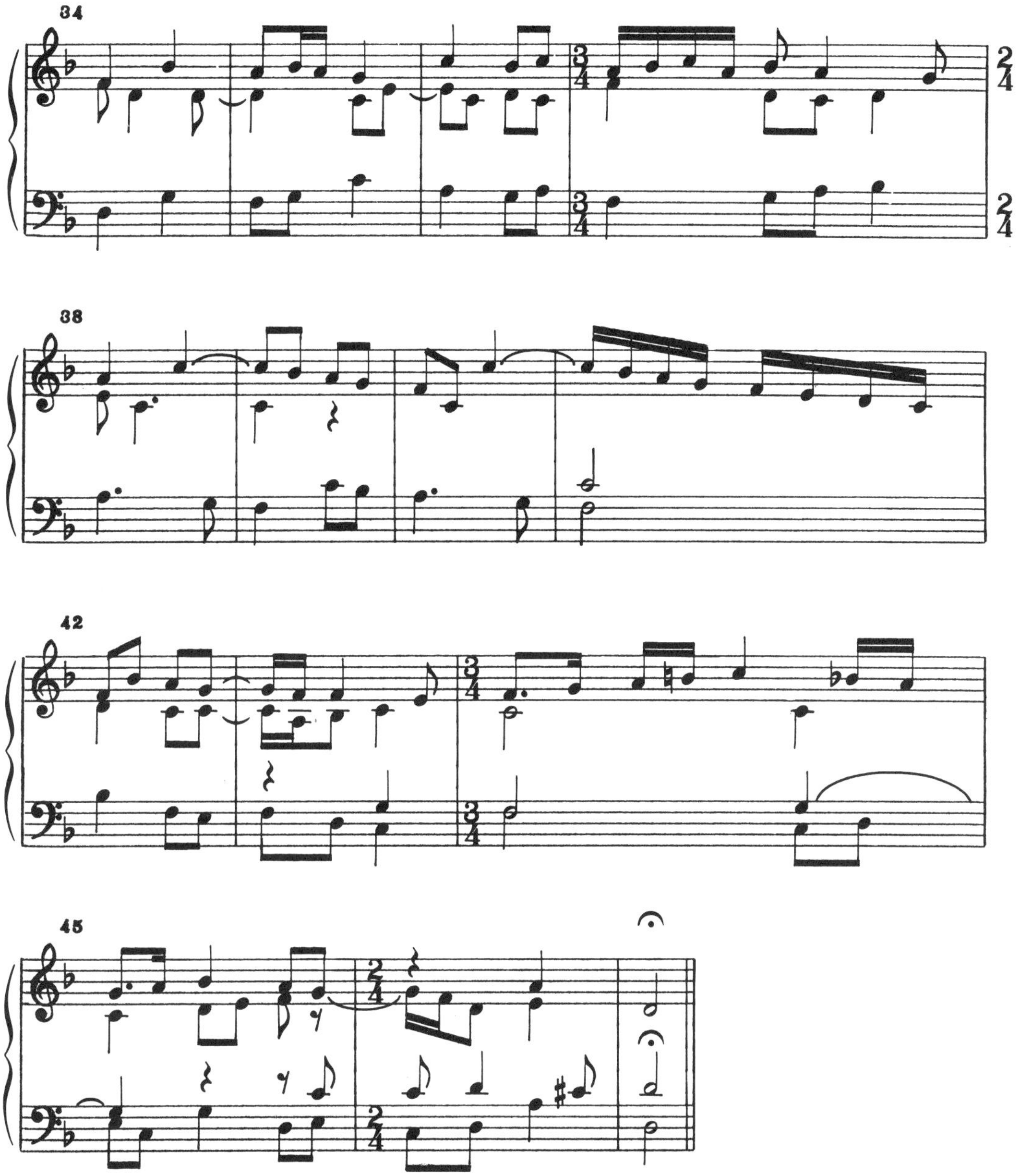
34
38
42
45

3. FANTASIA NO. 3 in Tone I (Fol. B iii^v)

Allegro Moderato

39

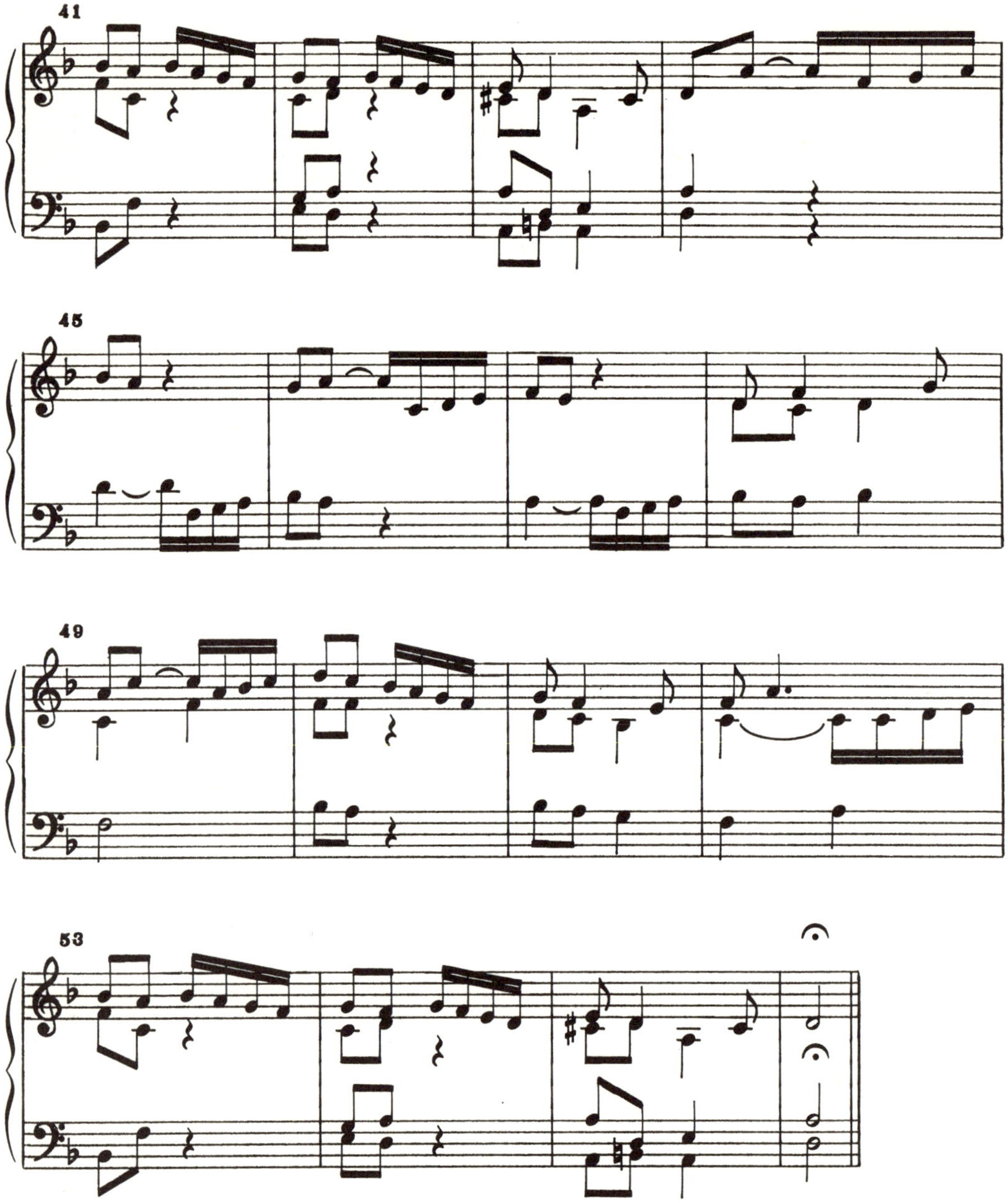
41
45
49
53

4. FANTASIA NO. 4 in Tone II (Fol. [B v^r])

Allegro

5. FANTASIA NO. 5 in Tone II (Fol. [B vi^r])

Allegro

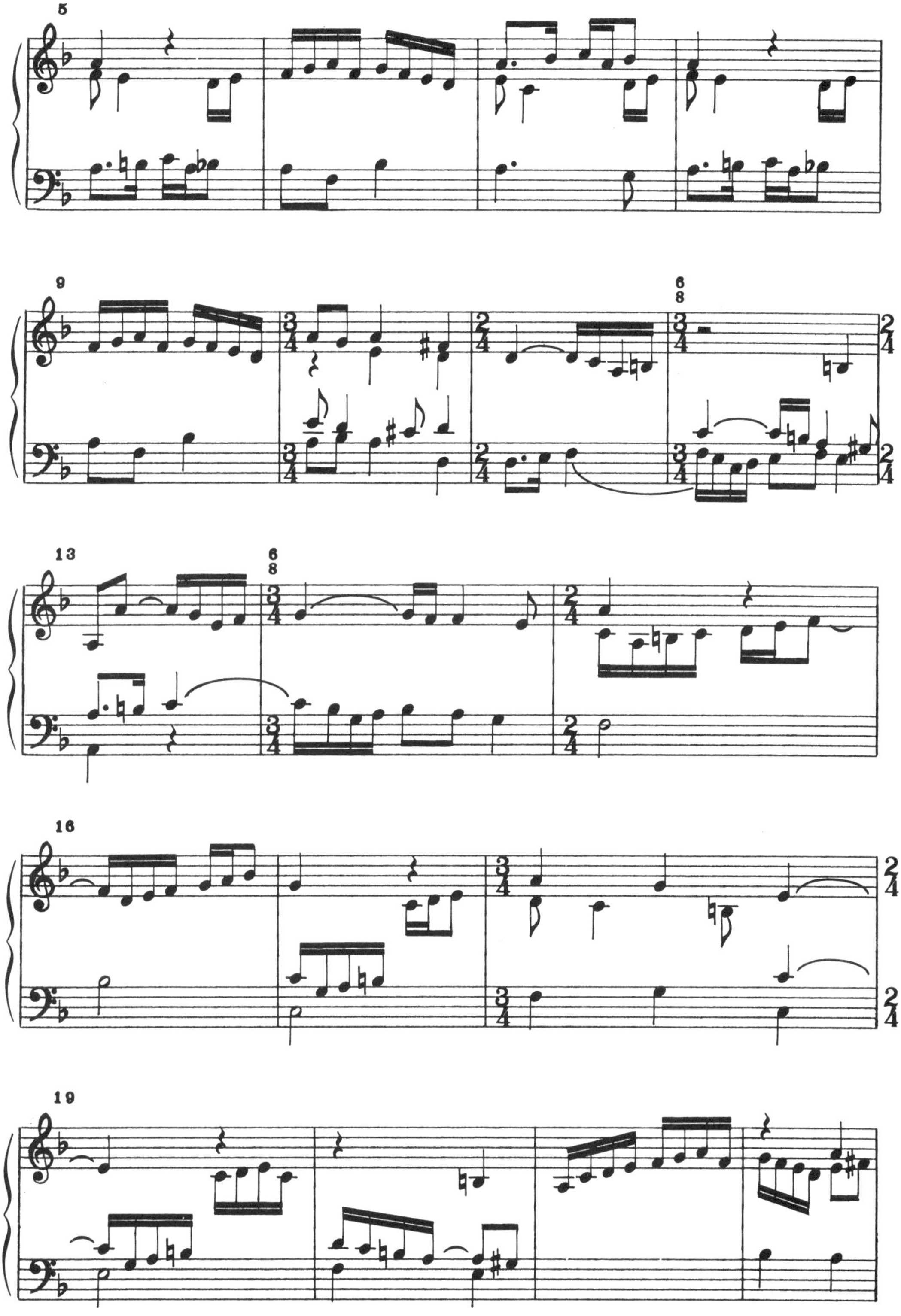
5
9
13
16
19

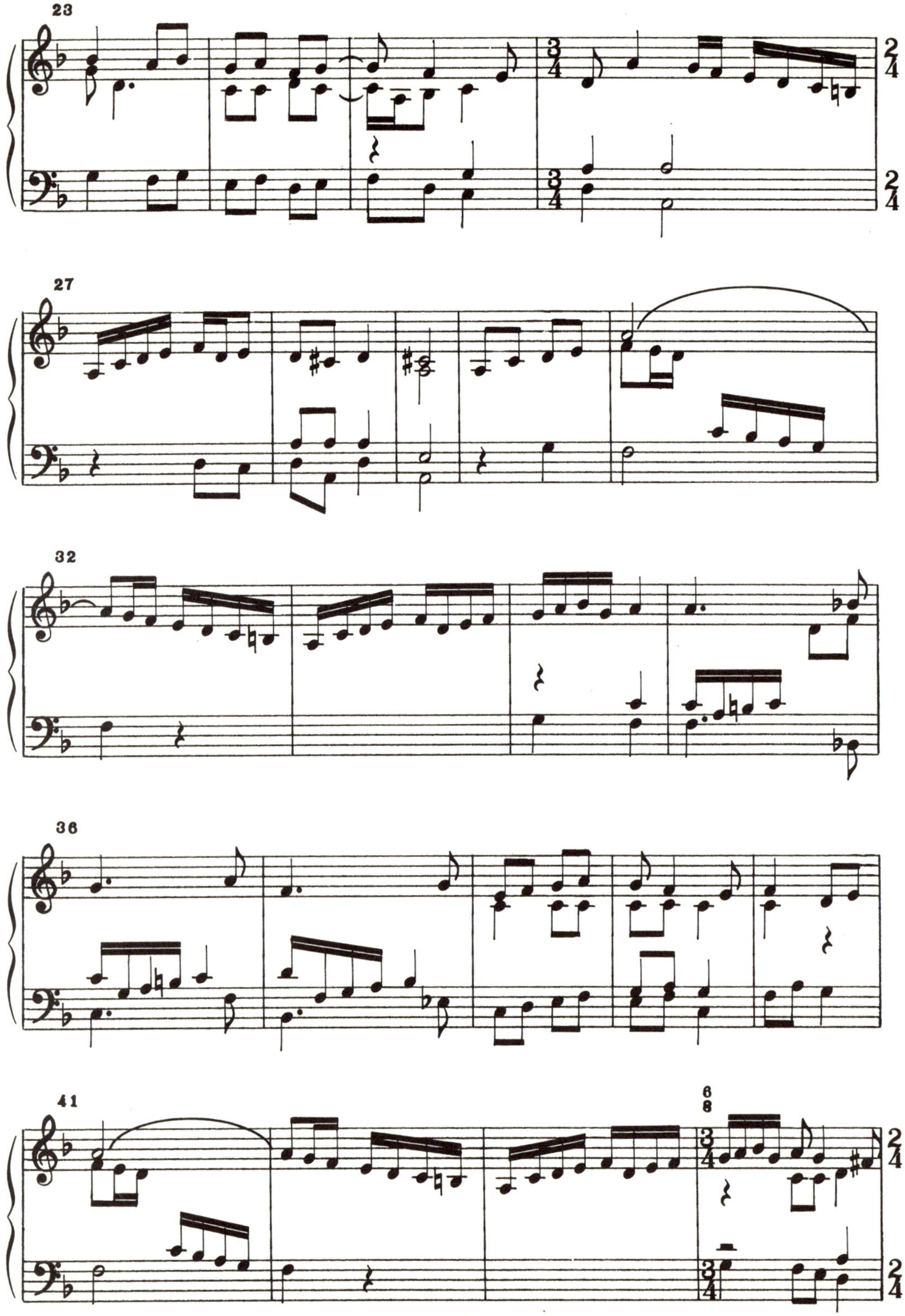
23
27
32
36
41

6. FANTASIA NO. 6 in Tones I and II (Fol. Cᵛ)

[Allegro]

46

47

✱ To be played on Courses 3 and 4 (i.e., strings tuned to g and b).

7. FANTASIA NO. 7 in Tone III (Fol. C iii^r)

Molto Allegro

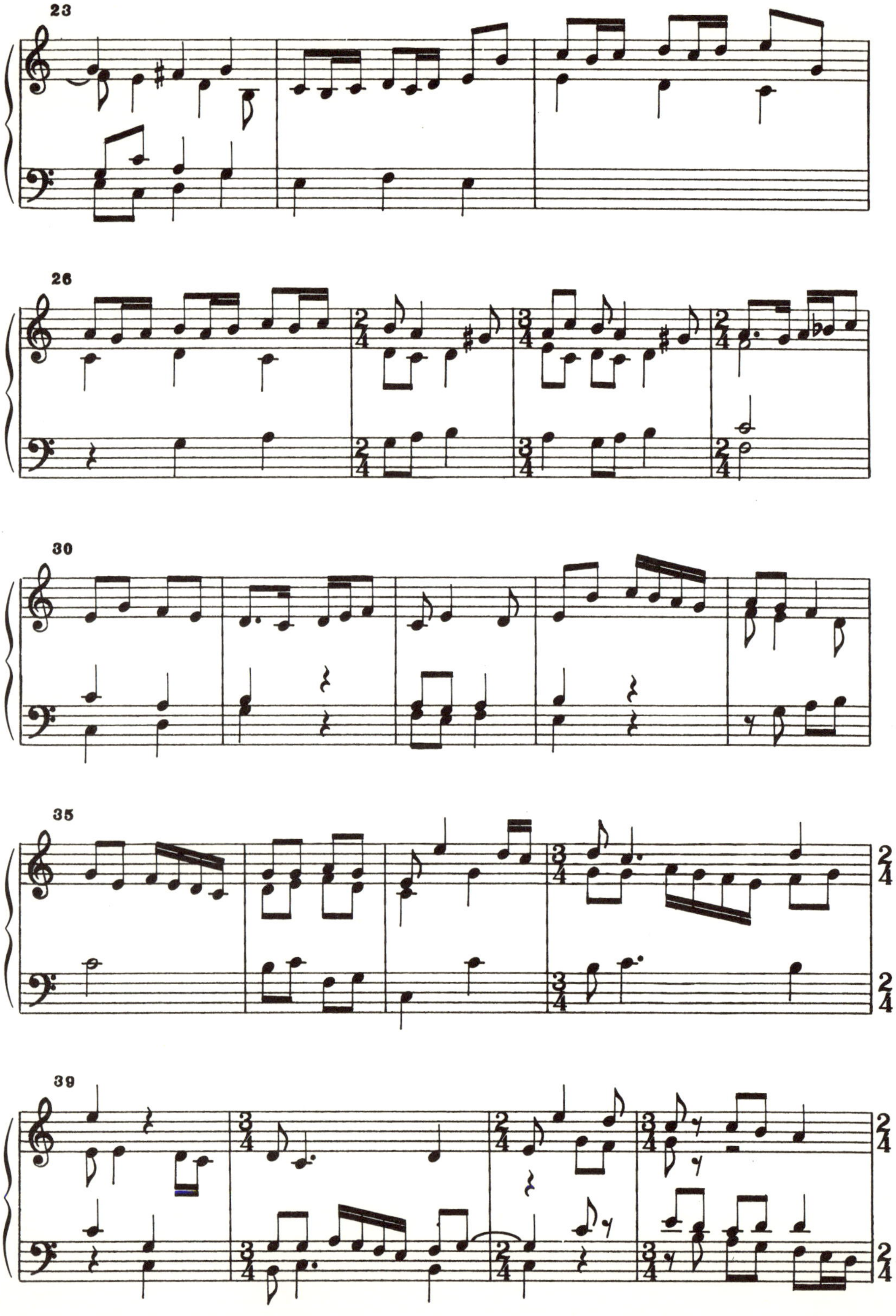
23
26
30
35
39

8. FANTASIA NO. 8 in Tone IV (Fol. [C iv^v])

Allegro

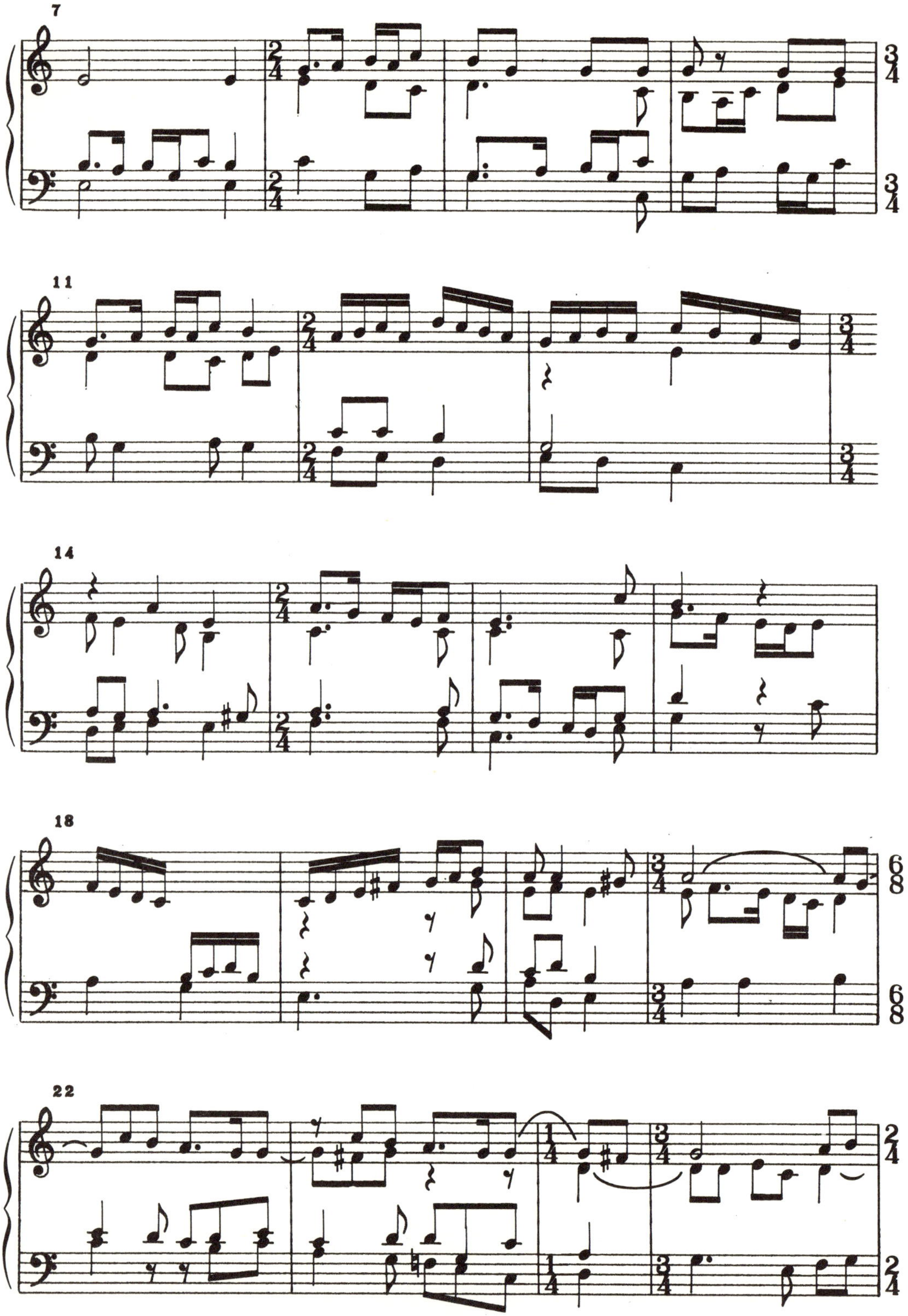
7
11
14
18
22

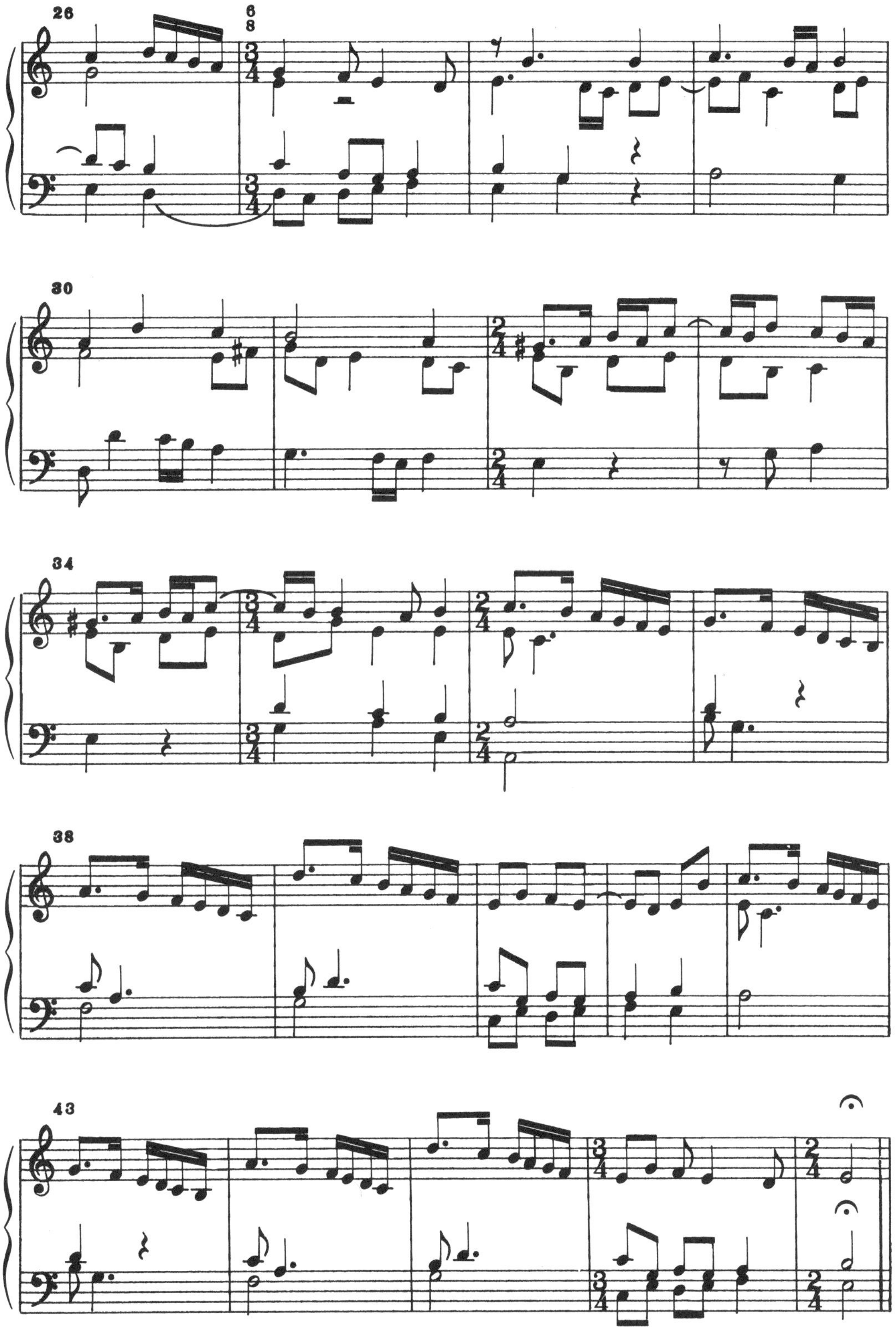
26
30
34
38
43

9. FANTASIA NO. 9 in Tones III and IV (Fol. [C v^v])

Allegro

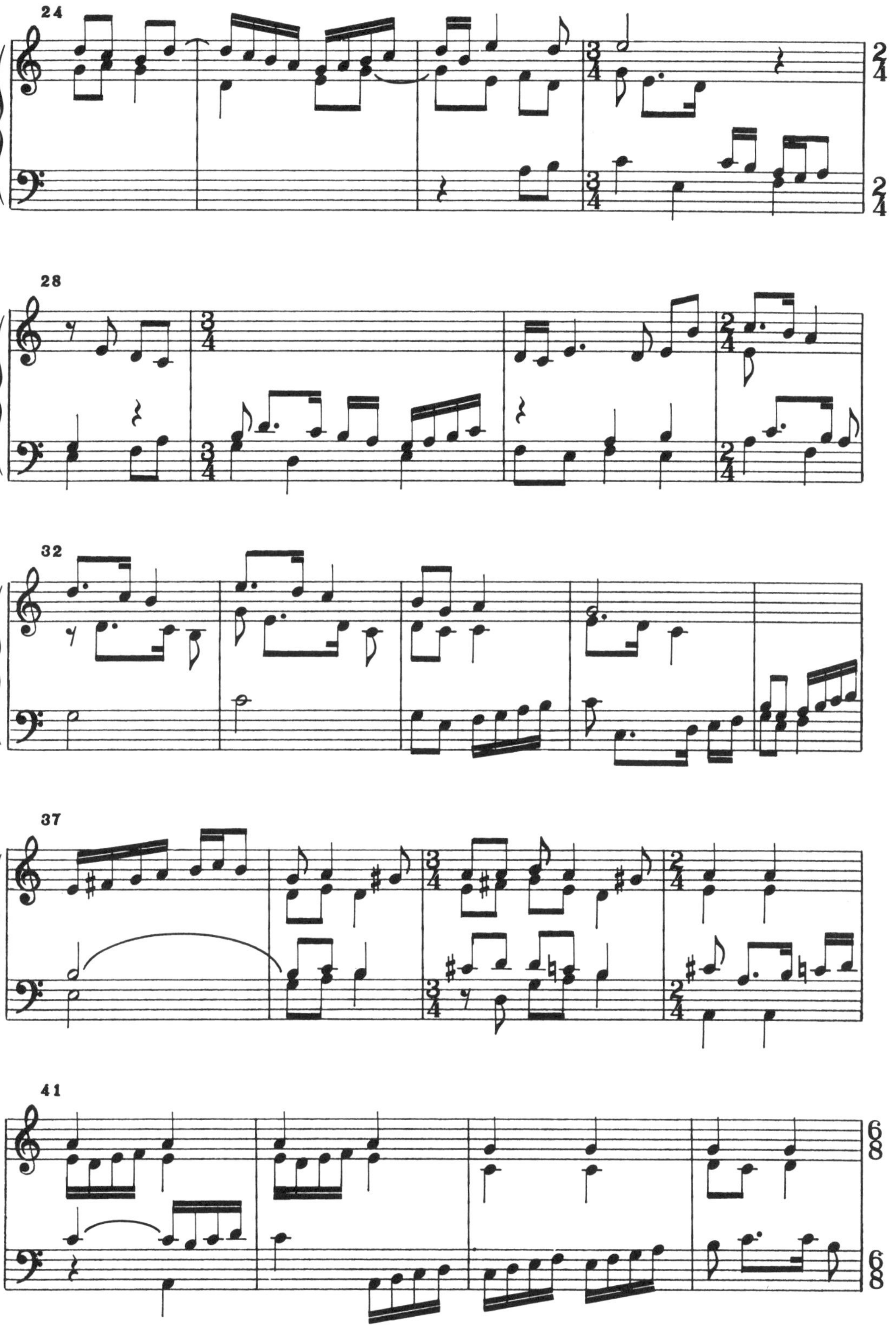
24
28
32
37
41

56

10. FANTASIA NO. 10 in Tones I and II (Fol. Dᵛ)

Moderato e Rubato

58

11. FANTASIA NO. 11 in Tones I and II (Fol. D ii^{iv})

Moderato e Rubato

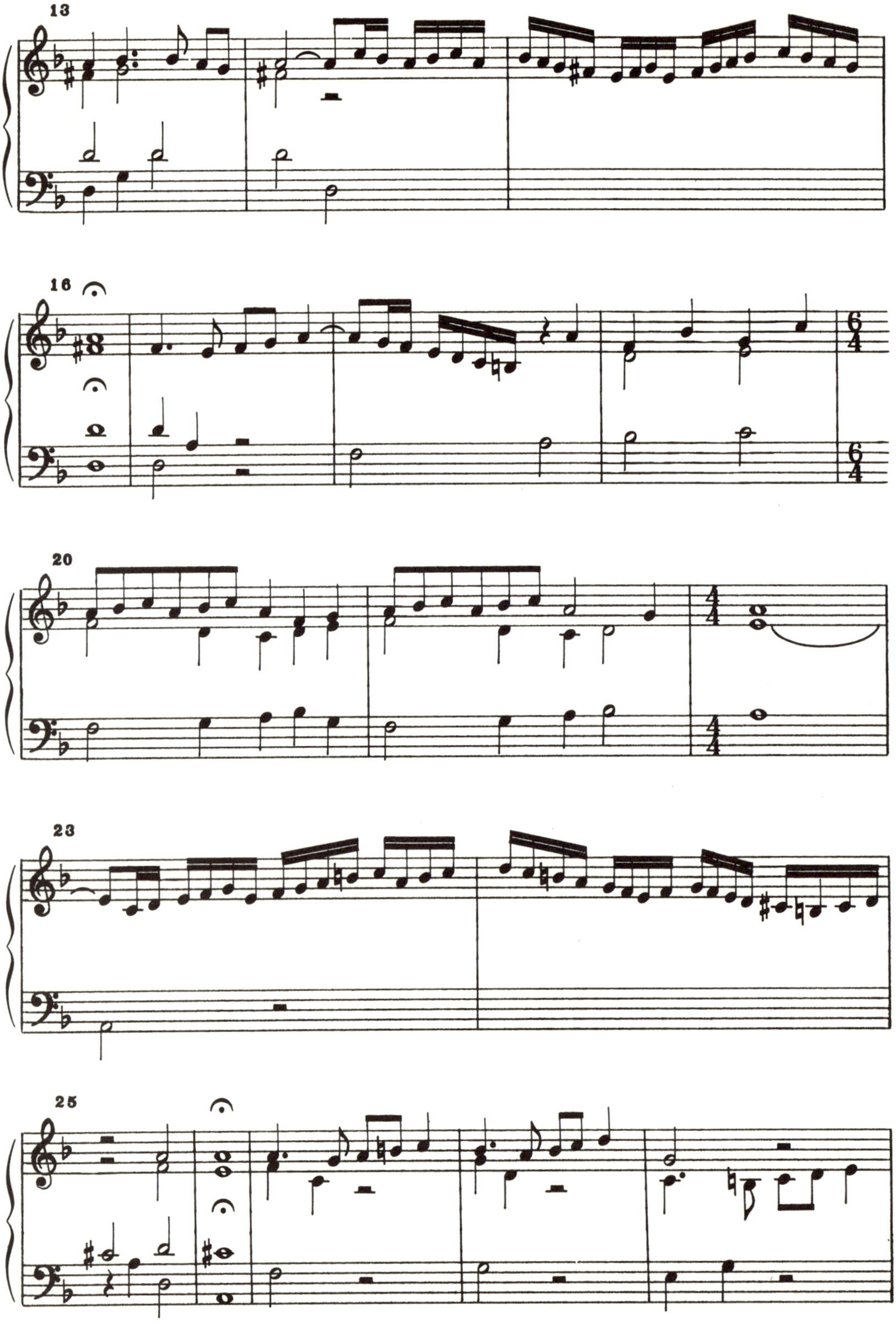
13
16
20
23
25

61

12. FANTASIA NO. 12 in Tones III and IV (Fol. [D iv^r])

Moderato e Rubato

[sic]

63

64

13. FANTASIA NO. 13 in Tone I (Fol. [D vʳ])

Moderato e Rubato

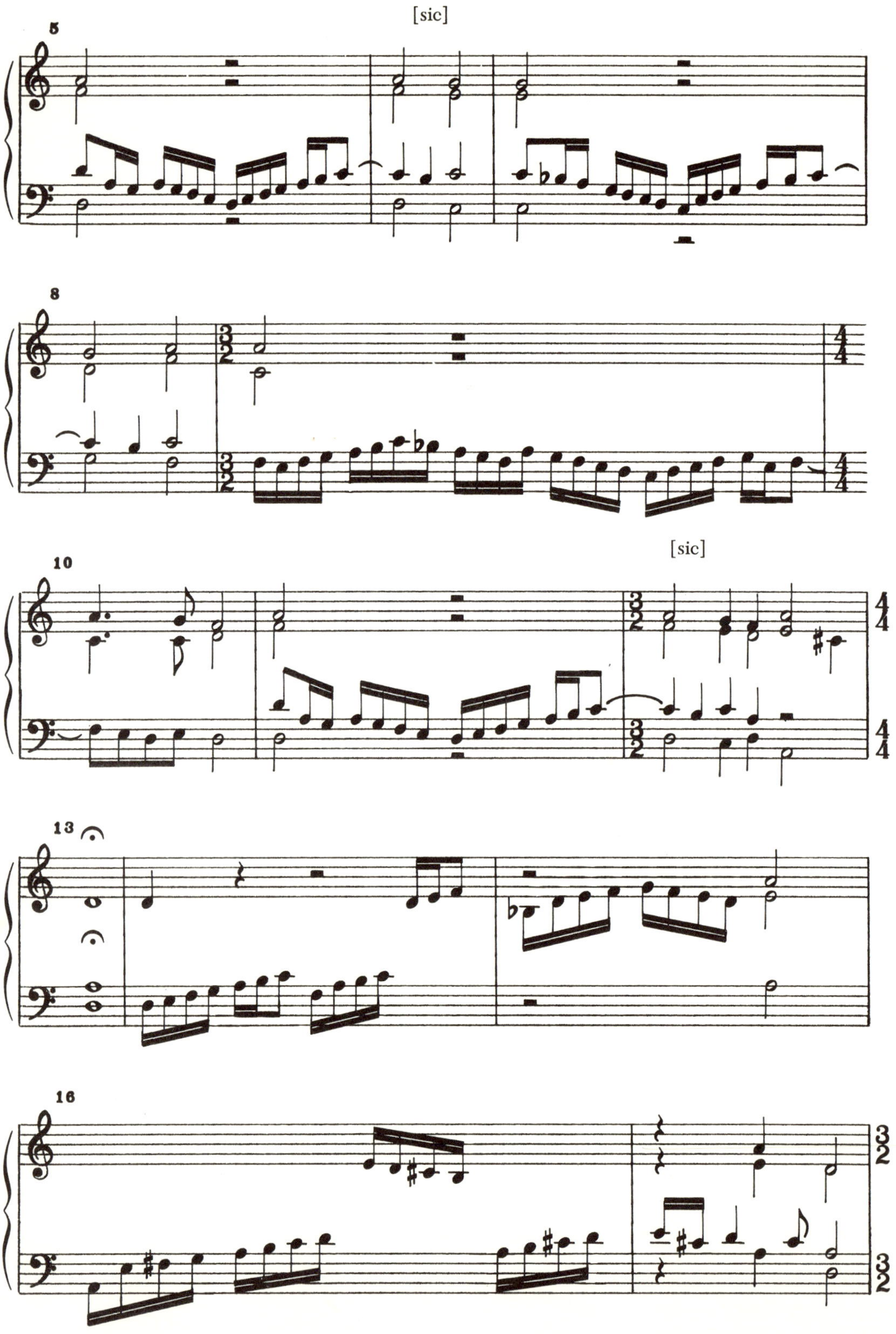
[sic]
5
8
10
[sic]
13
16

67

14. FANTASIA NO. 14 in Tones III and IV (Fol. [D vi^r])

Moderato e Rubato

15. FANTASIA NO. 15 in Tones V and VI (Fol. E^r)

Moderato e Rubato

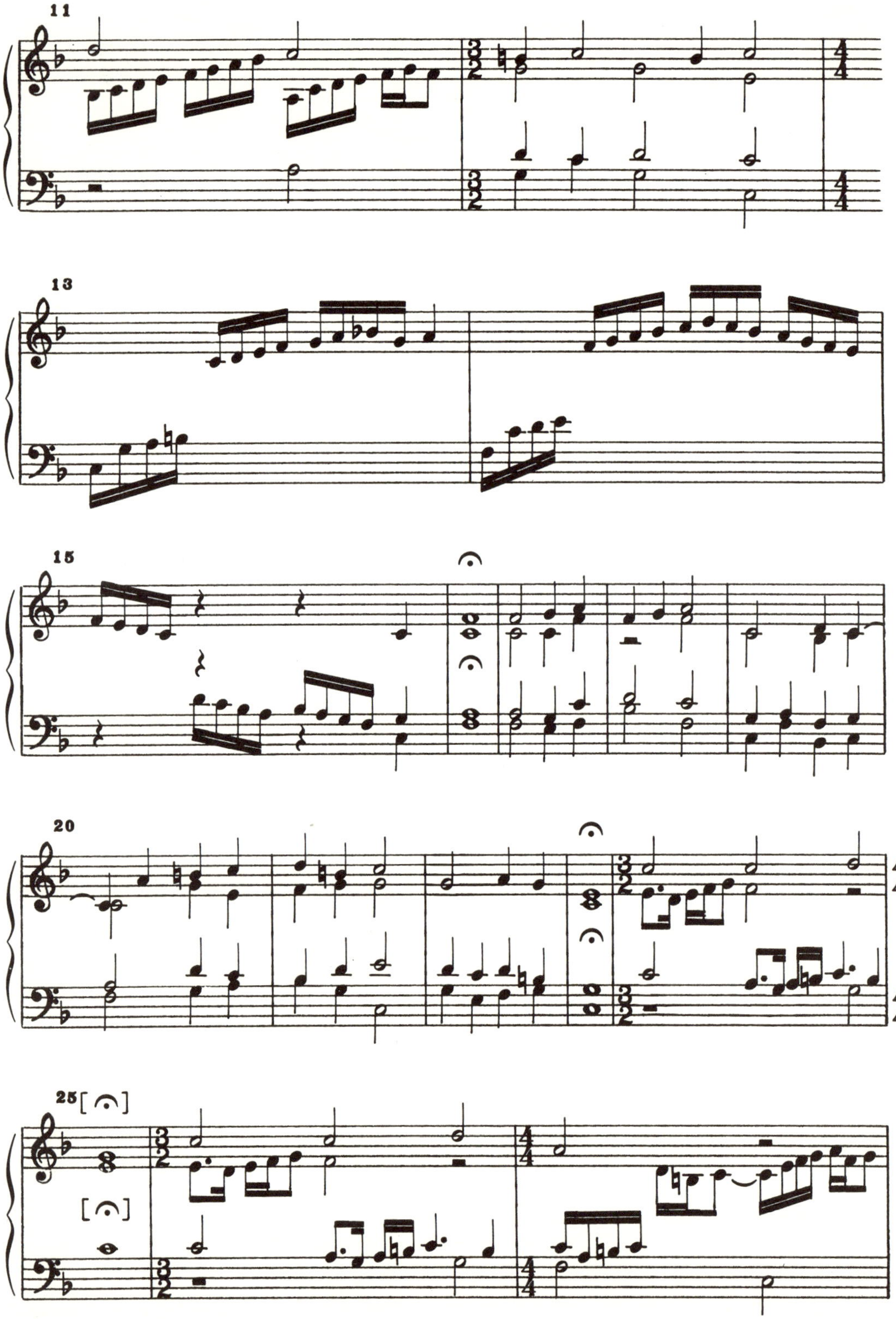
11
13
15
20
25

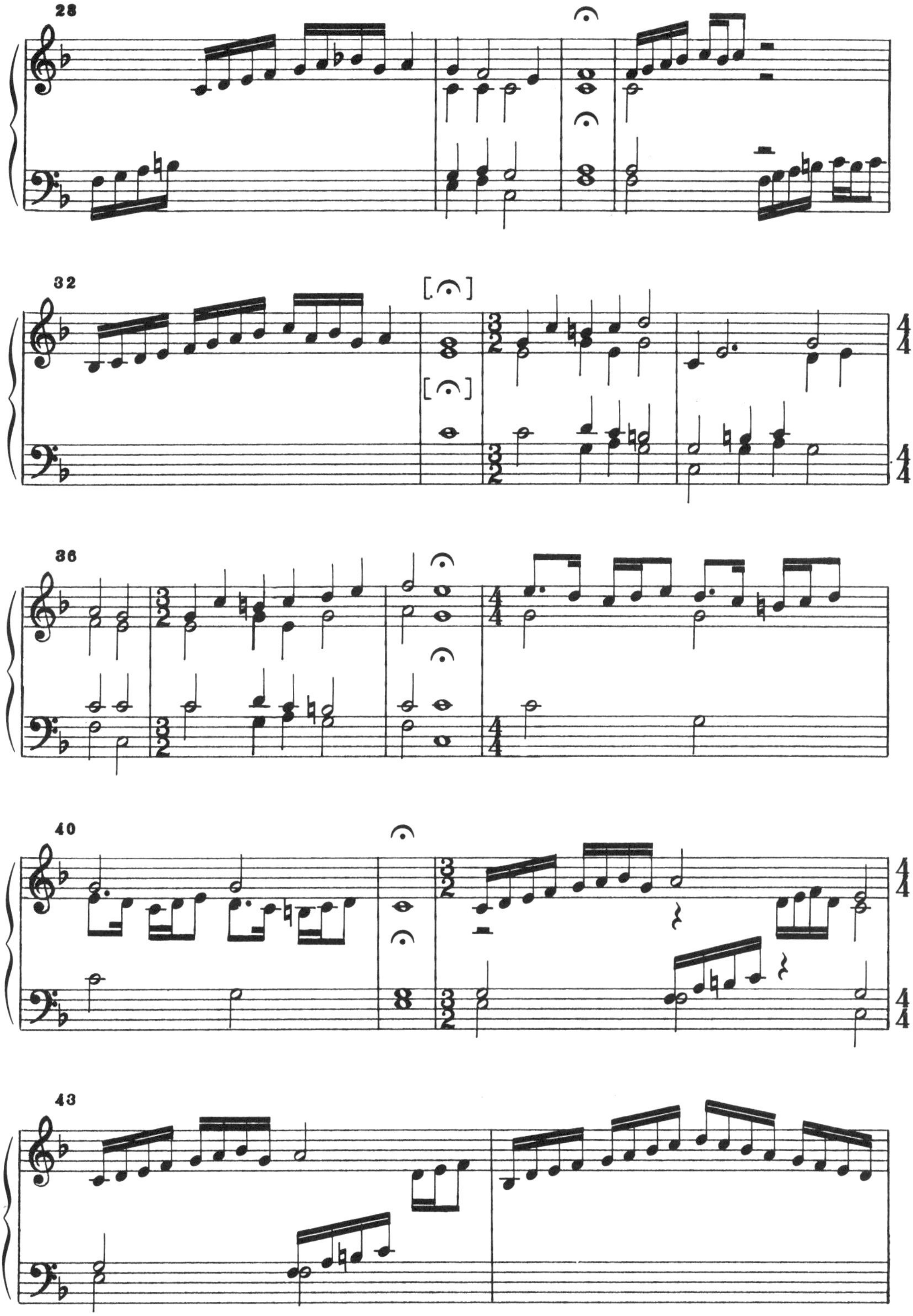
28
32
36
40
43

72

16. FANTASIA NO. 16 in Tones V and VI (Fol. E ii^v)

Moderato e Rubato

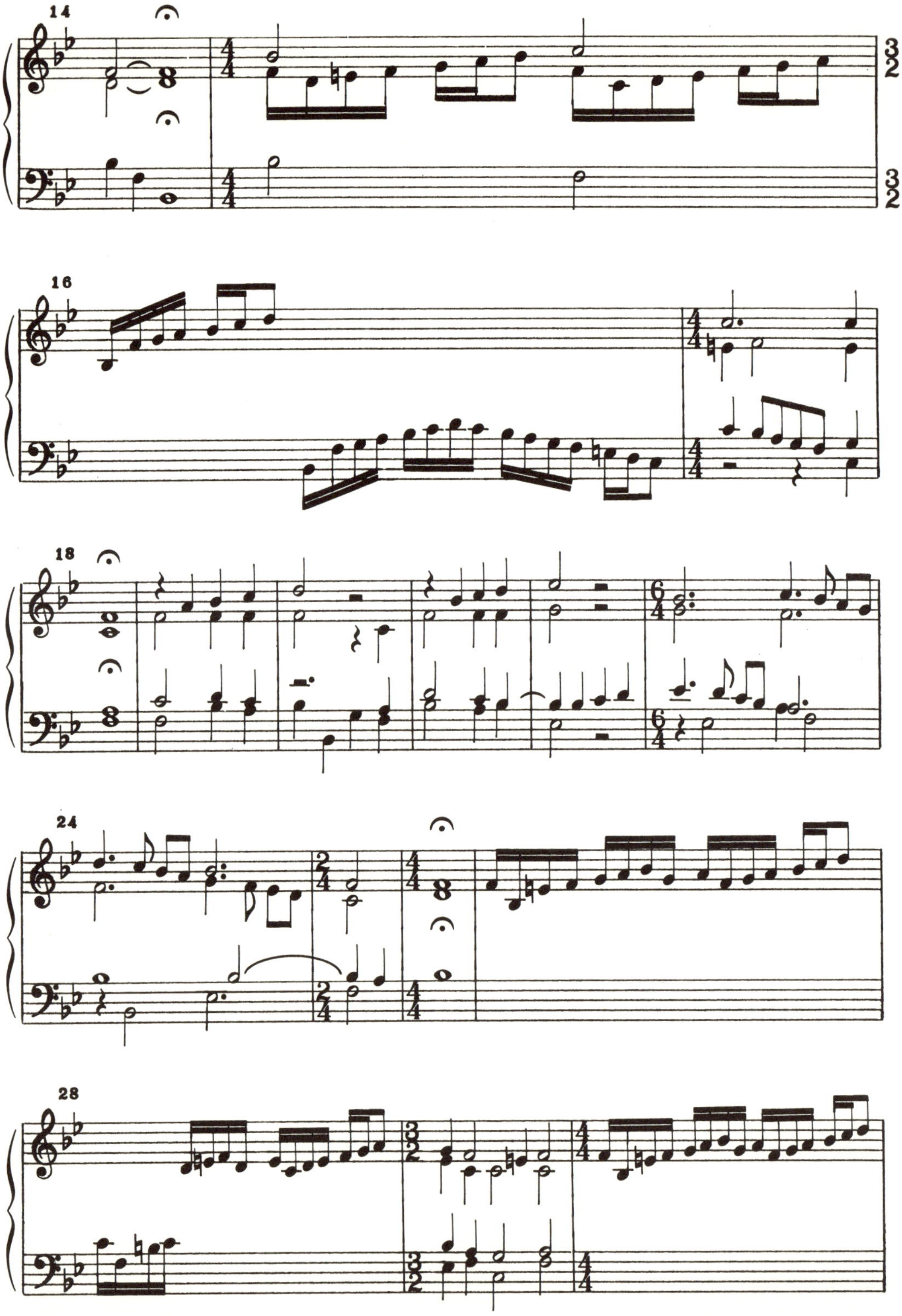
14
16
18
24
28

75

17. FANTASIA NO. 17 in Tones V and VI (Fol. [E iv^r])

Moderato e Rubato

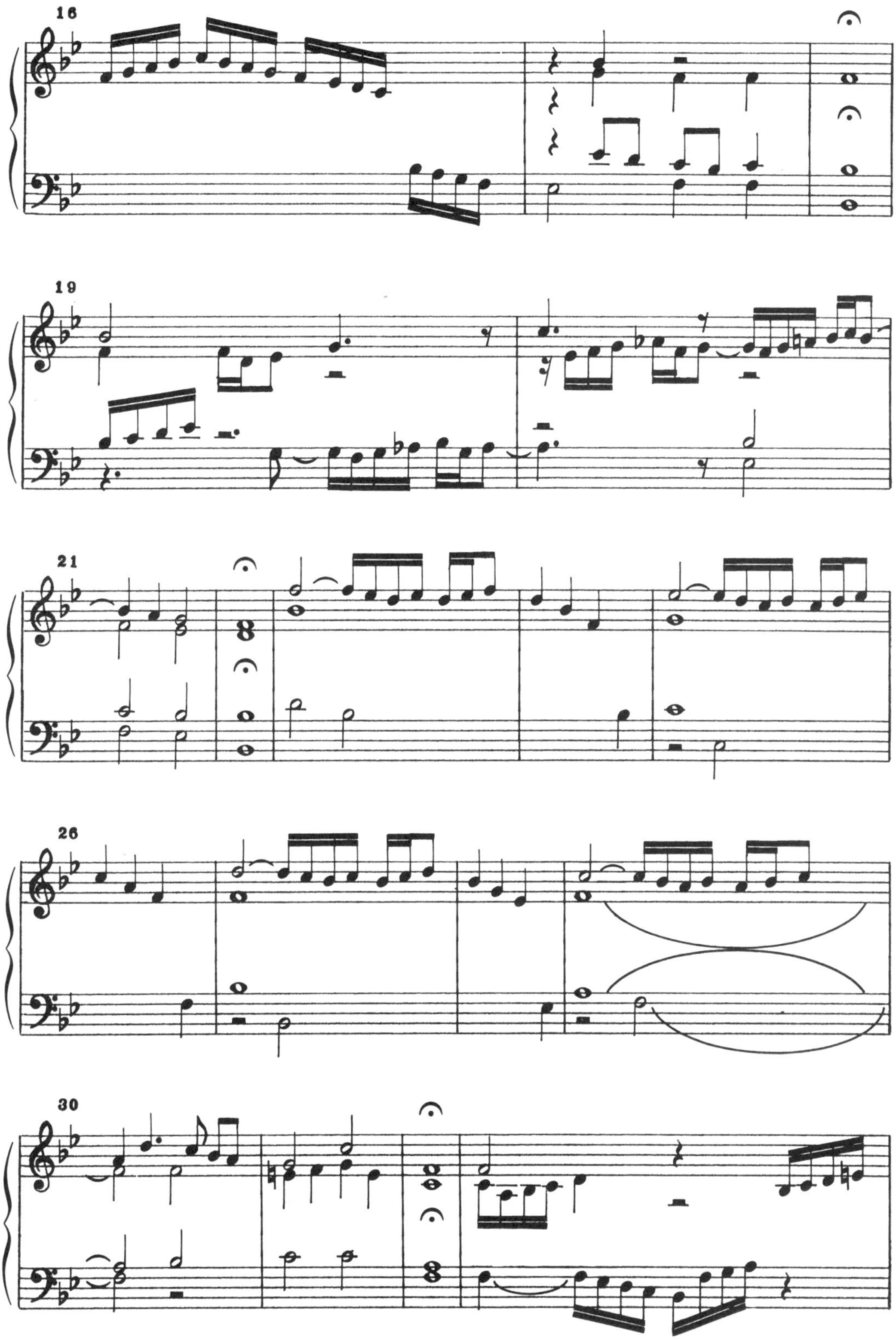

16
19
21
26
30

18. FANTASIA NO. 18 in Tones VII and VIII (Fol. [E v^r])

Moderato e Rubato

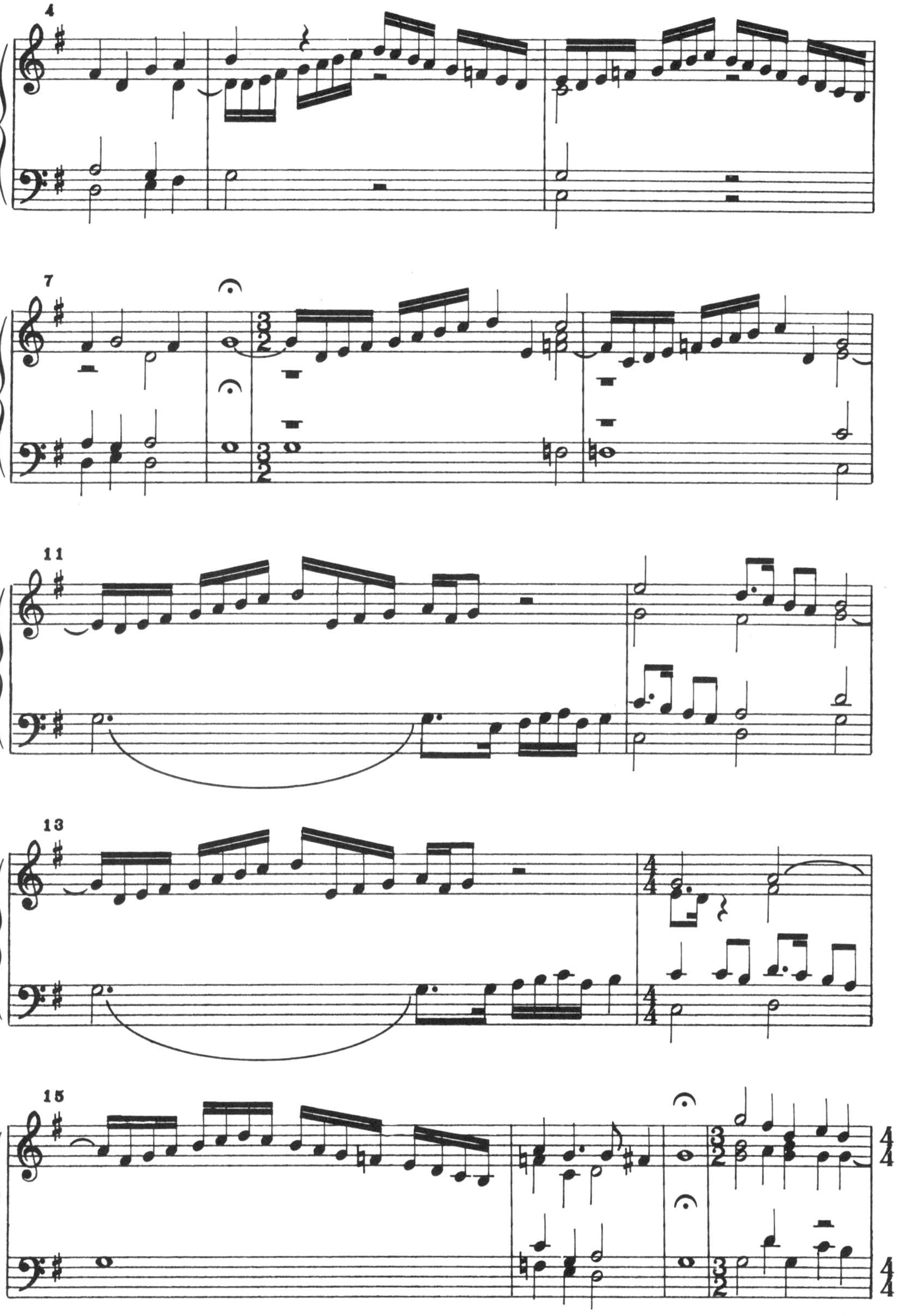
4
7
11
13
15

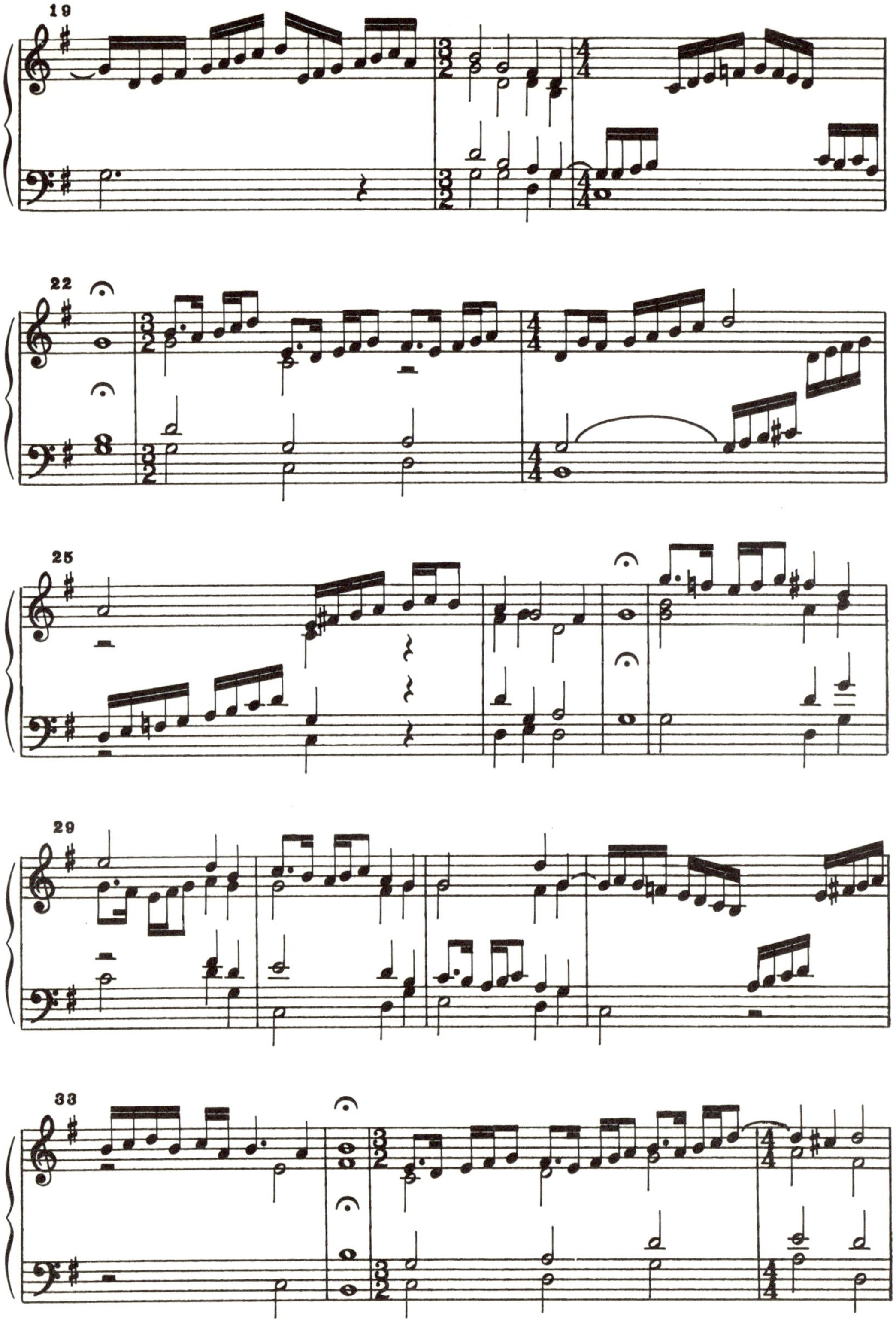
19
22
25
29
33

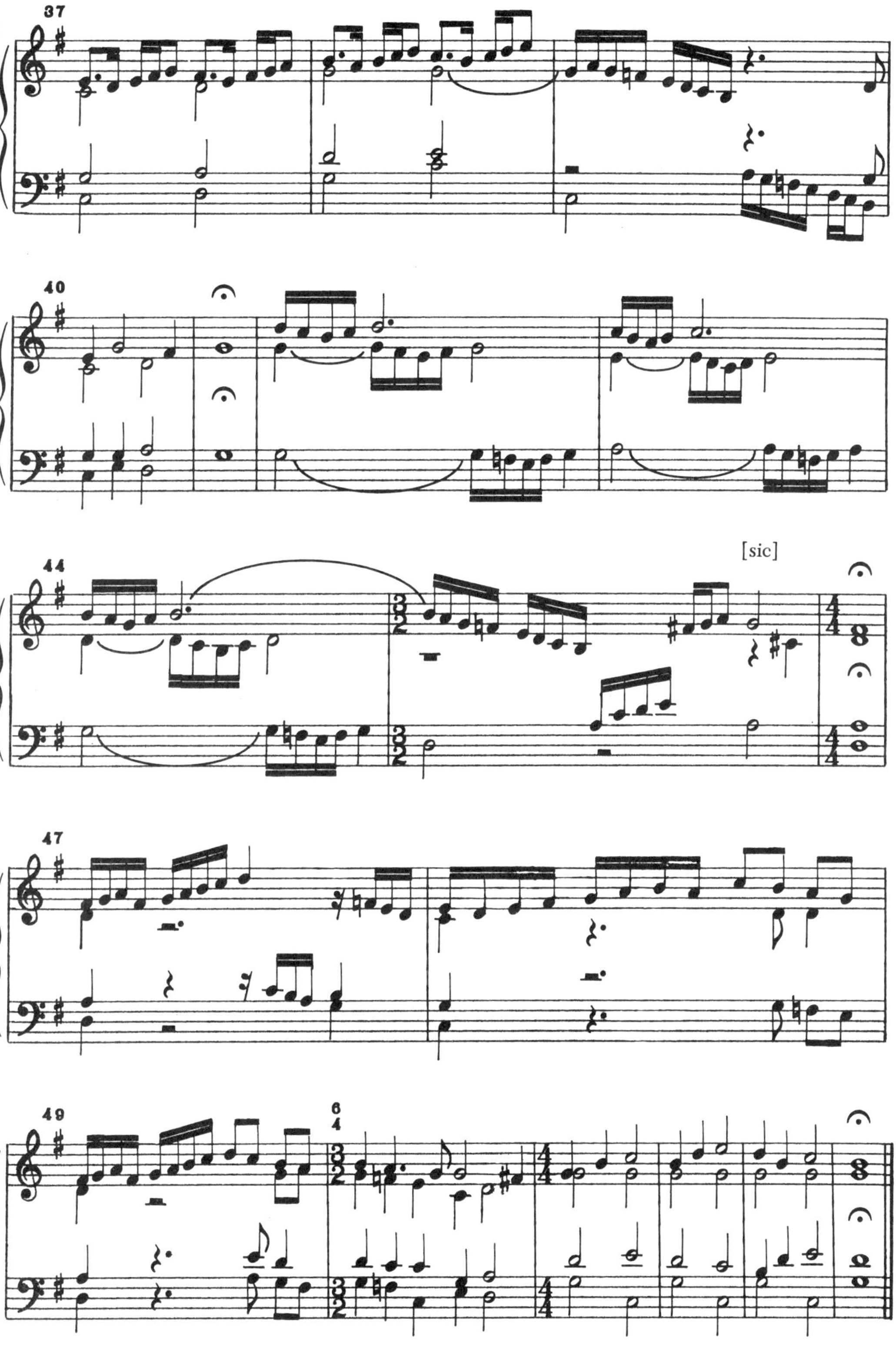
[sic]

19. FANTASIA NO. 19 in Tone V (Fol. F^v)

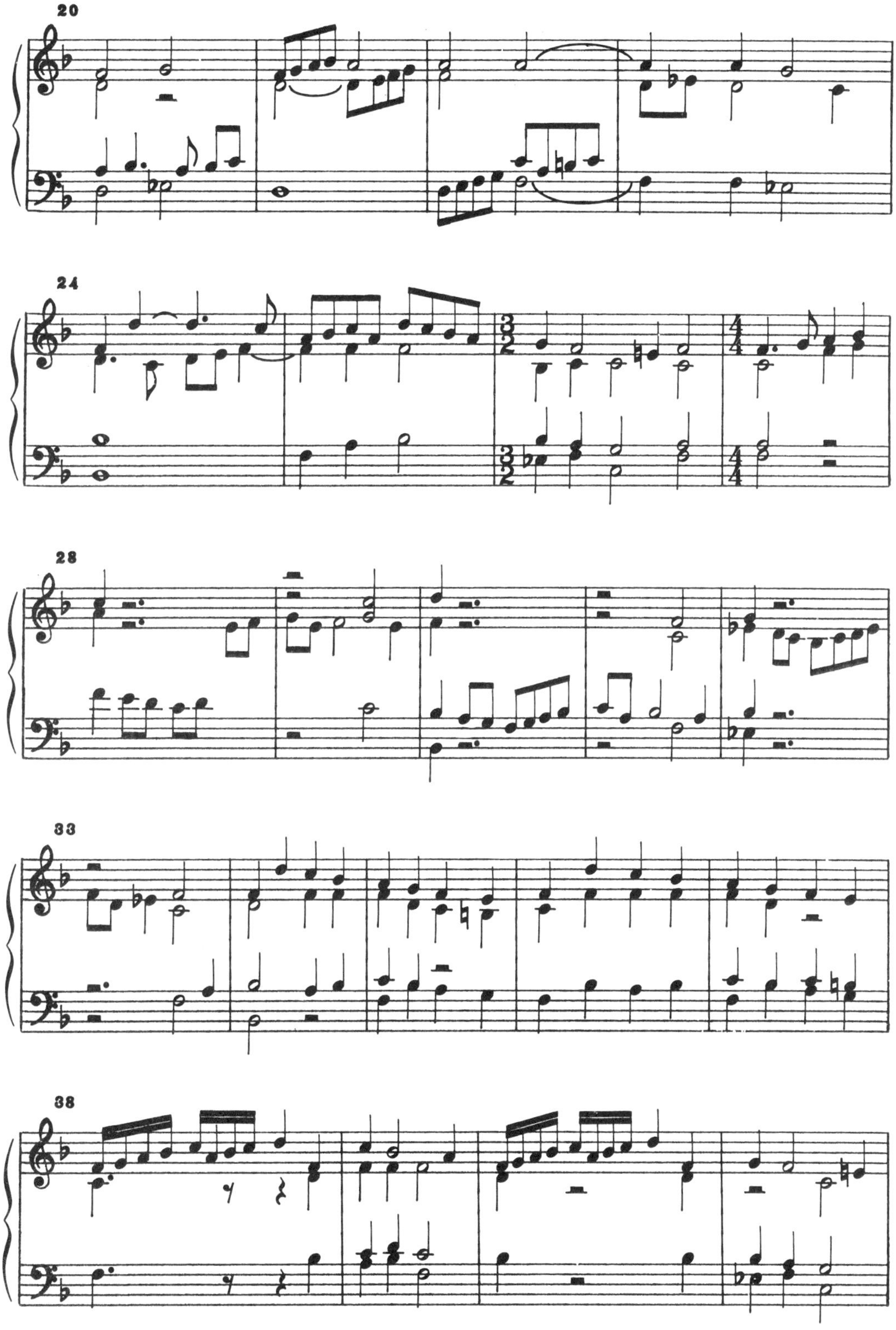
20
24
28
33
38

84

85

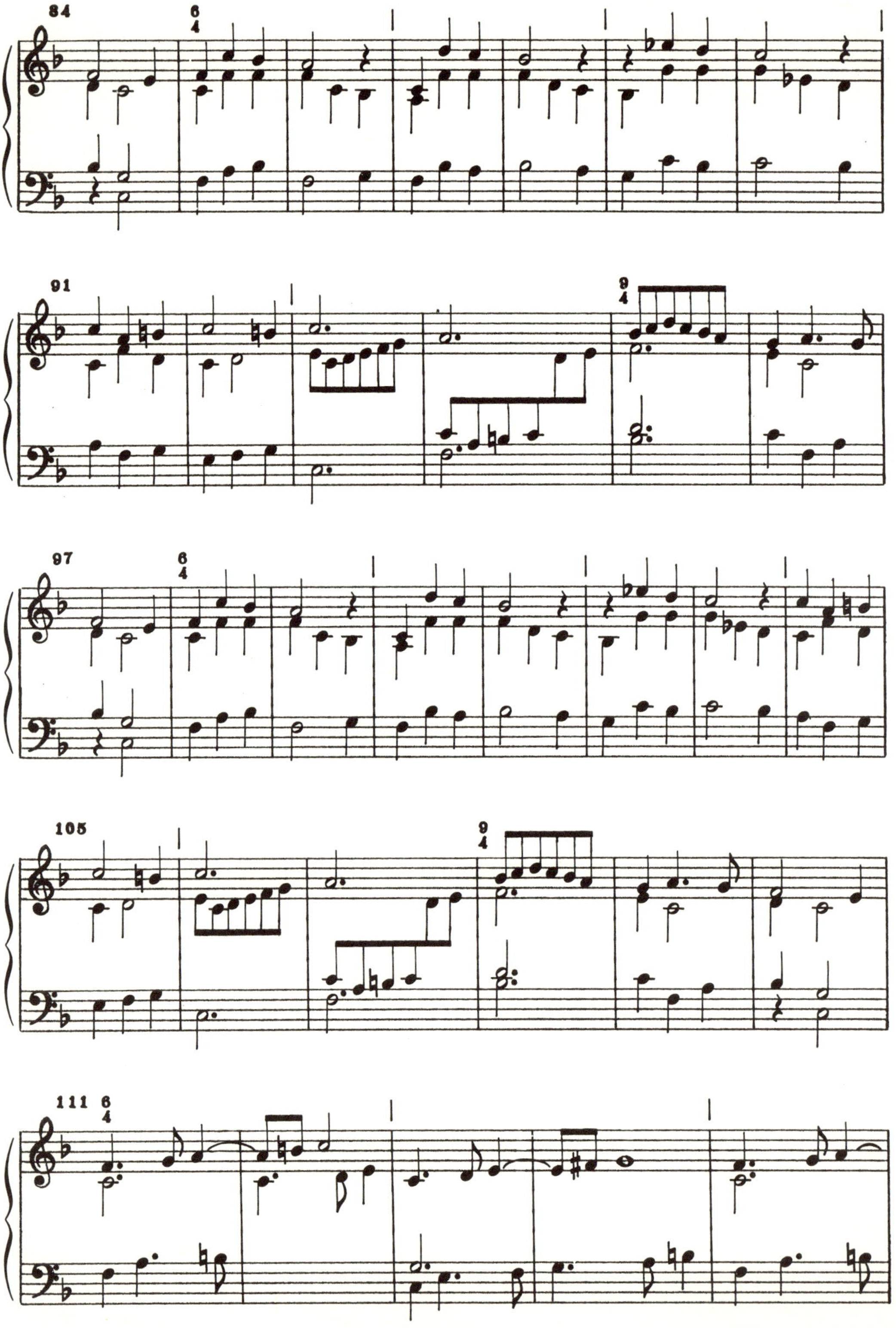
84
6
4
91
9
4
97
6
4
105
9
4
111
6
4

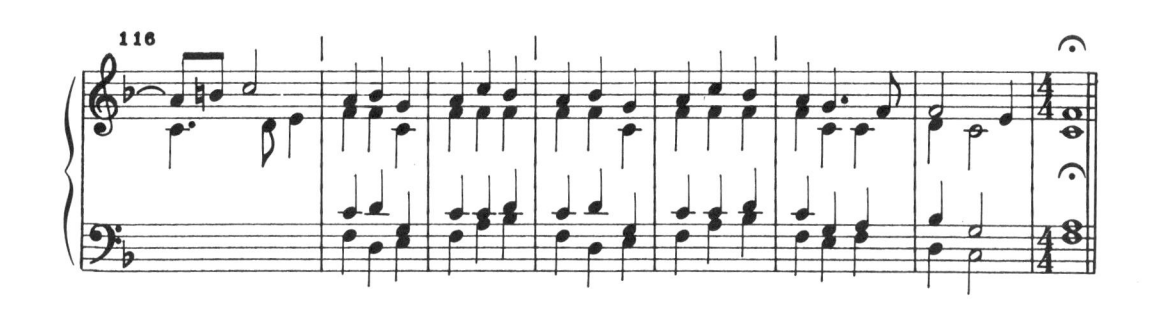

20. FANTASIA NO. 20 in Tone VI (Fol. [F iv^r])

[Moderato]

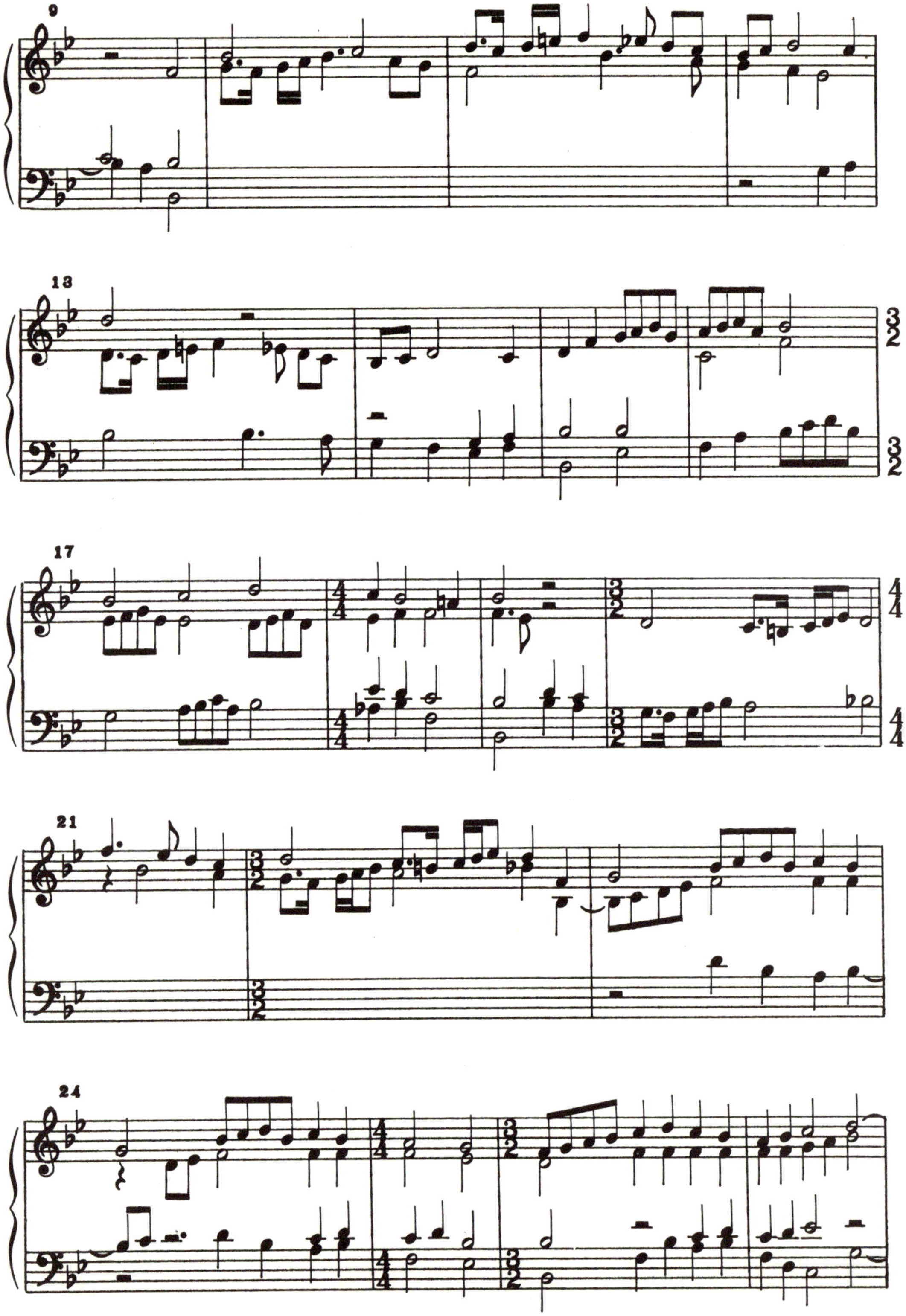
9
13
17
21
24

89

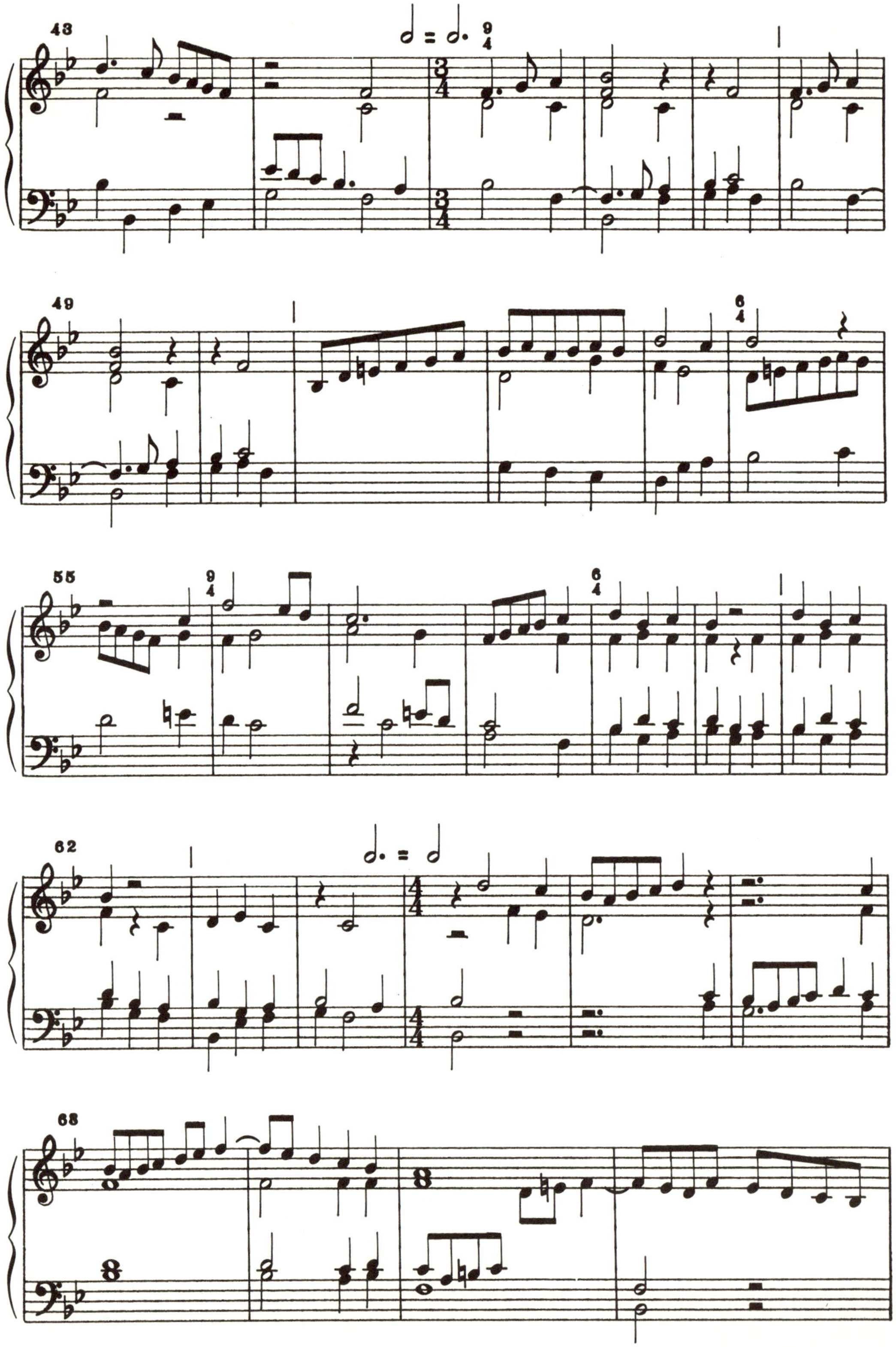
43
49
55
62
68

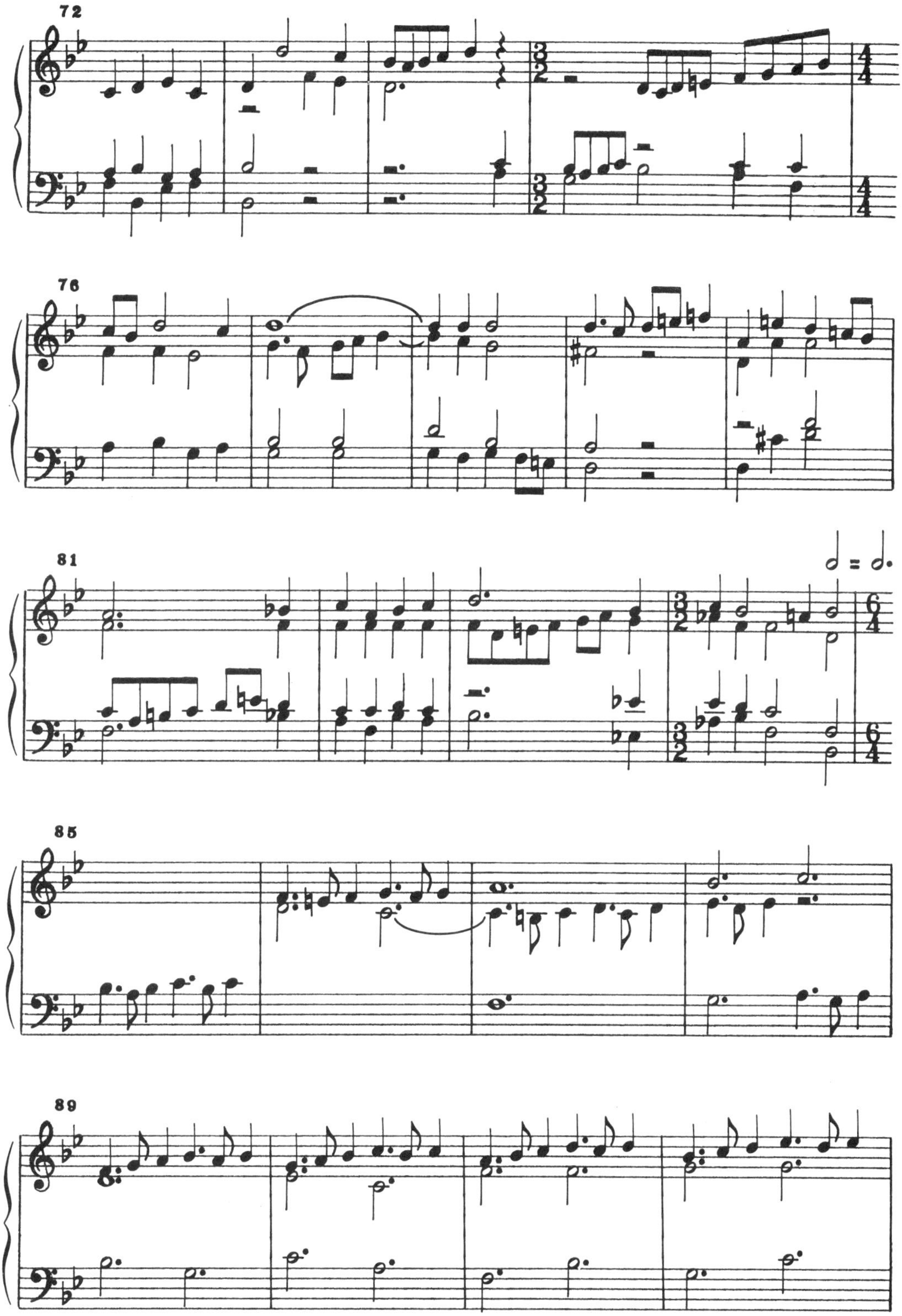
72
76
81
85
89

92

21. FANTASIA NO. 21 in Tone VII (Fol. [F vi^v])

[Moderato]

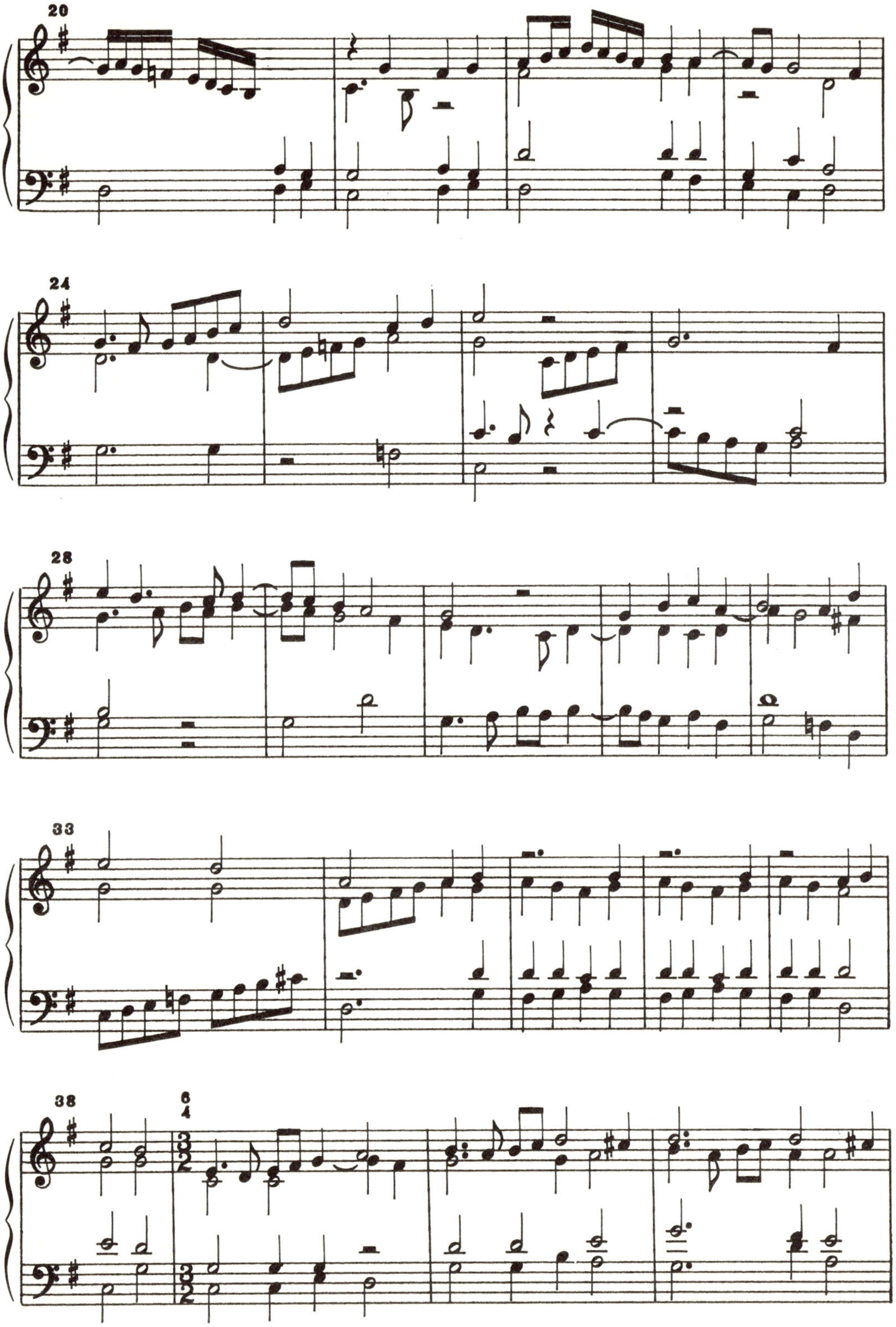
20
24
28
33
38

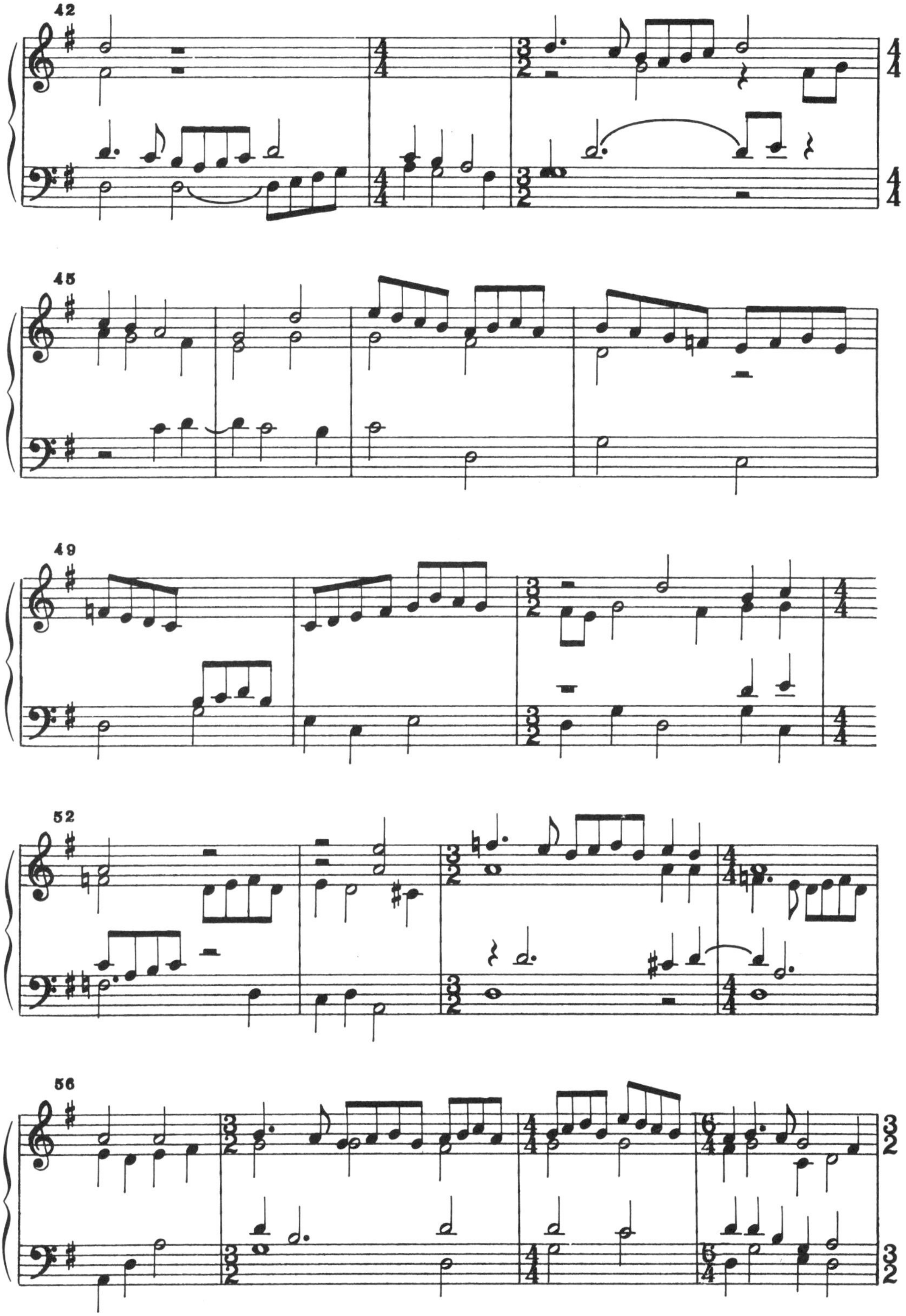
42
45
49
52
56

22. FANTASIA NO. 22 in Tone VIII (Fol. G iiʳ)
Moderato

97

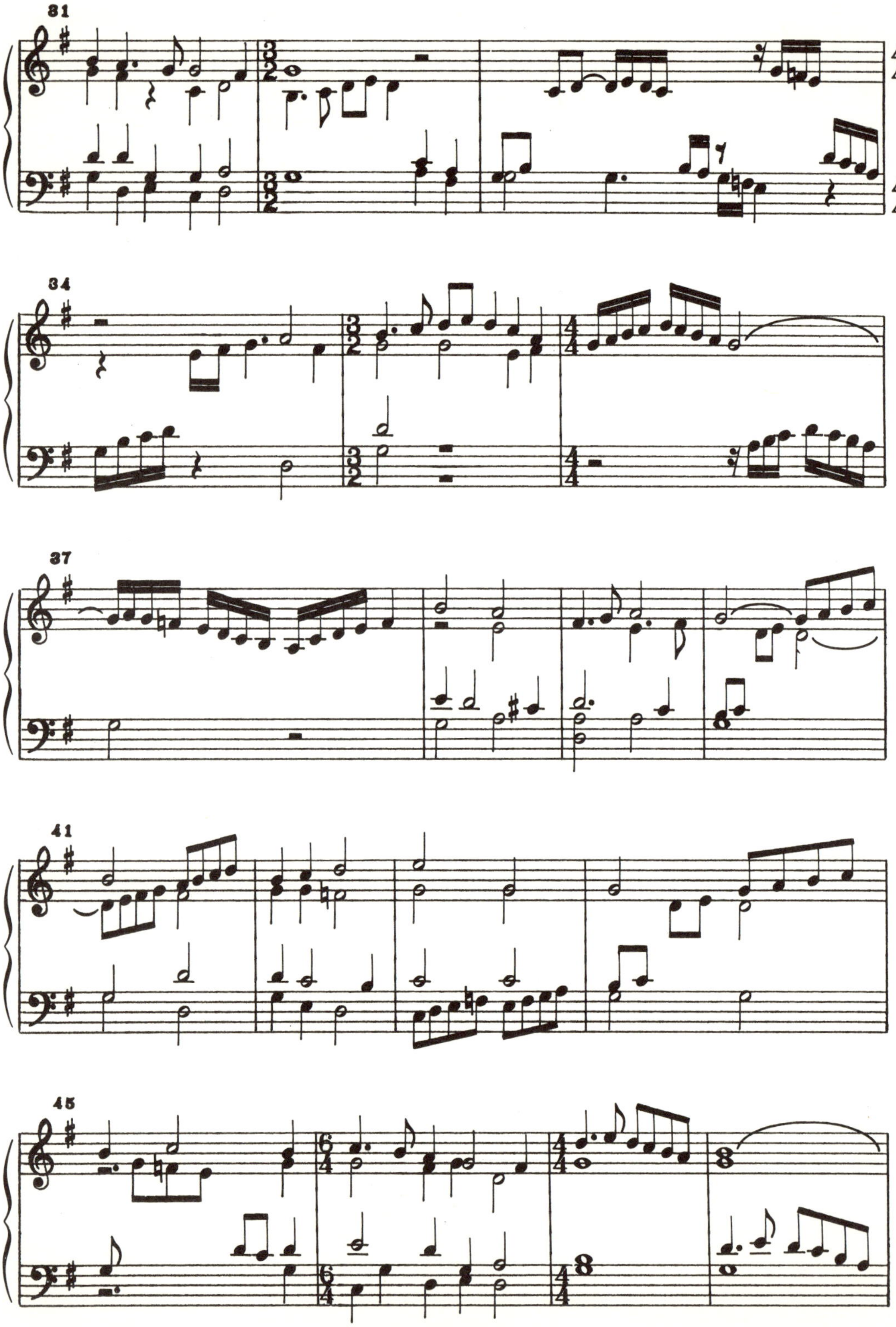
31
34
37
41
45

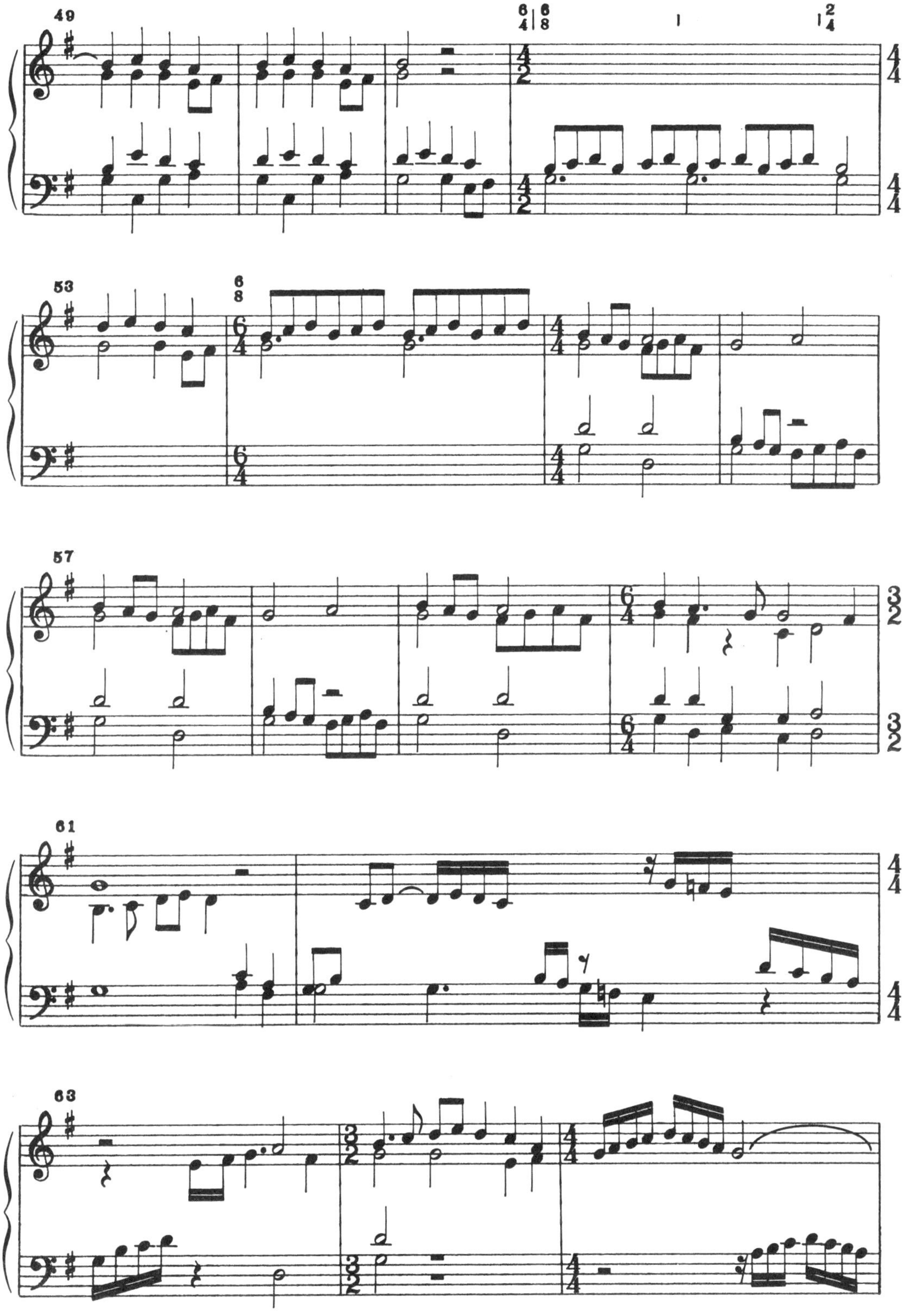
49
53
57
61
63

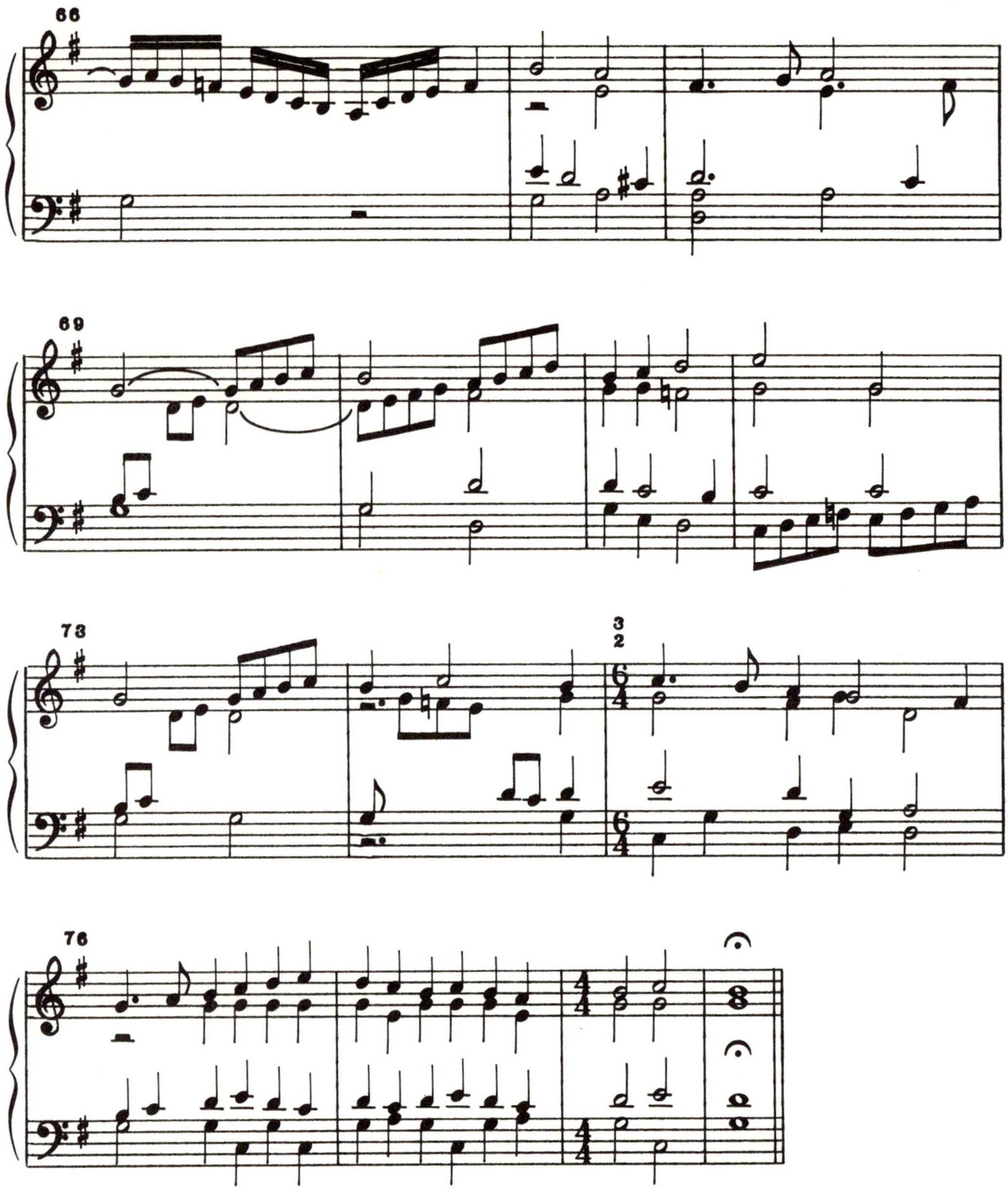
66
69
73
3
2
76

23. PAVAN NO. 1 in Tones I and II (Fol. G iii^v)

Allegro Moderato

24. PAVAN NO. 2 in Tones III and IV (Fol. [G iv^r])

Allegro Moderato

✸ To be played on Courses 2 and 3 (i.e., strings tuned to b and e').

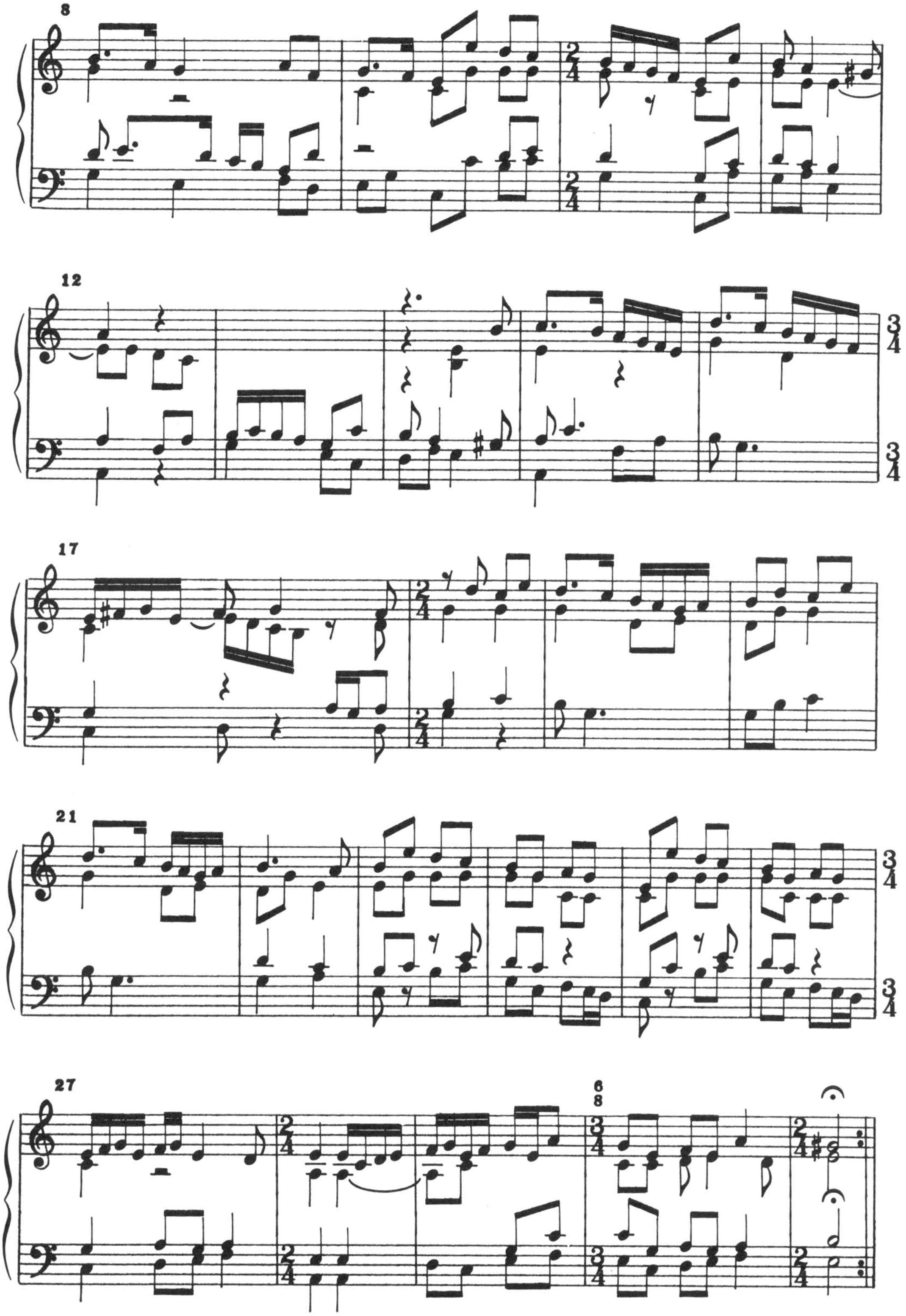
8
12
17
21
27

25. PAVAN NO. 3 in Tones V and VI (Fol. [G v^r])

Allegro Moderato

26. PAVAN NO. 4 in Tones VII and VIII (Fol. [G v^v])

Allegro Moderato

106

27. PAVAN NO. 5 in Tone VIII, *"La bella franceschina"* (Fol. [G vi^r])

Allegro Moderato

28. PAVAN NO. 6 in Tone VIII (Fol. [G vi^v])

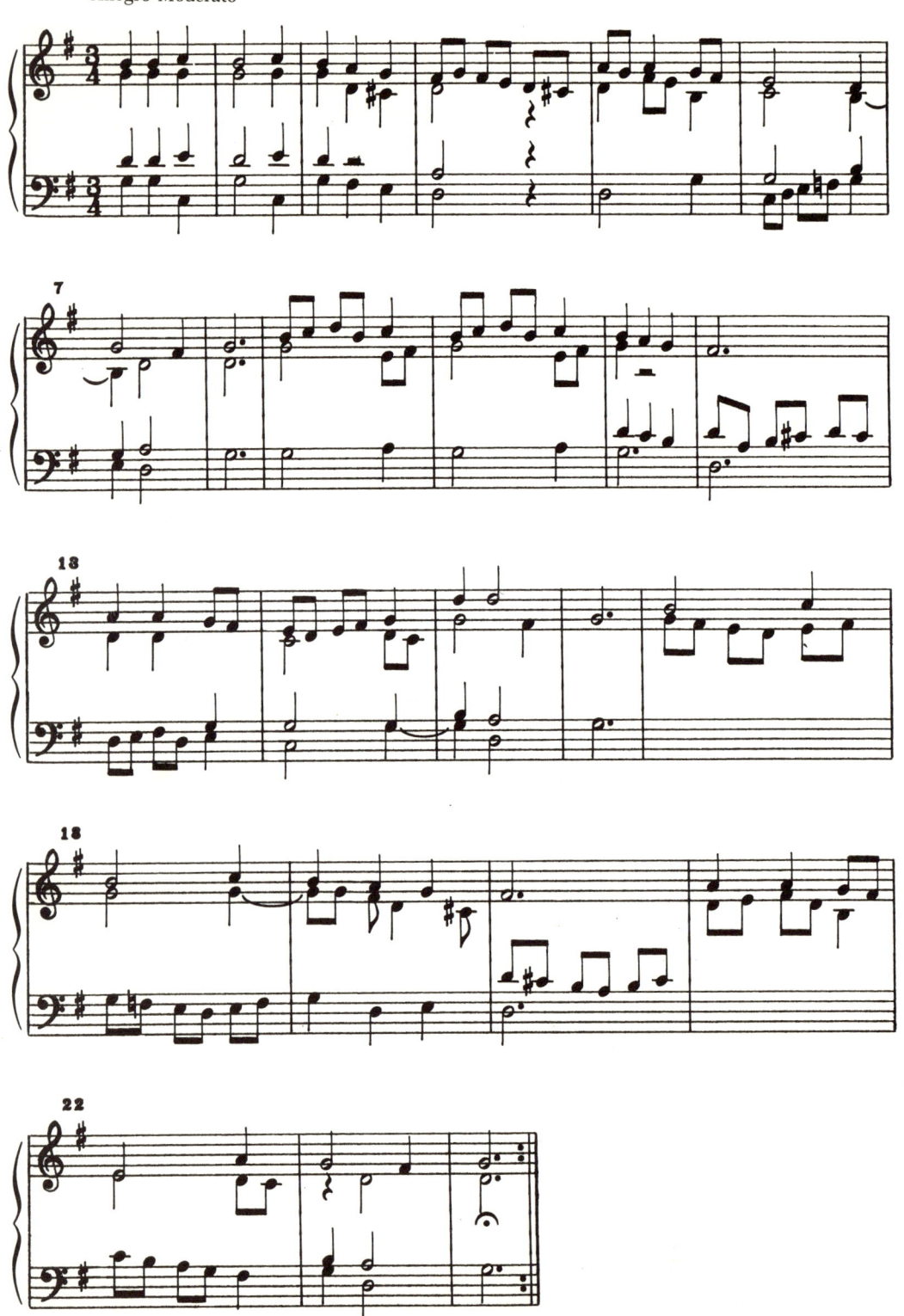

Allegro Moderato

29. VILLANCICO NO. 1, *"Toda mi vida hos amé"* (Fol. H^r) ✱

1. To- da mi vi- da hos a- me. Si me a- ma- ys yo no lo se.
4. Y por siem- pre hos a- ma- re.

2. Bien se que te- neys a- mor al des- a- mor y al ol- vi- do.
3. Se que soy a- bo- rre- ci- do ya que sa- be el dis- fa- vor.

Fine

D.C. al Fine

✱ Two settings. Translations of all vocal lyrics may be found in the Critical Notes to this edition.

109

B. Allegro Moderato

1. To- da mi vi- da hos a- me-
4. Y por siem- pre hos a- ma- re-

Si me a- ma- ys yo no lo se.

Fine

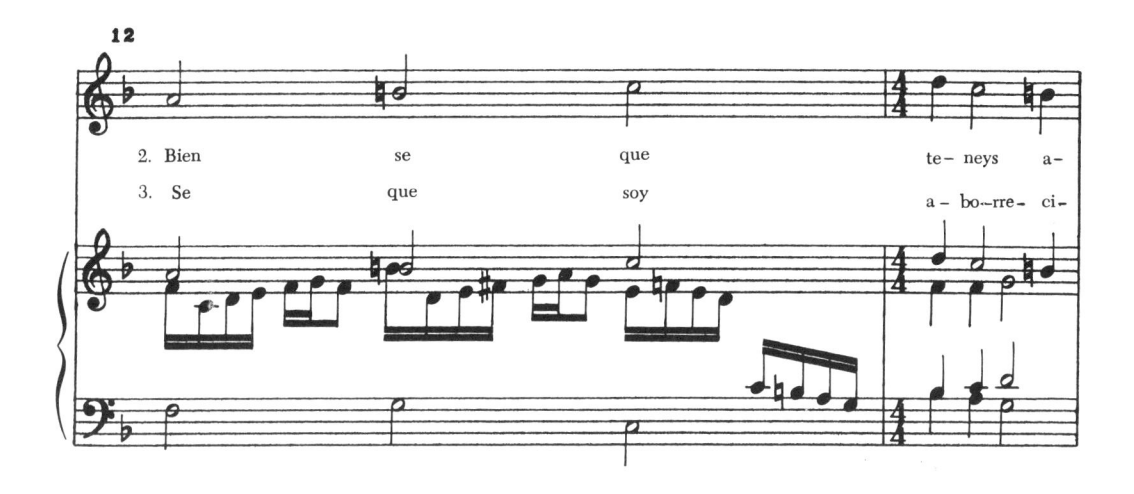

2. Bien se que te- neys a-mor al desque a- mor y al ol- vi- do.
3. Se que soy a- bo-rre- ci- do ya que sa- be el dis- fa- vor.

D.C. al Fine

30. **VILLANCICO NO. 2**, *"Sospiró una señora que yo ví"* (Fol. H^v) ✽

A. Molto Lento

1. Sos- pi- ro u- na se- ño- ra que yo vi.
4. Ya yo se que's bur- la- do- ra y aun- que as- si. O- xa-

lla fues- se por mi.
2. Sos- pi- ro u- na se- ño- ra
3. Que sos- pi- ra por te- ner

Fine

y'e me da- do a'n- ten- der.
gran pe- sar de quien llo- ra.

D.C. al Fine

✽ Two settings.

B. Allegro

1. Sos- pi- ro u- na se- ño- ra que yo vi. O- xa- lla fues- se por
4. Ya yo se que's bur- la- do- ra y aun- que a- si.

2. Sos- pi- ro u- na se- ño- ra y'e me da- do a'n- ten- der.
3. Que sos- pi- ra por te- ner gran pe- sar de quien llo- ra.

Fine

D.C. al Fine

31. VILLANCICO NO. 3, *"Agora viniesse un viento"* (Fol. H ii^r)

Allegro Moderato

1. A—go—ra vi—nies—se un vien—to. Que me e—
4. Y me hi—zies—se tan con—ten—

chas—se a—cu—lla den—tro.
2. A—go—ra
3. Que me e—chas—

Fine

vi—nies—se un vien—to tan bue—no co—mo
se a—cu—lla den—tro en fal—das de mi

115

D.C. al Fine

32. VILLANCICO NO. 4, *"Quien amores ten"* (Fol. H. ii^r) ✱

A. Lento

1. Quien a- mo- res ten a fin que los ben.
4. A fin que los ben e non par- ta de- lla.

✱ Two settings:

116

Que nan he vein- to que va y ven. Fine

2. Quien a-
3. E ten

mo— res ten a— lla en Cas- te-
seu a— mor en da— ma don— ze—

lla.
lla.

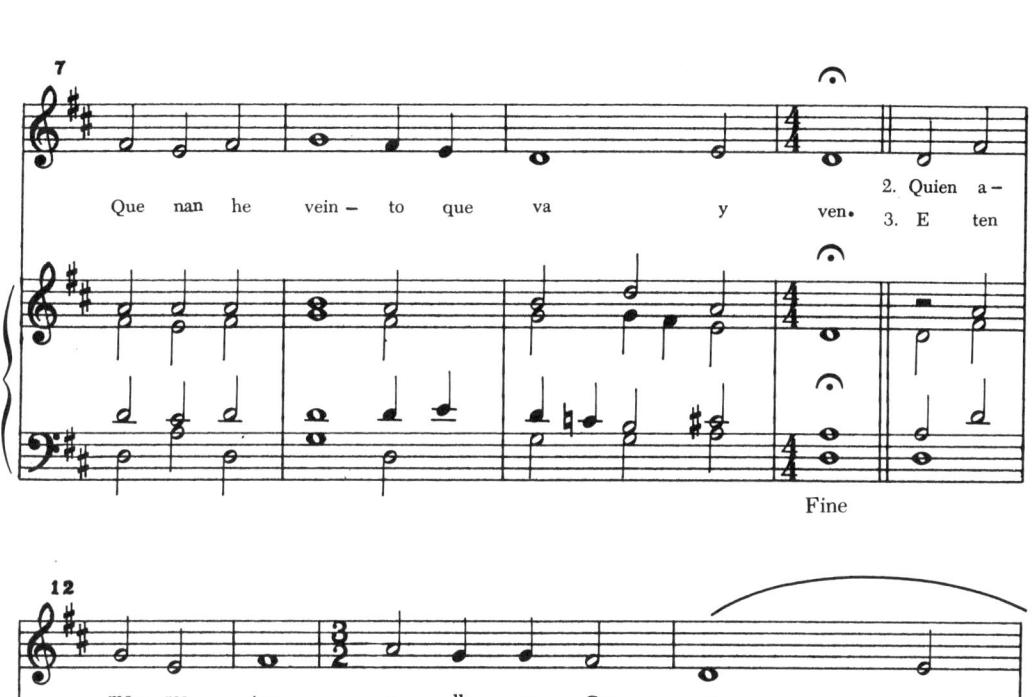

D.C. al Fine

B. Allegro

1. Quien a— mo— res ten
4. A fin que los ben

a fin que los ben.
e non par— ta de— lla.

[sic]

Que nan he vein— to que va y ven.

Lyrics:

Que nan he vein- to que va y ven. Que nan he vein- to que va y ven.

2. Quien a- mo- res ten a- lla en Cas-
3. E ten seu a- mor en da- ma don-

Fine

33. VILLANCICO NO. 5, *"Falai miña amor"* (Fol. H iii[r])

Allegro Moderato

1. Fa- la- i , mi- ña a- mor, fa- la- i-
4. Pois te- ne- ys po- der fa- la- i-

me. Si no me fa— lla— ys, ma—
me.

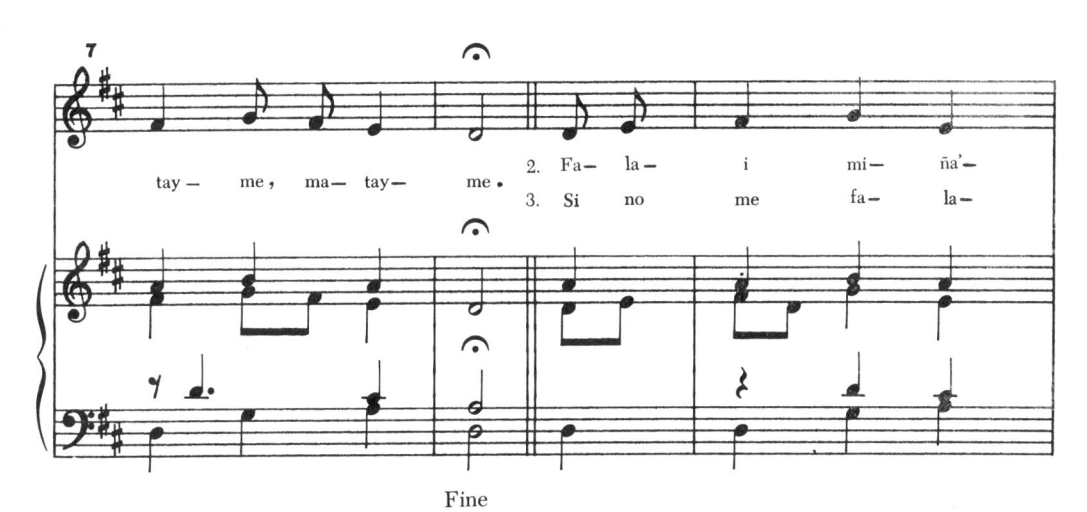

tay— me, ma—tay— me. 2. Fa— la— i mi— ña'—
3. Si no me fa— la—

Fine

mor que os fa— ço sa— ber.
ys que nan te— ño ser.

D.C. al Fine

121

34. VILLANCICO NO. 6, *"Poys dezeys que me quereys ben"* (Fol. H iiiʳ) ✻

A. [Lento]

1. Poys de- zeys que me que- re- ys ben por- que days fa- lla a nin- gen. 2. Vos de- zeys que me a- ma- ys.
4. Si vos a nin- gen fa- lla- ys, yo non vos que- i- re mas ben. 3. Yo vos veg- go que bur- la- ys.

Fine

D.C. al Fine

✻ Two settings.

122

B. [Allegro]

1. Poys de- zeys que me que- re- ys
4. Si vos a nin- gen fa- la-

ben por- que days fa- lla a nin-
ys, yo non vos que- i- re mas

gen. 2. Vos de- ze- ys que me a- ma- ys.
ben. 3. Yo vos veg- go que bur- la- ys.

Fine   D.C. al Fine

35. ROMANCE NO. 1, *"Durandarte, Durandarte"* (Fol. H iii^v)

13

a - cor - dar -
a - go - ra

18 [sic]

se te de-vria a
des- co- no- ci- do

21

d'a- quel buen tiem- po pas- sa-
di, ¿por- que me has ol- vi- da-

3. Pa— la— bras son li— son— ge— ras, se—
4. Pues a— mas— tes a Ga— y— fe— ros quan—

ño— ra, de vu— es— tro gra— do, que si
do yo fu— y des— te— rra— do, y por

yo mu- dan- ça hi- ze- haveys me lo vos cau- sa- do.
no su- frir ul- tra- ge mo- ri- re de- ses- pe- ra- do.

36. ROMANCE NO. 2, *"Sospirastes Baldovinos"* (Fol. H iv^v)

Moderato

1. Sos — pi — ras — tes Bal — do — vi — nos
2. No ten — go mie — do a los mo — ros

las co —
ni en

sas que yo mas que — ri — a
Fran — cia ten — go a — mi — ga

15
o te—
mas tu
17
neys mie— do a los mo— ros
mo— ra y yo cris— tia— no
21
o en Fran—
ha— ze— mos

25
cia te— ne— ys a— mi— ga.
muy ma— la vi— da.
29
6
4
2
4
3. Si te vas con—
4. Y ve— ras la
34
mi— go en Fran— ci— a
flor del mun— do

todo nos sera a-le-gri-a
de mejor cava-lle-ri-a

ha-re jus-tas y tor-ne-os
yo se-re tu ca-va-lle-ro

por ser— vir— te ca— dal— di— a.
tu se— ras mi lin— da a— mi— ga.

37. SONNET NO. 1, *"Amor che nel mio pensier vive"* [Petrarch] (Fol. [H v^v])

Moderato [sic]

A — mor, che nel mi — o pen — sier vi — ve e re —

gna, il su—o seg— gio mag— gior nel mi—o cor

te— ne, tal—hor ar— ma—to ne la fron— te

ve— ne, i—vi si lo— ca et i—vi

pon su- a in- se- gna. Quel- la che a- ma- re et sof- fe- rir ne 'n- se- gna et vol che 'l gran de- si- o, l'ac- ce- sa spe- ne, ra- gion, ver- go- gna, et re- ve-ren- za a- fre- ne, di no- stro ar- dir fra se stes-

sa si sde- gna. **On-** **de** **A-** mor pa- ven- to- so

fug- ge al co- re, las-

san- do o- gni su- a in- pre- sa, et pian- ge et tre- ma, i- vi s'a- scon- de et non ap- par piu fo- re. Che pos- s'io far, te- men- do il mio signore, se non star seco infin a l'hora extrema? Che bel fin fa chi ben amando more.

38. SONNET NO. 2, *"Porta chiascun nela fronte signato"* (Fol. [H vi^v])

Moderato

Por— ta chia— scun ne— la fron— te si— gna— to il su— o de— sti— no e di che na— sce a'l mon— do. Chi a— ma— ro et tri— sto, chi liet— to et gioc— con— do. Et

✱ To be played on Courses 5 and 6 (i.e., strings tuned to A and d).

140

va do-len-te al fon— do, ben-che si-a di buon san-gue nat-to. Chi se de-let-ta pe-re-gri-no an-da-re; chi ser-ve a gen-til ho-mo, chi a signo — re; chi cá—de in guer—ra; chi se a—ne—ga in ma—re; chi de—si—de—ra the—sor; chi fa—ma e ho—no—re.

A me da-to e per mi- o de-sti- no a- ma- re et mo-rir al fin per trop-po a- mo- re.

39. SONNET NO. 3, *"Nova angeleta"* [Petrarch] (Fol. [H vii^v])

za com- pa- gna et sen- za scor- ta mi vi-
de, un lac- cio che di se- ta or- di-
va te- se fra l'her- ba on- d'e ver- de'l ca- mi- no. Al-

[sic]

48
hor fui pre— so , et non mi spia—cque poi , si dol— ce lu— me u—
58
sci— a de— gli oc— chi suoi , u— sci— a de— gli oc—
66
chi suoi

40. FANTASIA NO. 23 in Tone I (Fol. J^r)

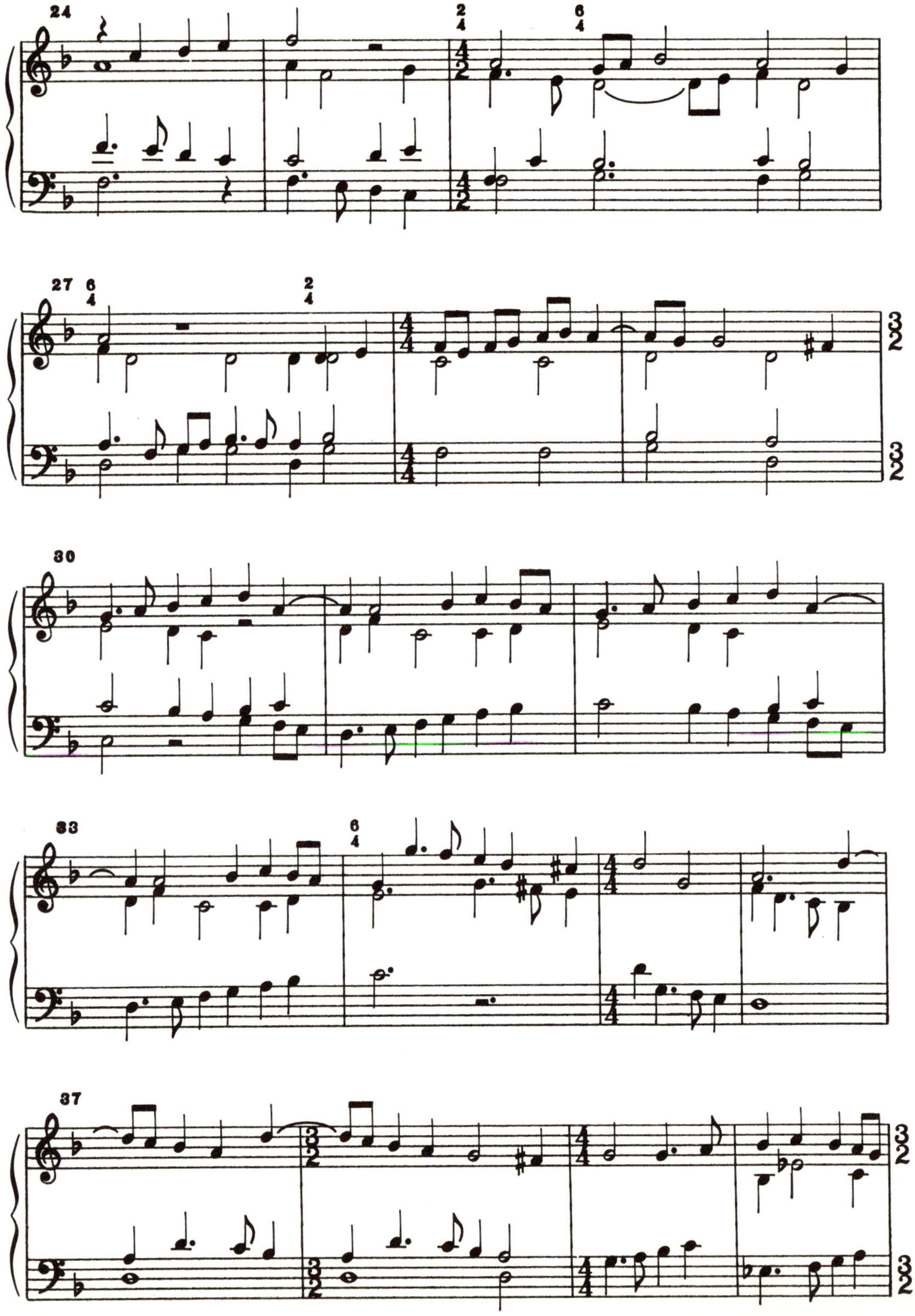
24
27
30
33
37

✸ To be played on Courses 4 and 5 (i.e., strings tuned to d and g).

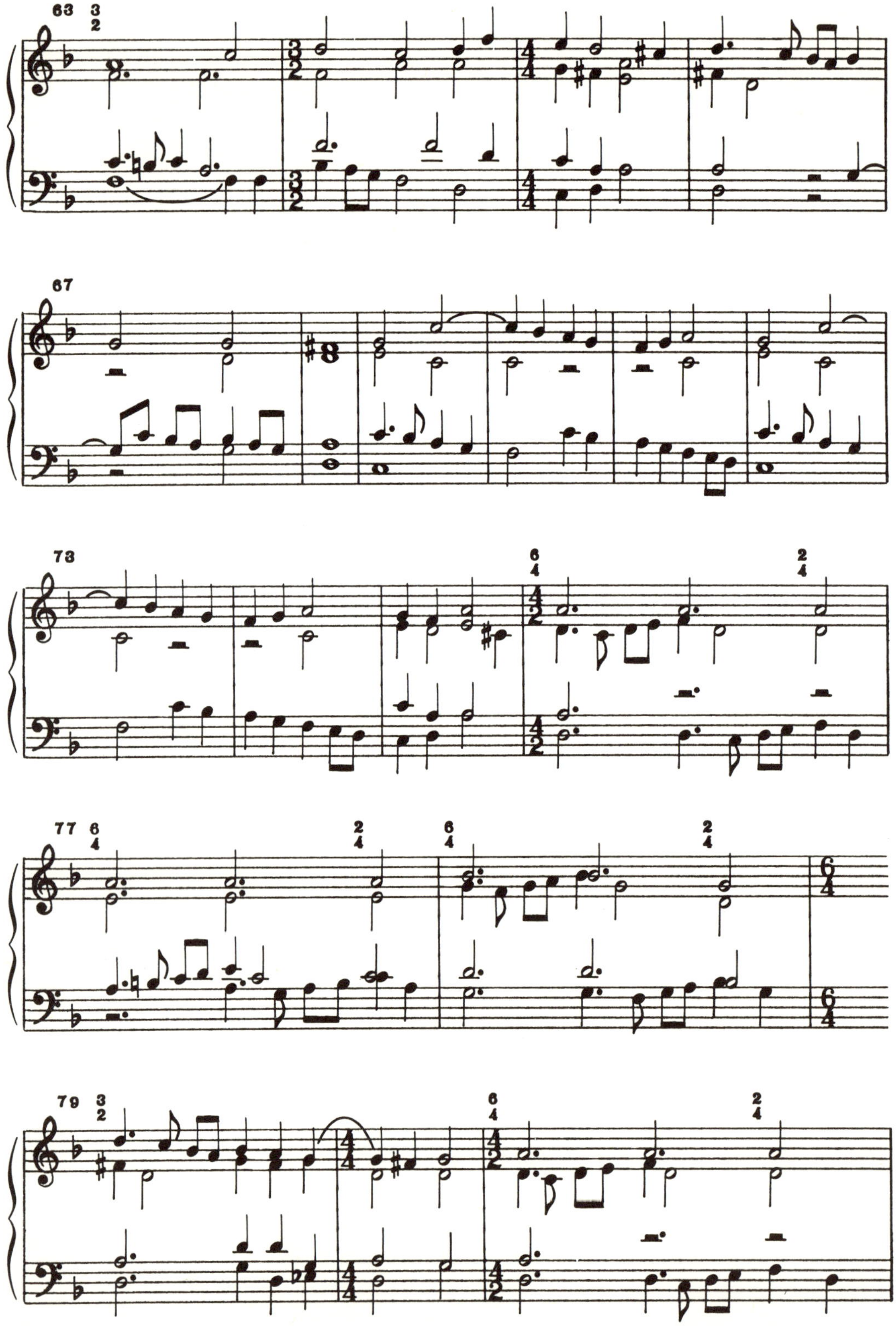
63
67
73
77
79

41. FANTASIA NO. 24 in Tone II (Fol. J iii^r)

✽ To be played on Courses 4 and 5 (i.e., strings tuned to d and g).

152

Accel?

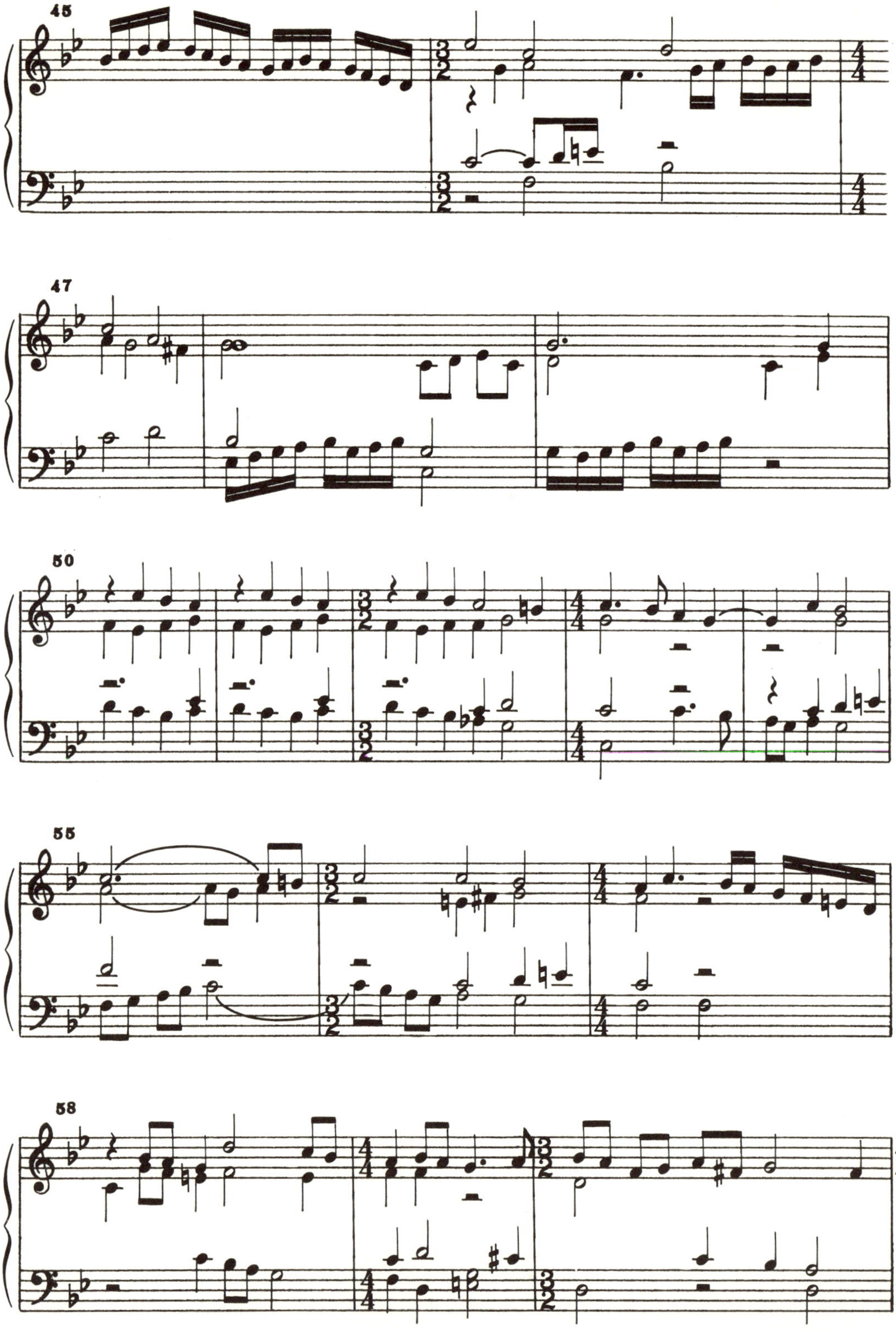
45
47
50
55
58

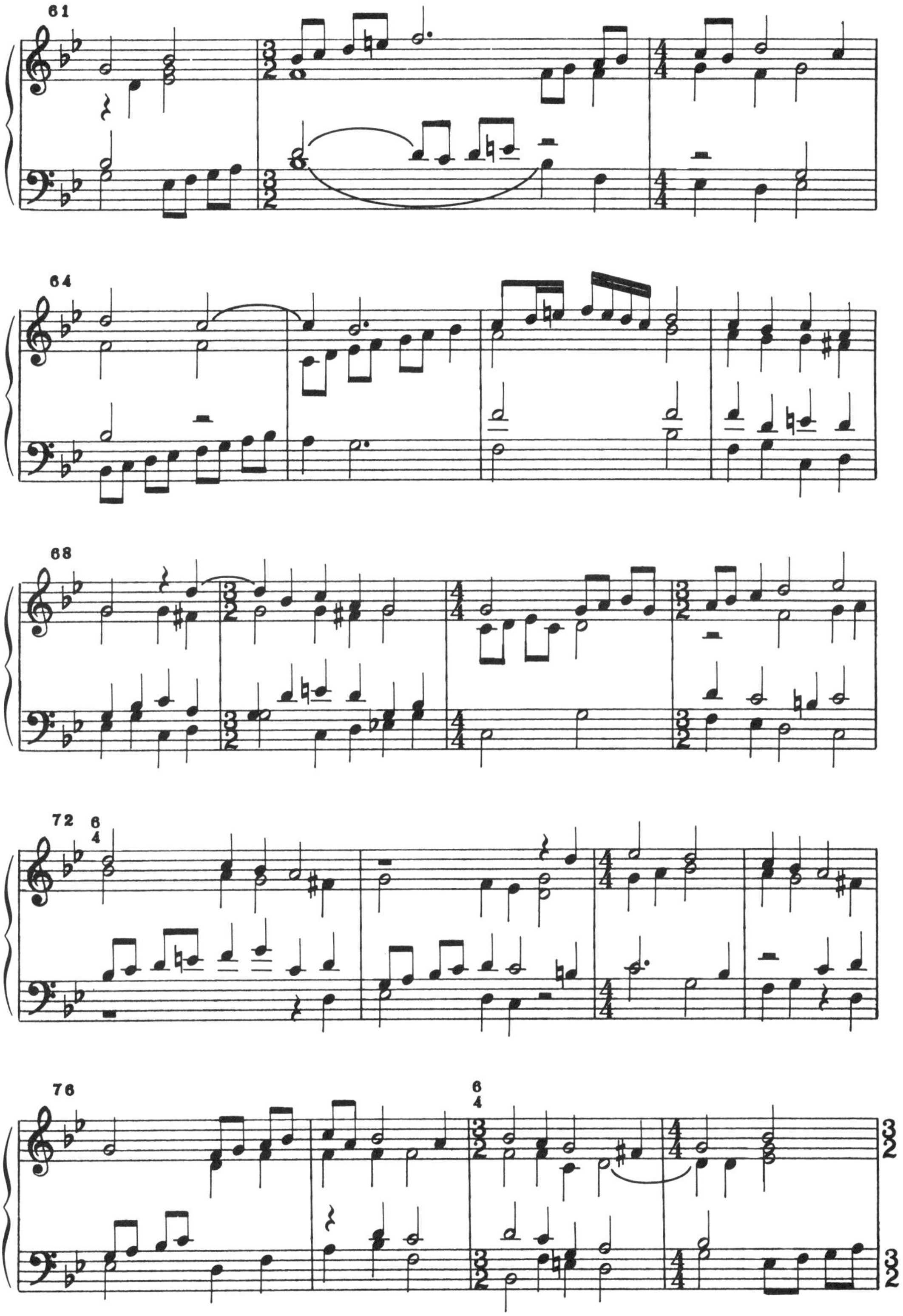
61
64
68
72
76

42. FANTASIA NO. 25 in Tones I and II (Fol. [J vʳ])

Moderato

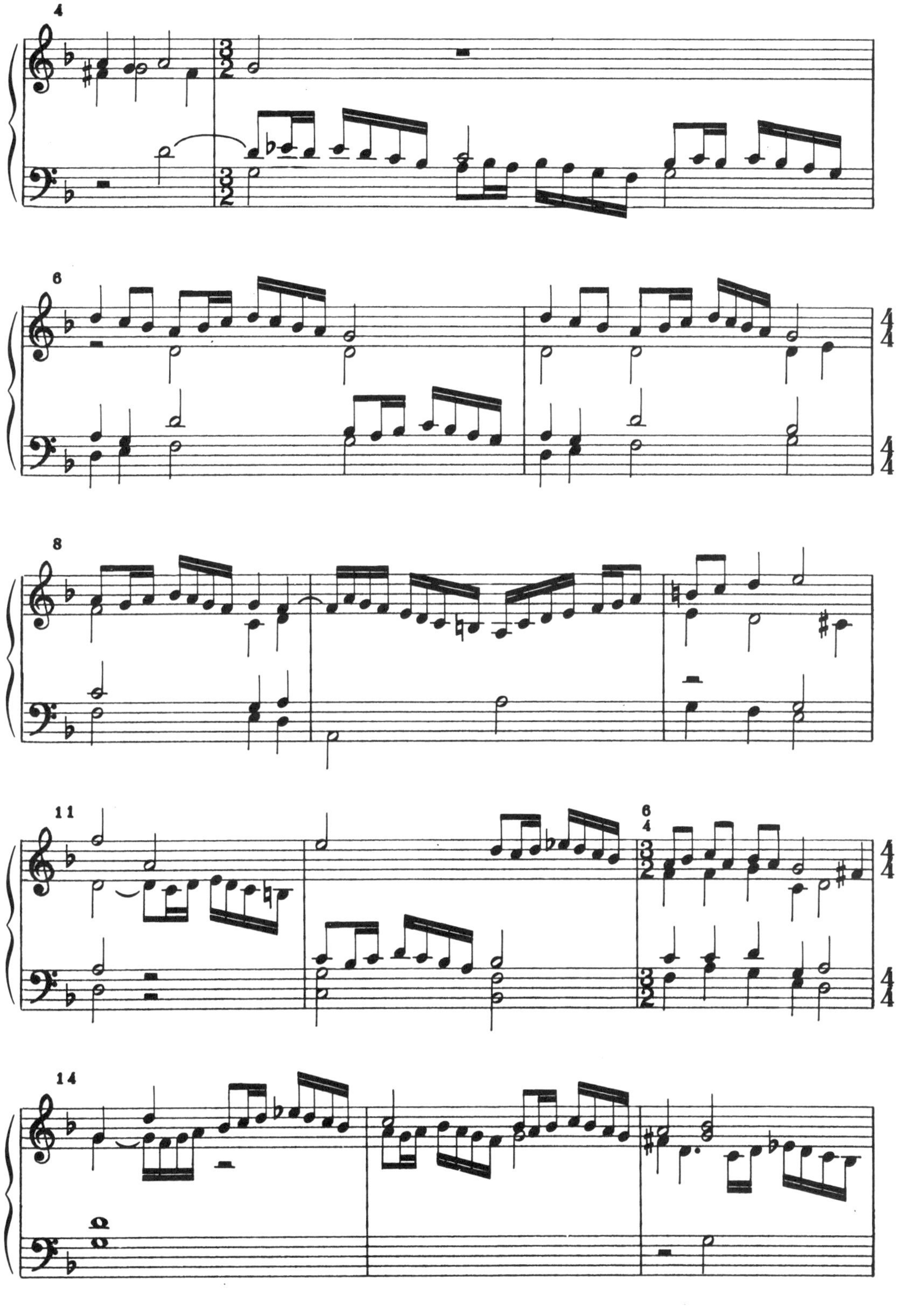
4
6
8
11
14

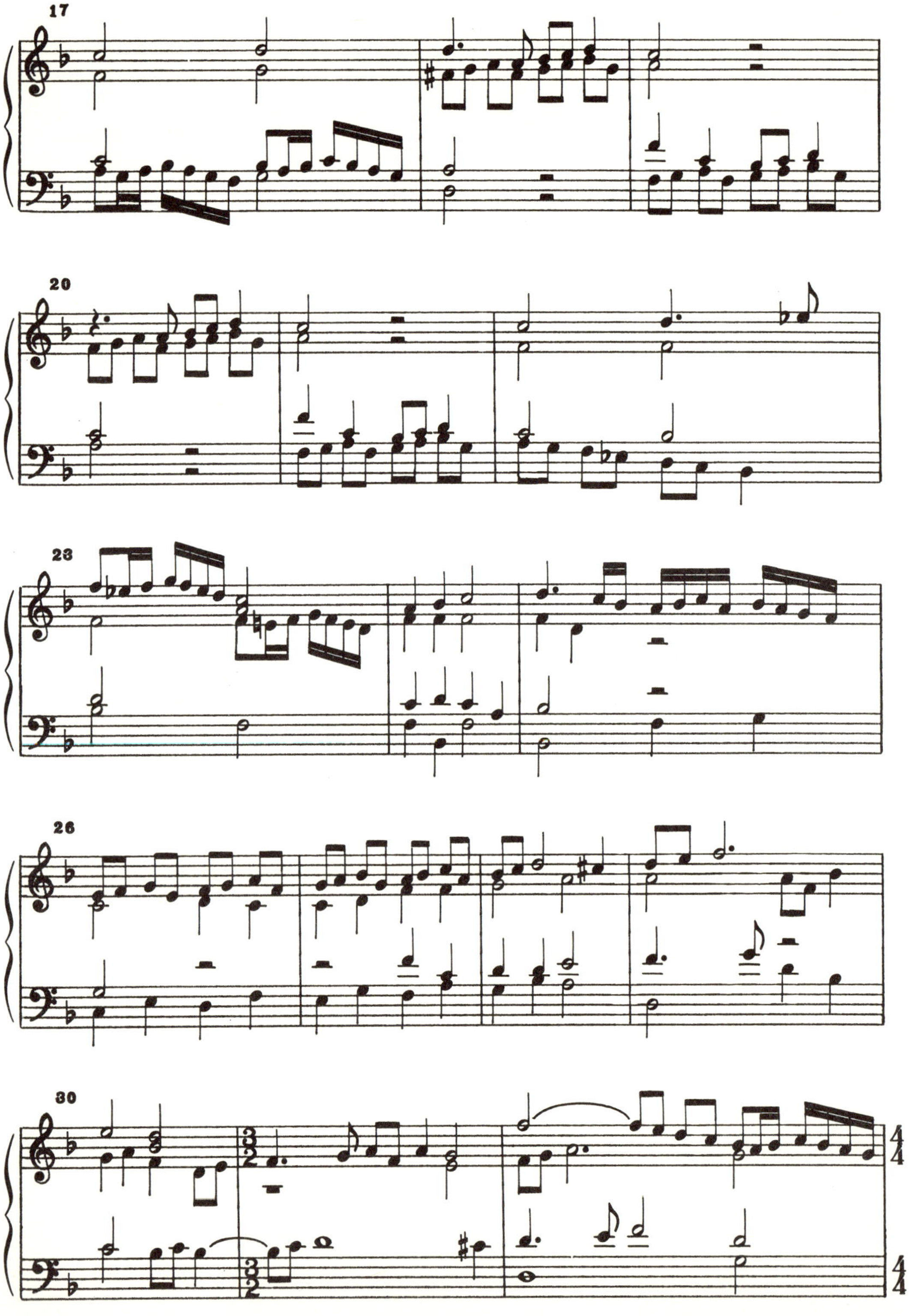
17
20
23
26
30

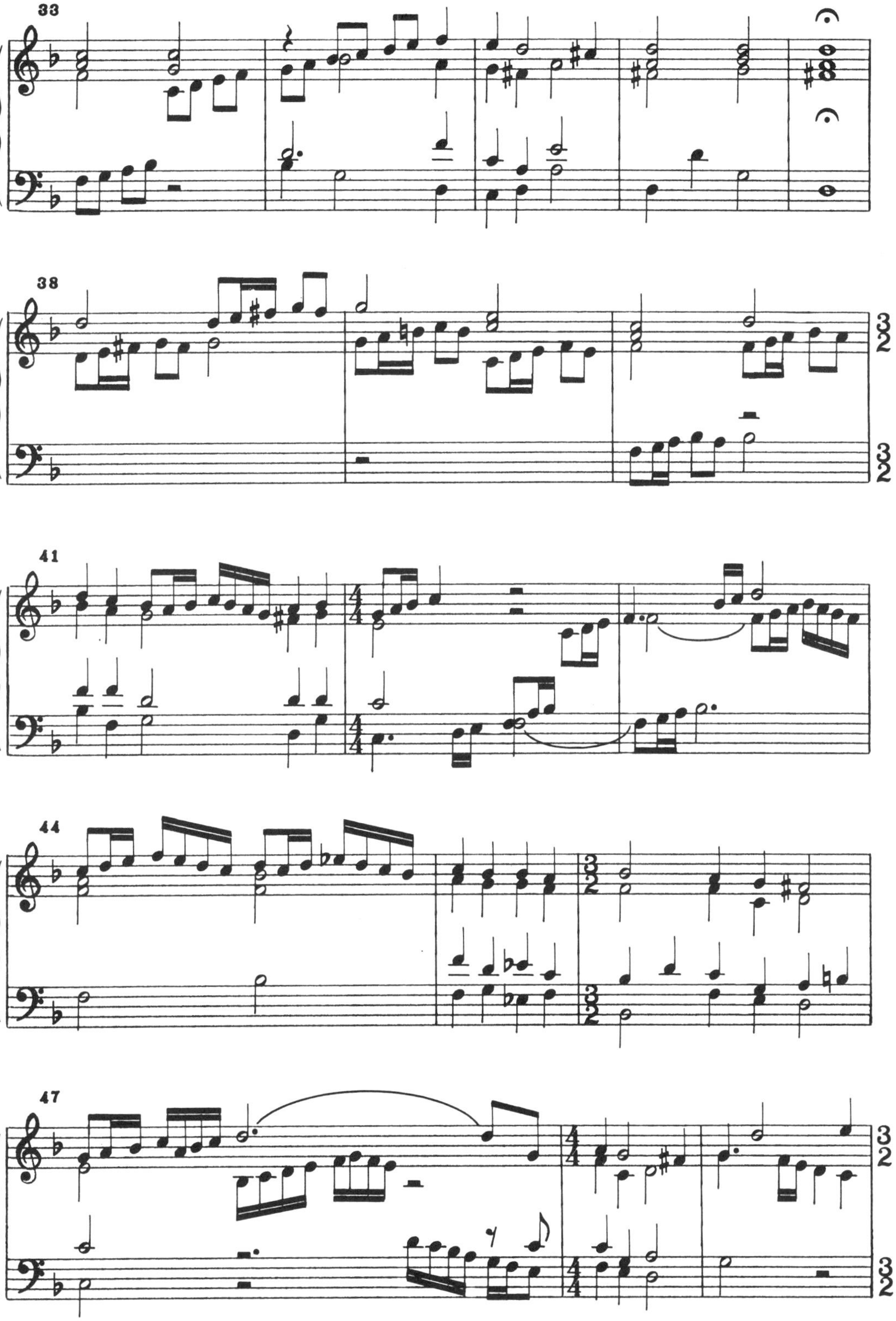
33
38
41
44
47

160

43. FANTASIA NO. 26 in Tones III and IV (Fol. Kᵛ)

Moderato

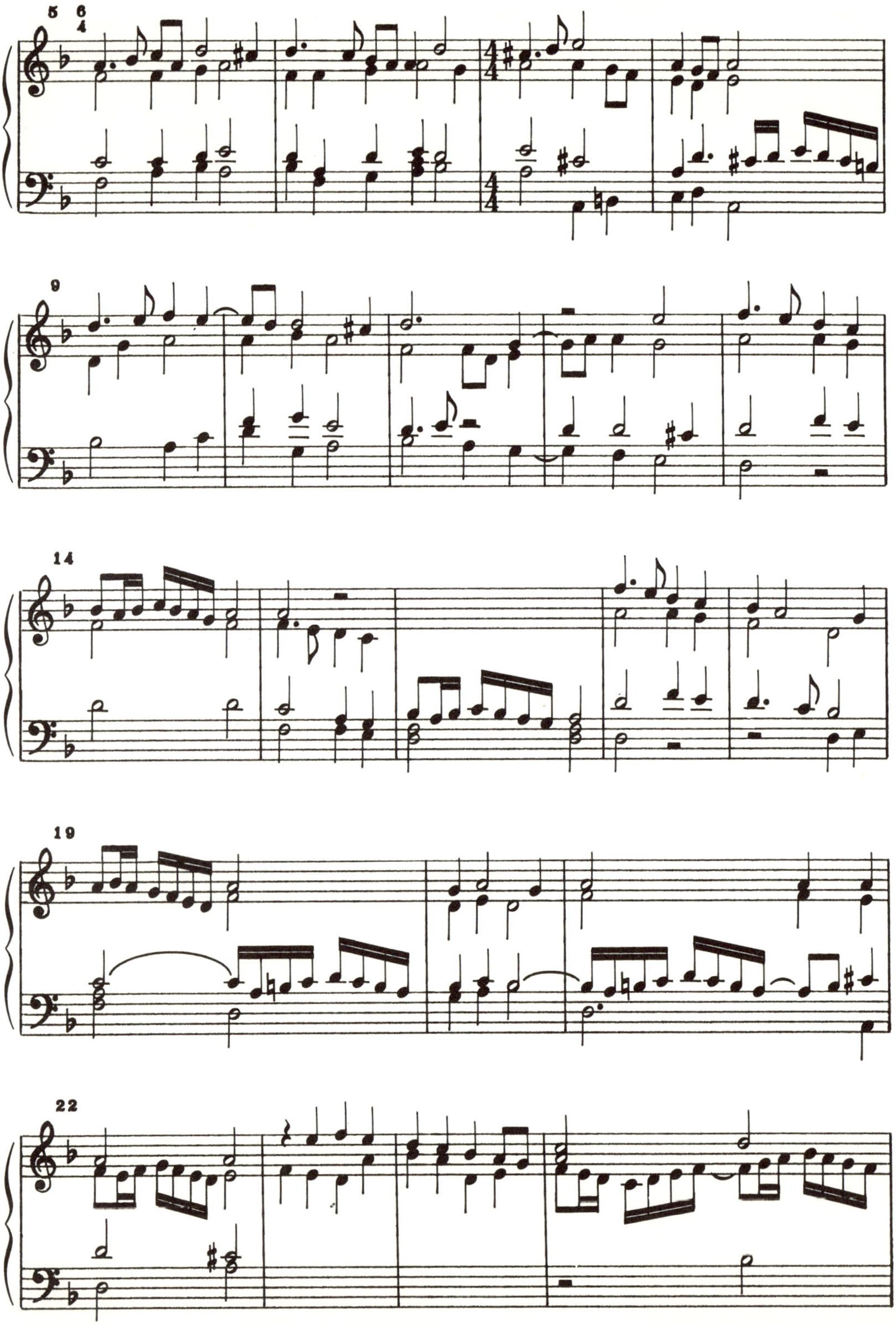
5
6
4
9
14
19
22

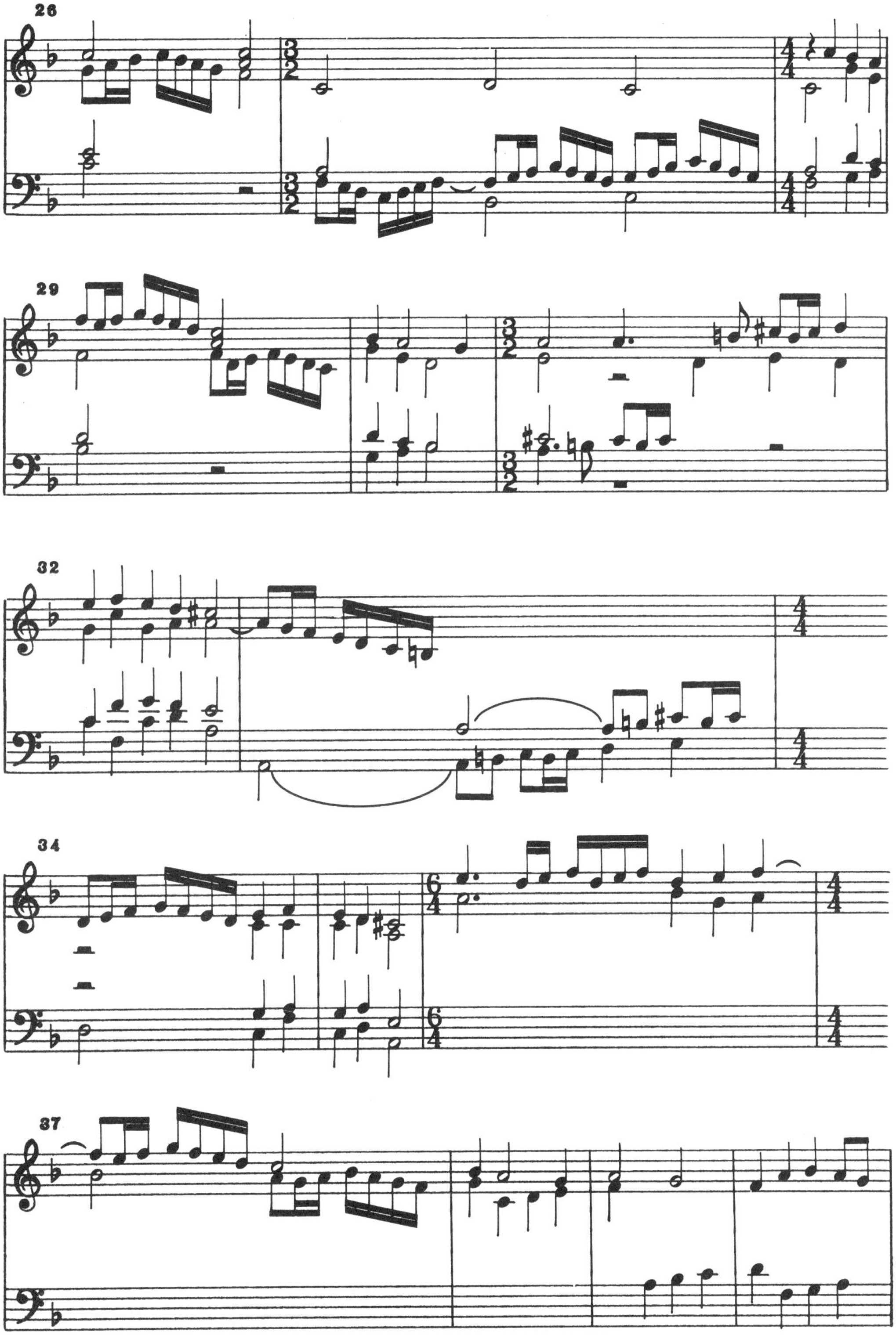
26
29
32
34
37

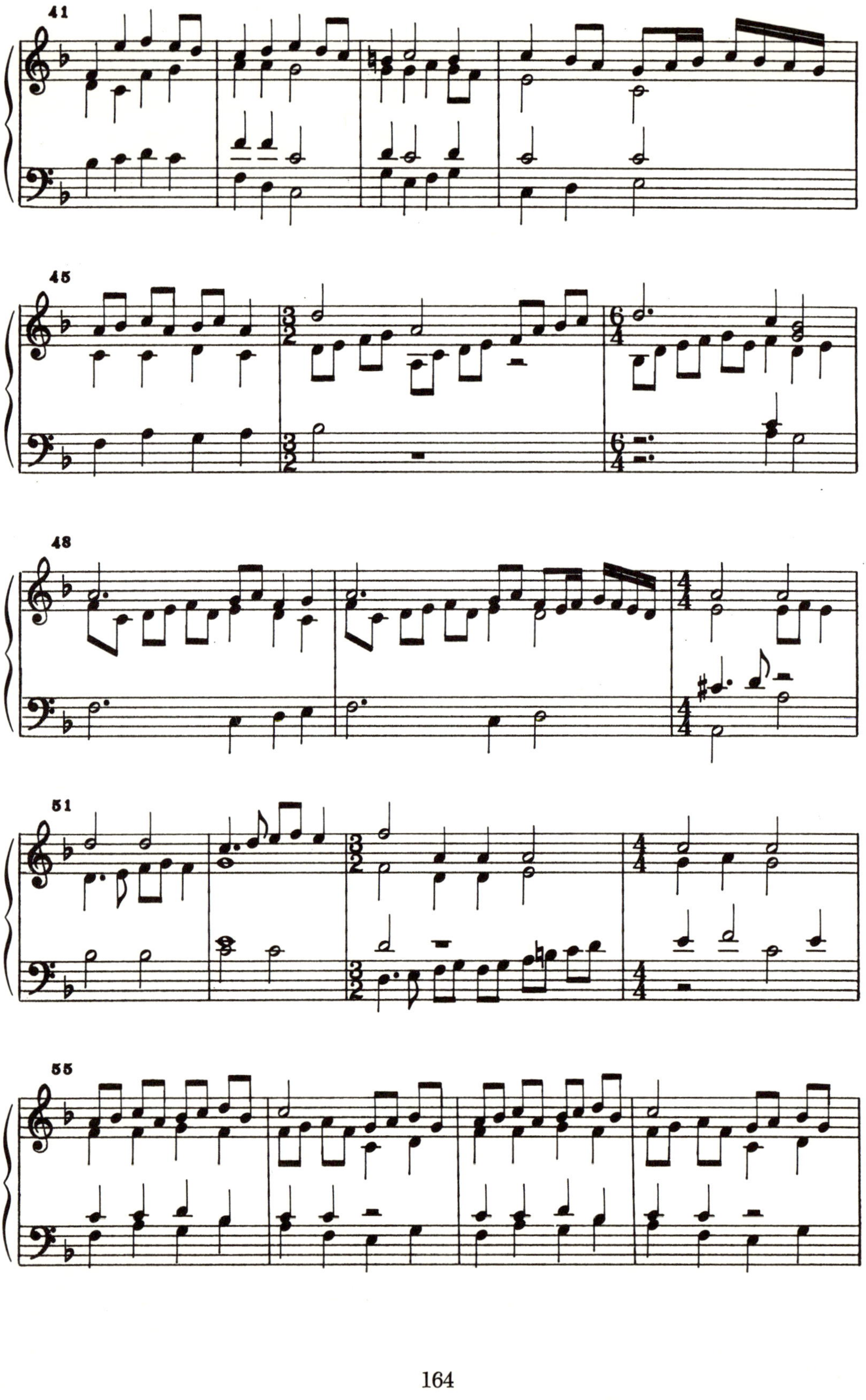
41
45
48
51
55

44. FANTASIA NO. 27 in Tone III (Fol. K iii^r)

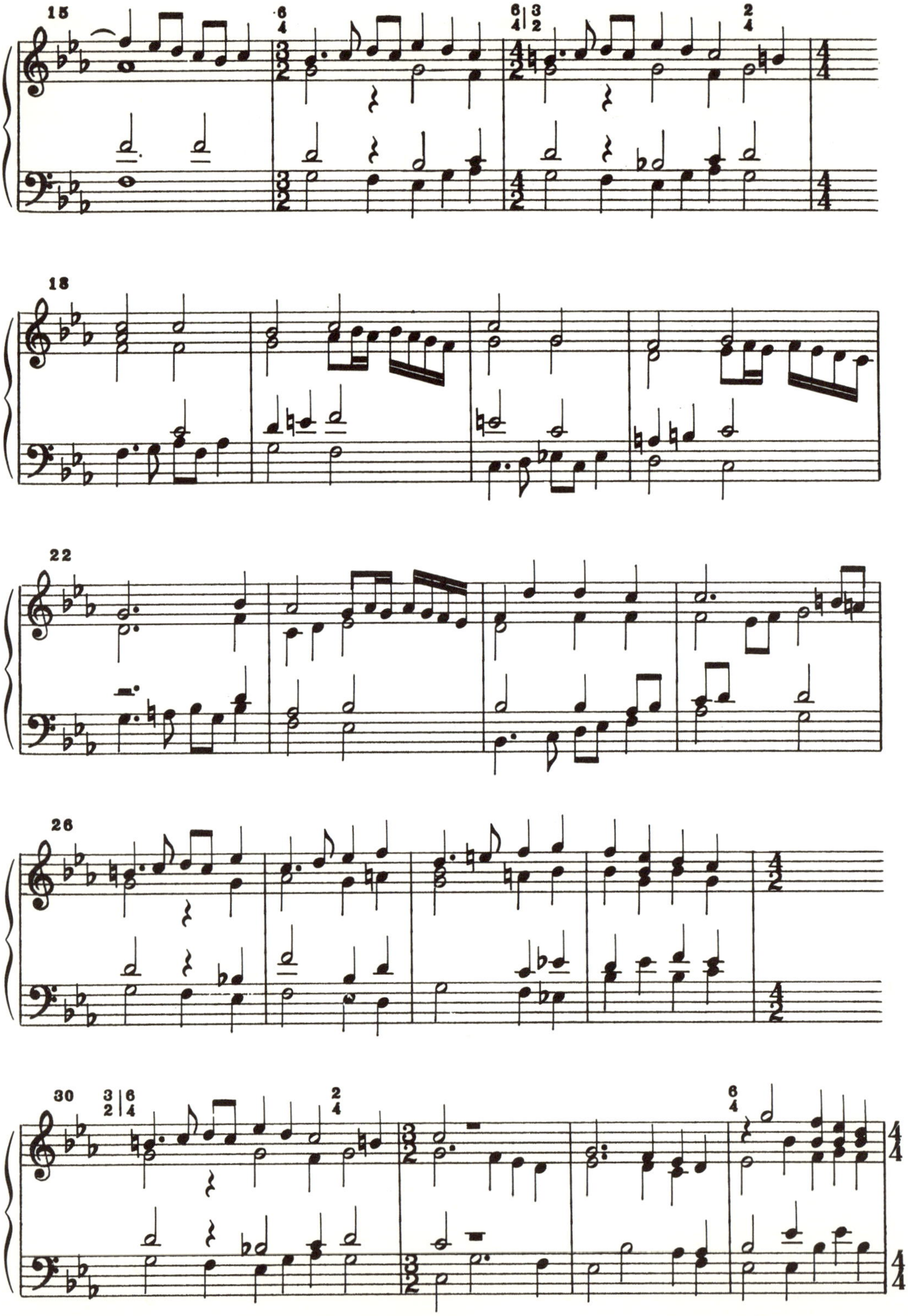
15
18
22
26
30

✽ To be played on Courses 4 and 5   (i.e., strings tuned to d and g).

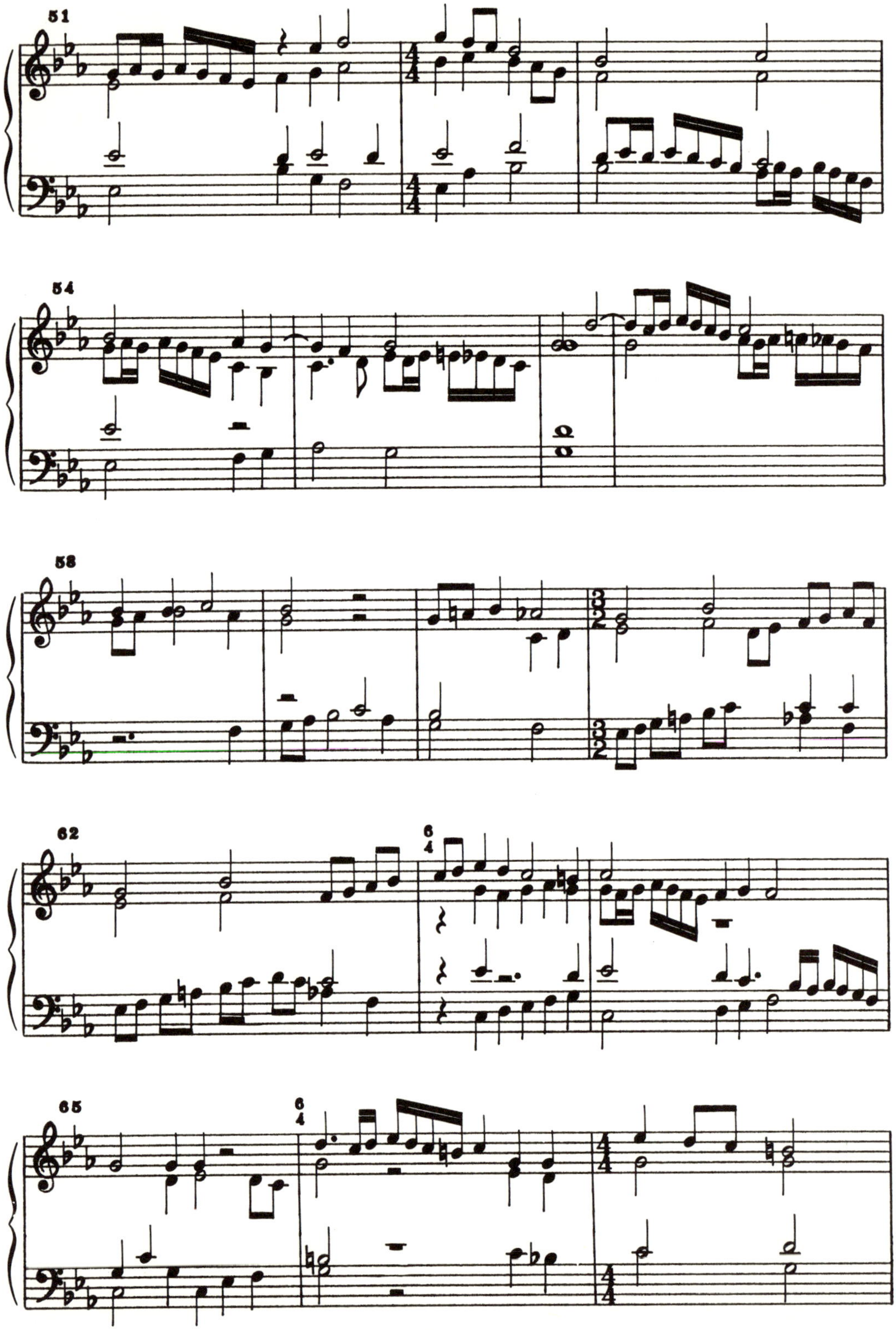
51
54
58
62
65

[sic]

[sic]

45. FANTASIA NO. 28 in Tone IV (Fol. [K v^r])

171

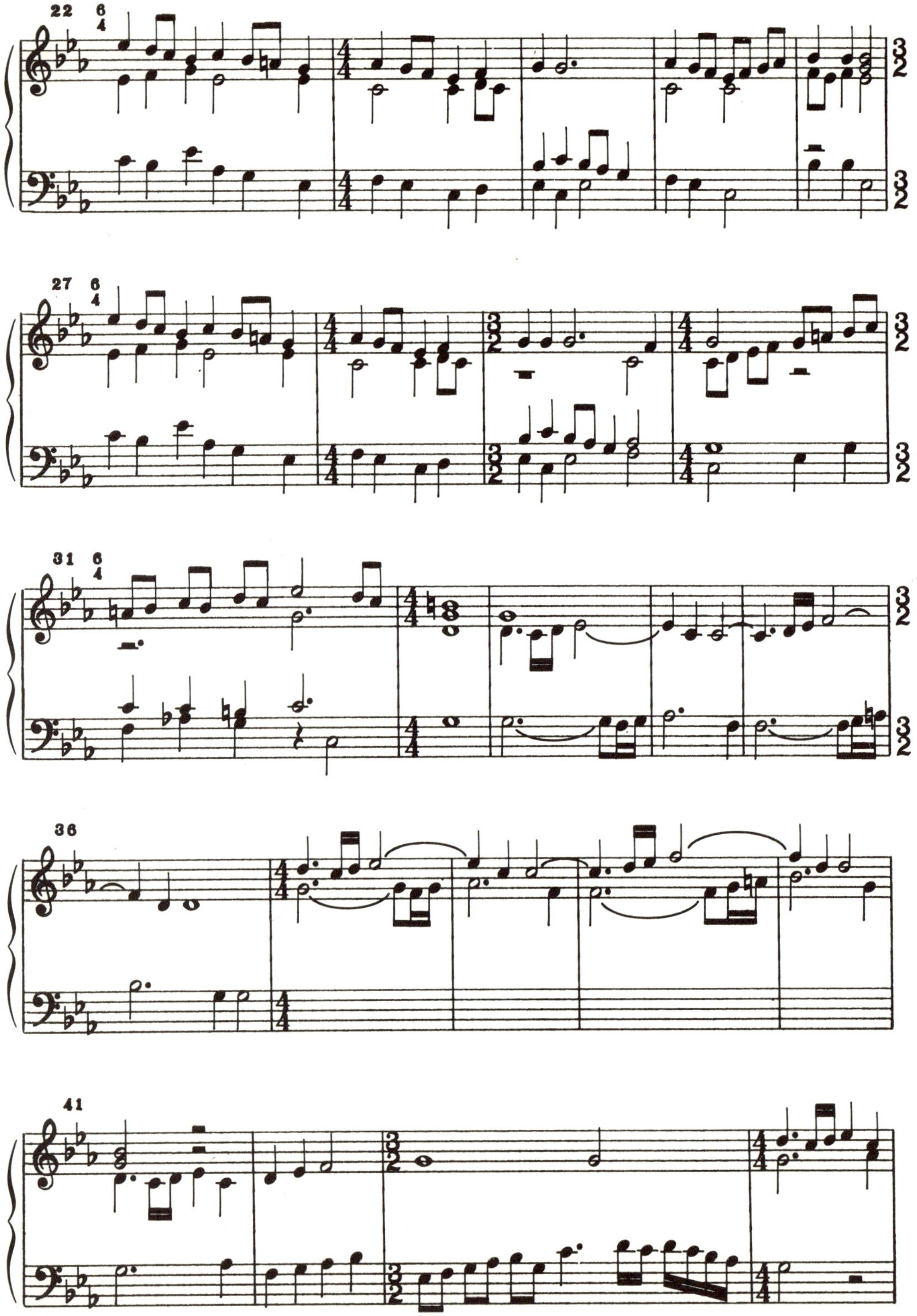
22
27
31
36
41

173

174

175

46. FANTASIA NO. 29 in Tones III and IV (Fol. L^r)

✱ To be played on Courses 4 and 5 (i.e., strings tuned to d and g).

177

178

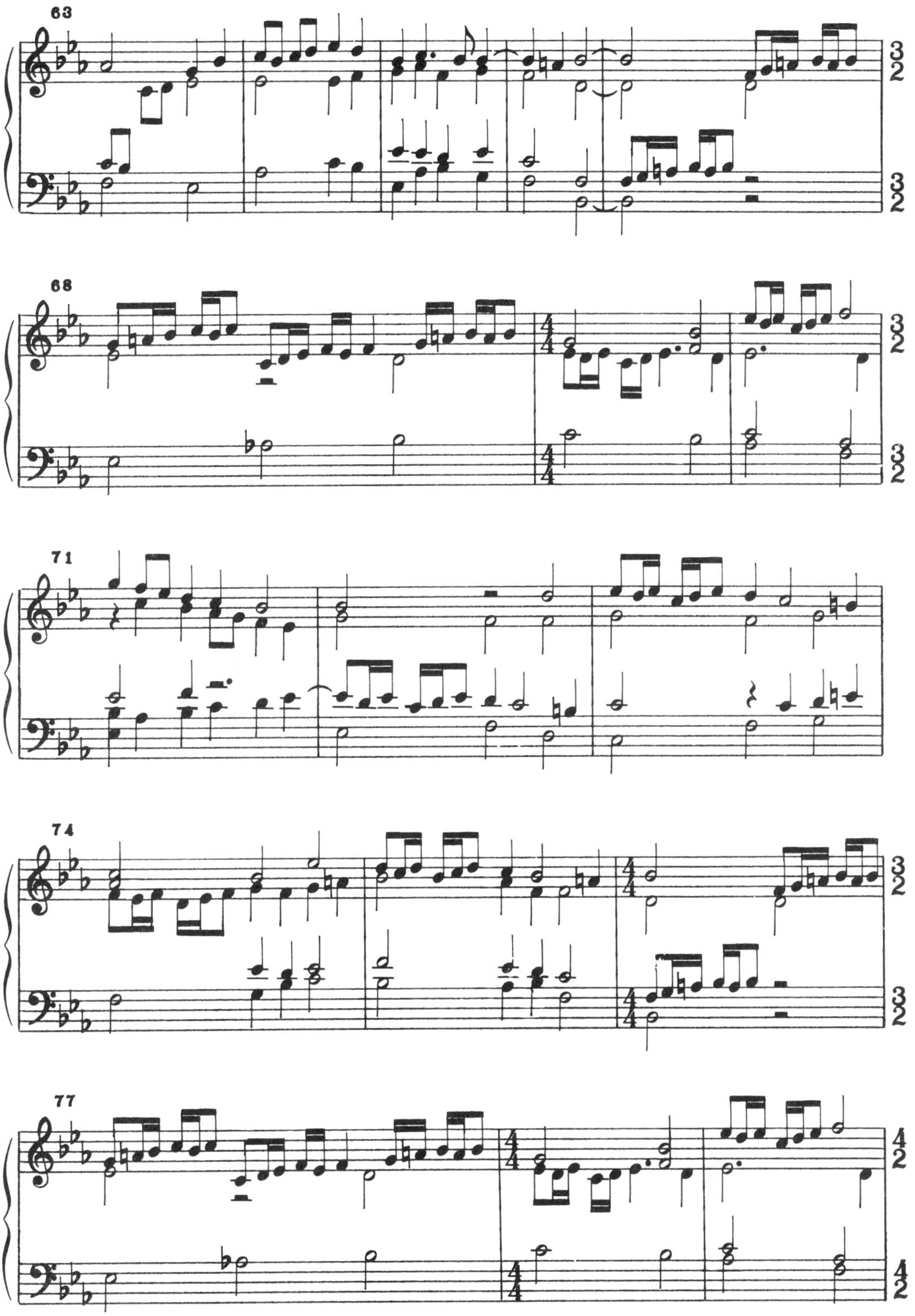
63
68
71
74
77

180

47. FANTASIA NO. 30 in Tones III and IV (Fol. L iii^v)

Allegro Moderato

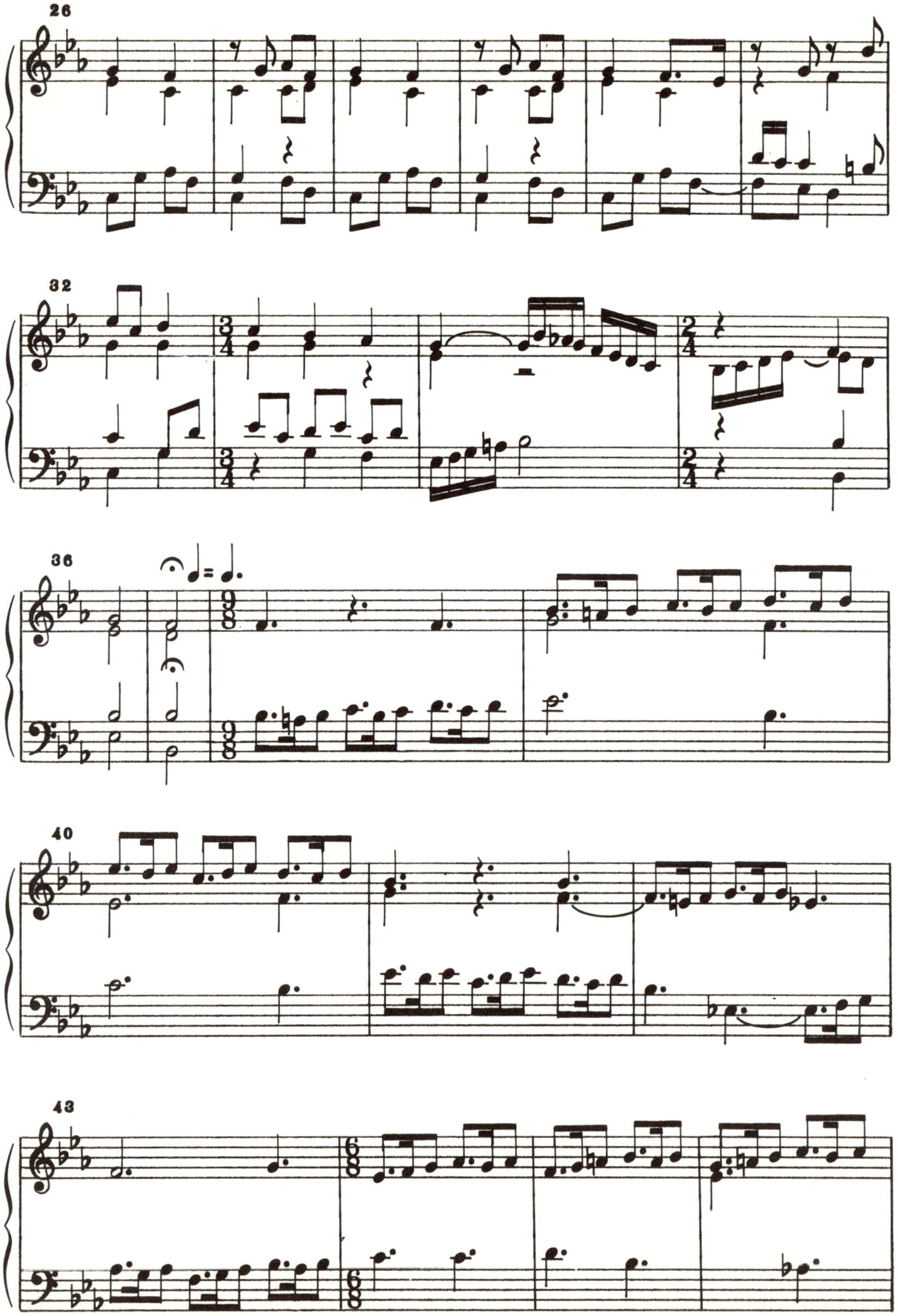
26
32
36
40
43

183

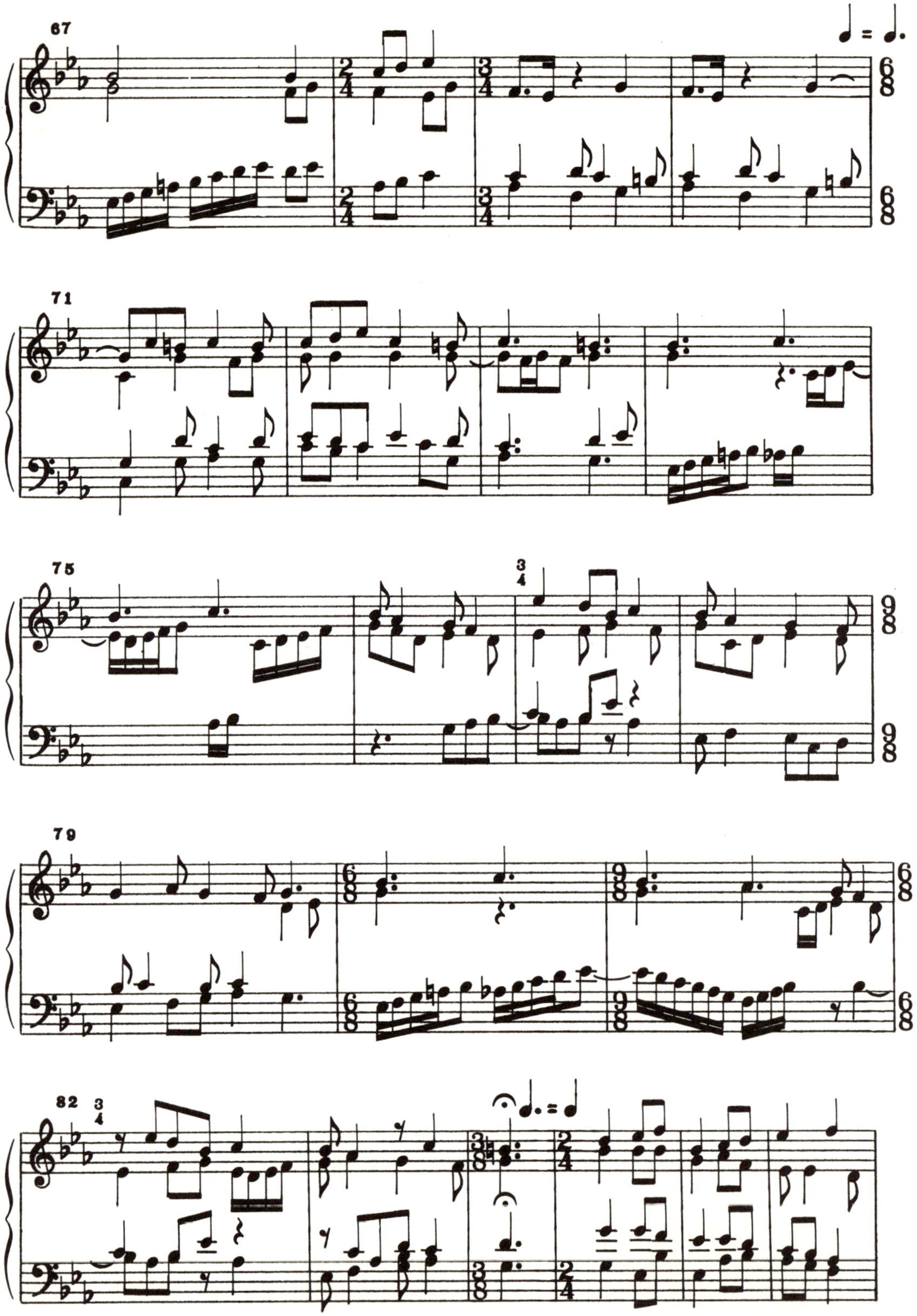
67
71
75
79
82

48. FANTASIA NO. 31 in Tone VI (Fol. [L vʳ])

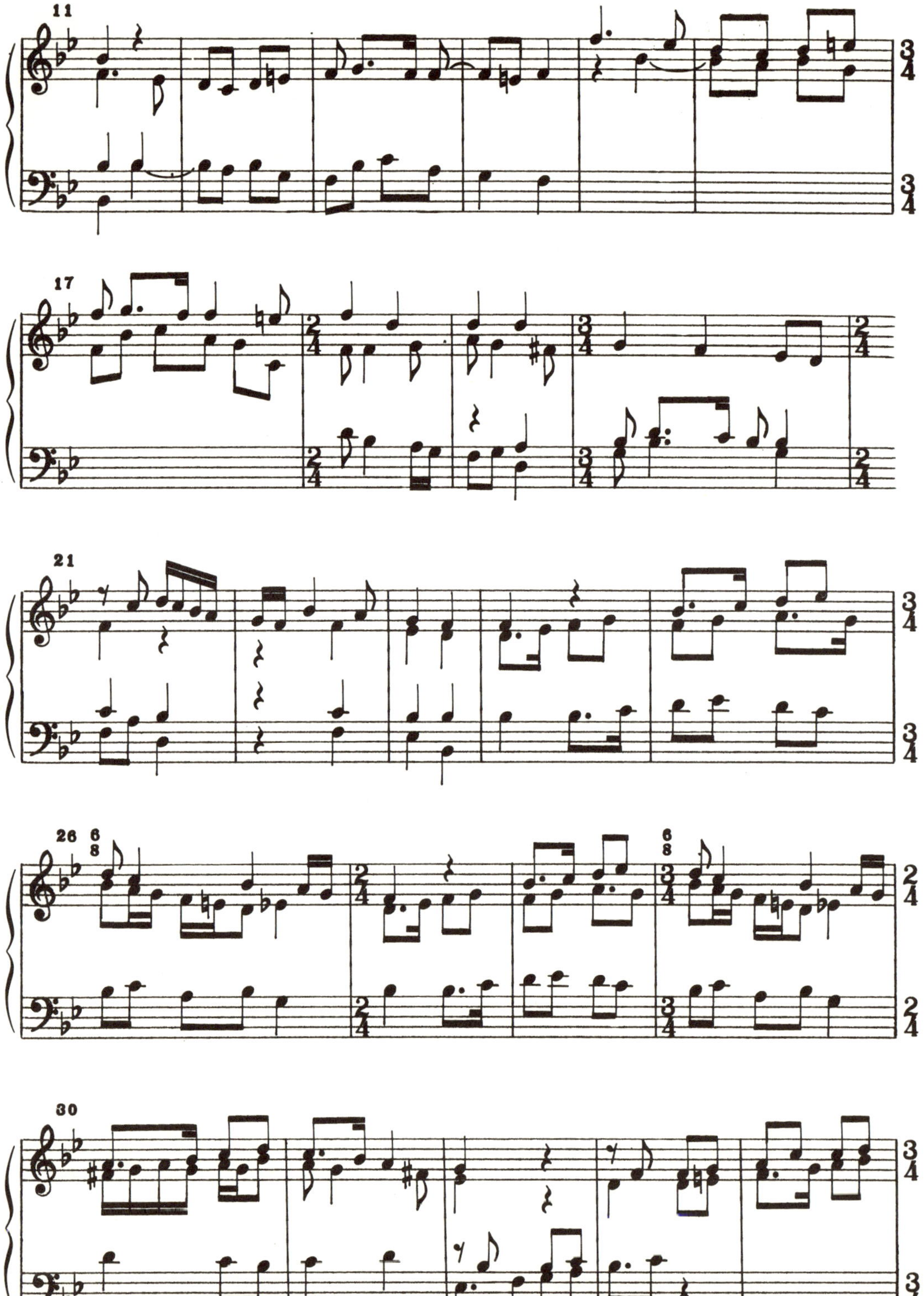
11
17
21
26
30

187

188

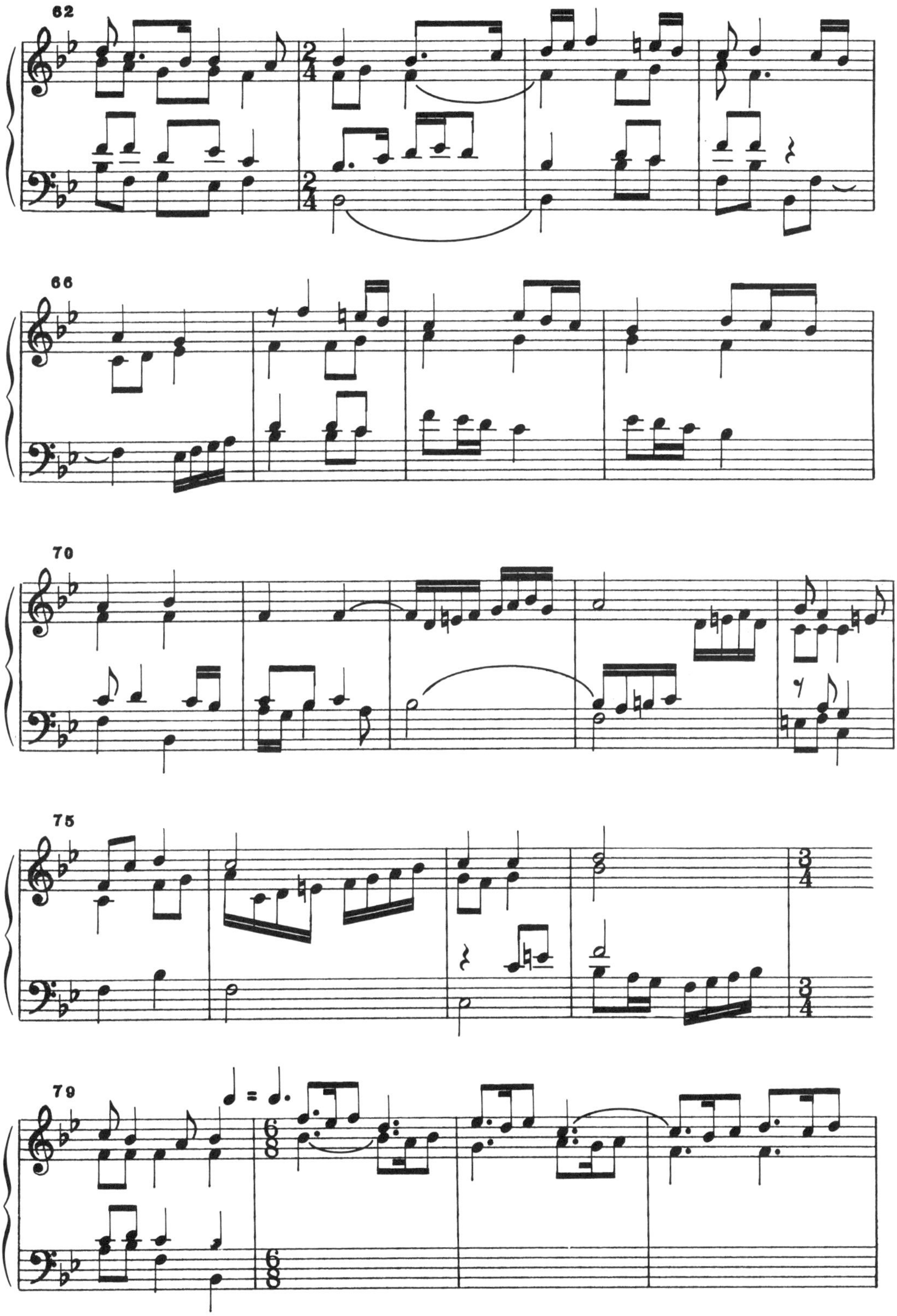
62
66
70
75
79

190

49. FANTASIA NO. 32 in Tone VI (Fol. M^r)

Allegro Moderato

[sic]

192

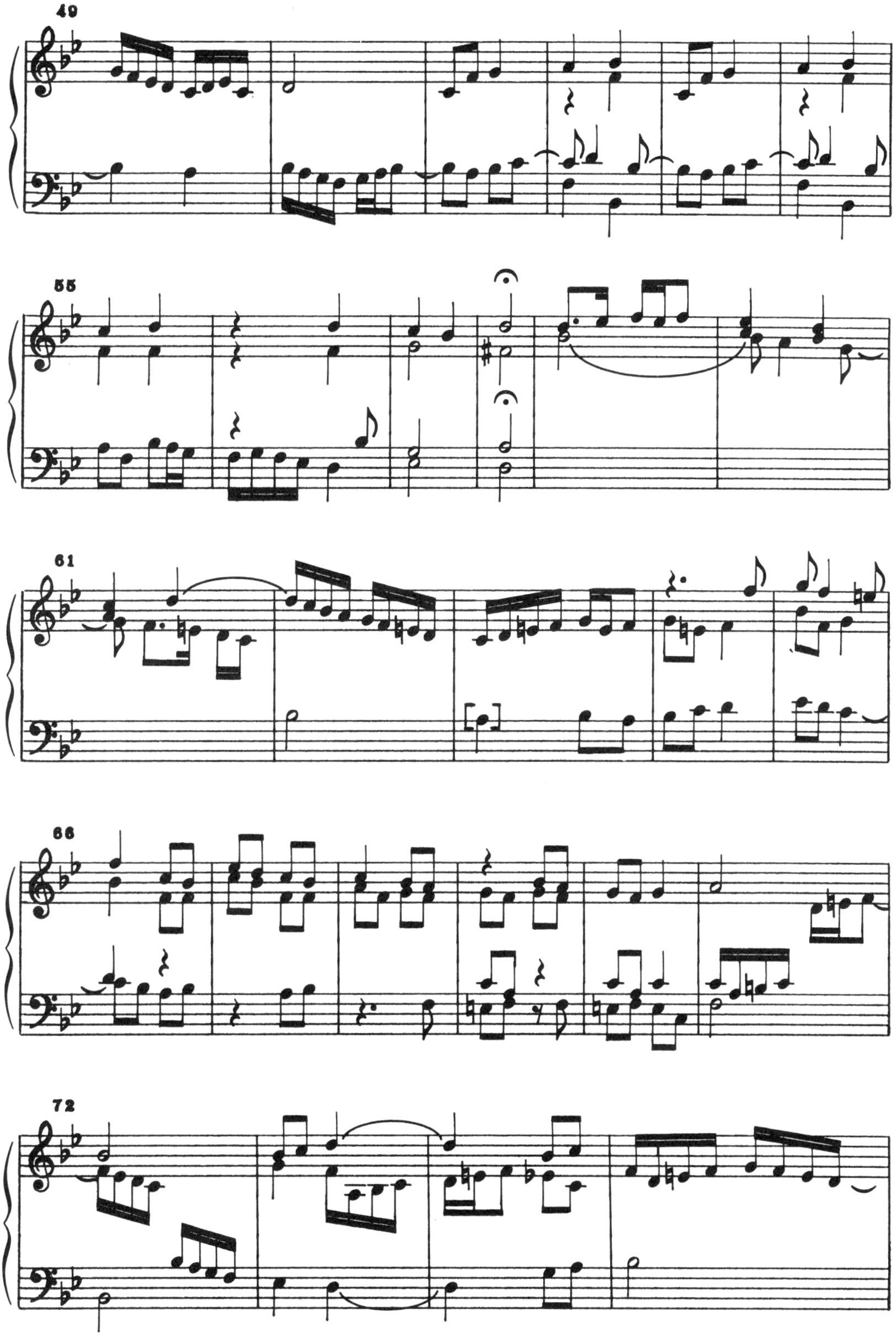
49
55
61
66
72

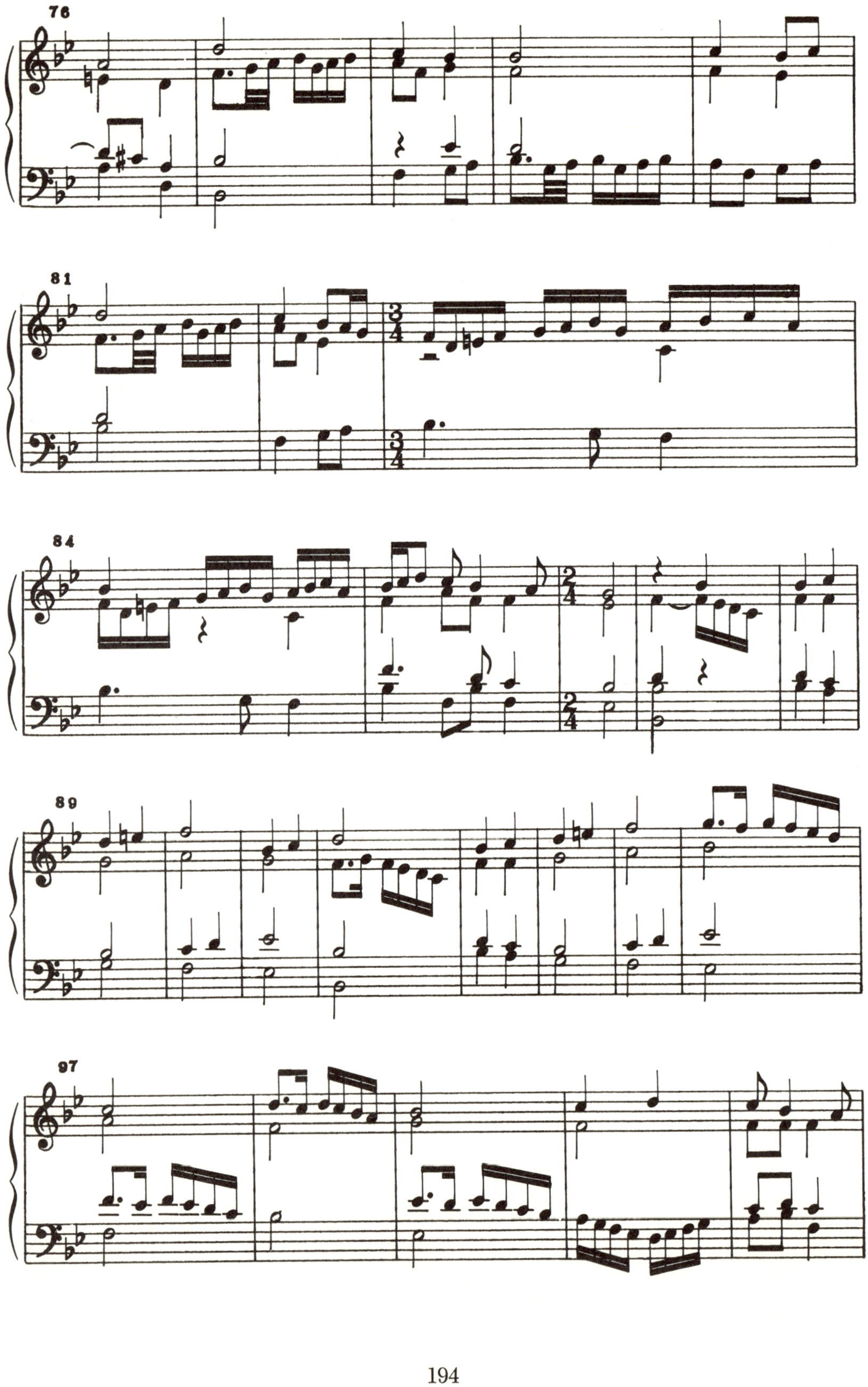
76
81
84
89
97

50. FANTASIA NO. 33 in Tone VI (Fol. M ii^v)

196

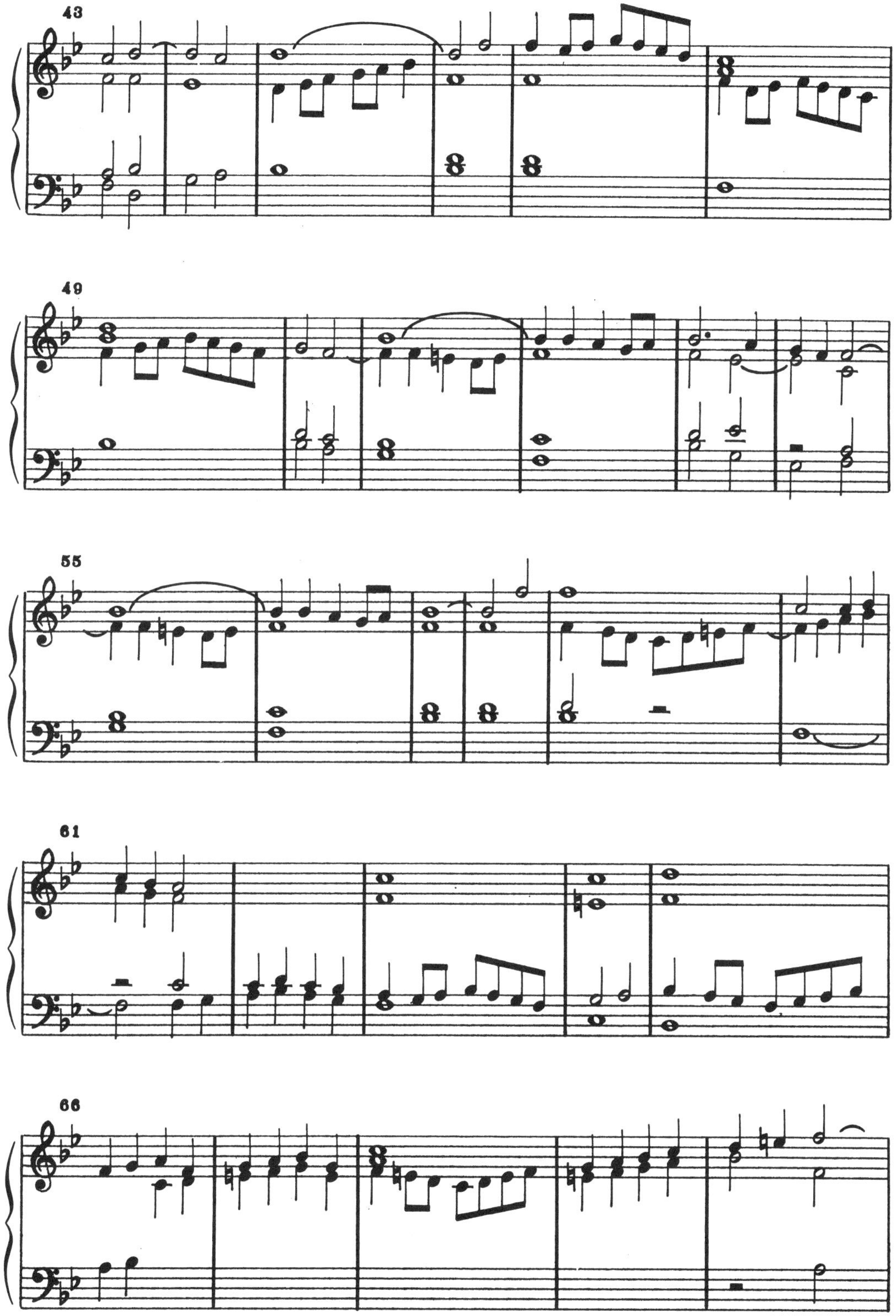
43
49
55
61
66

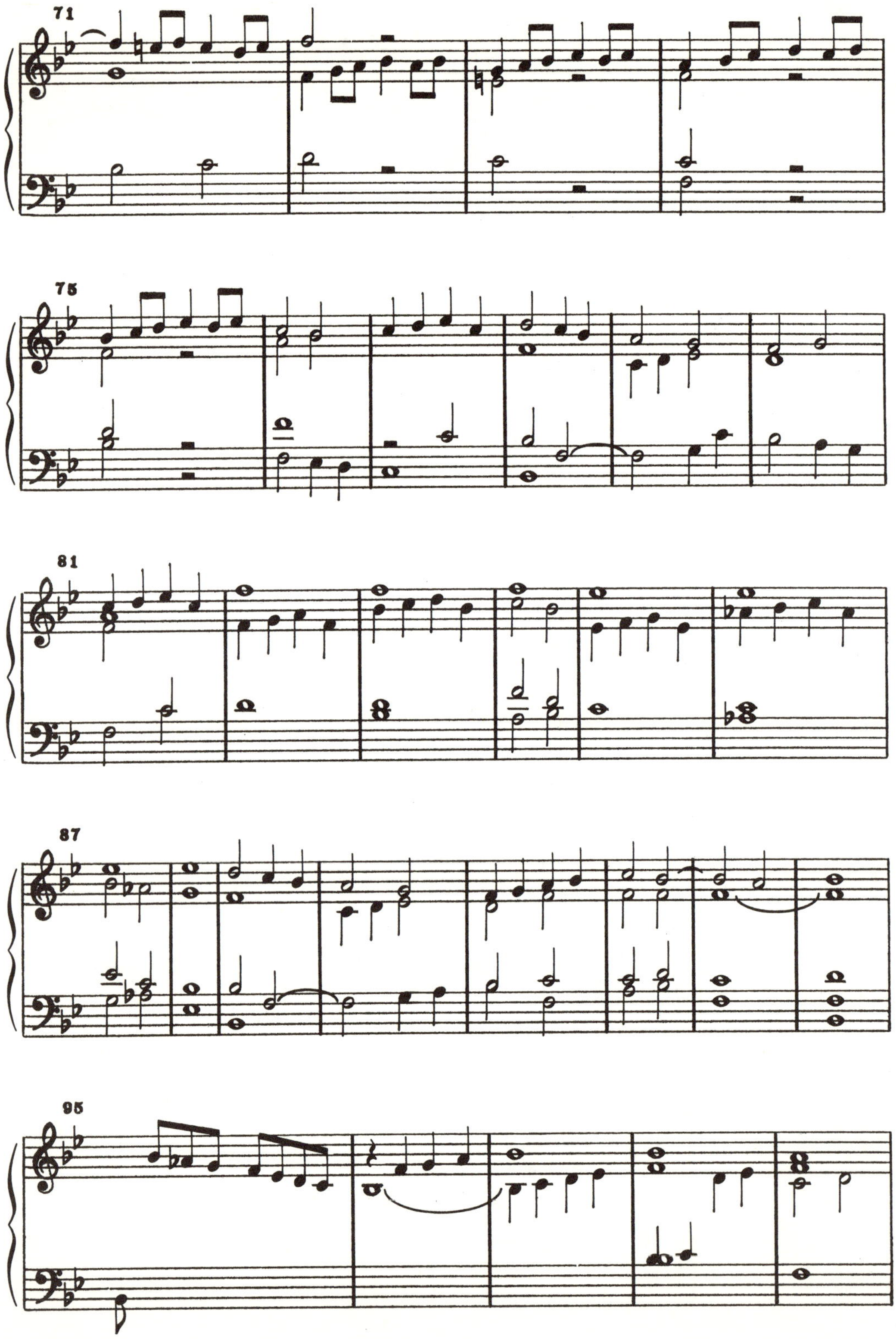
71
75
81
87
95

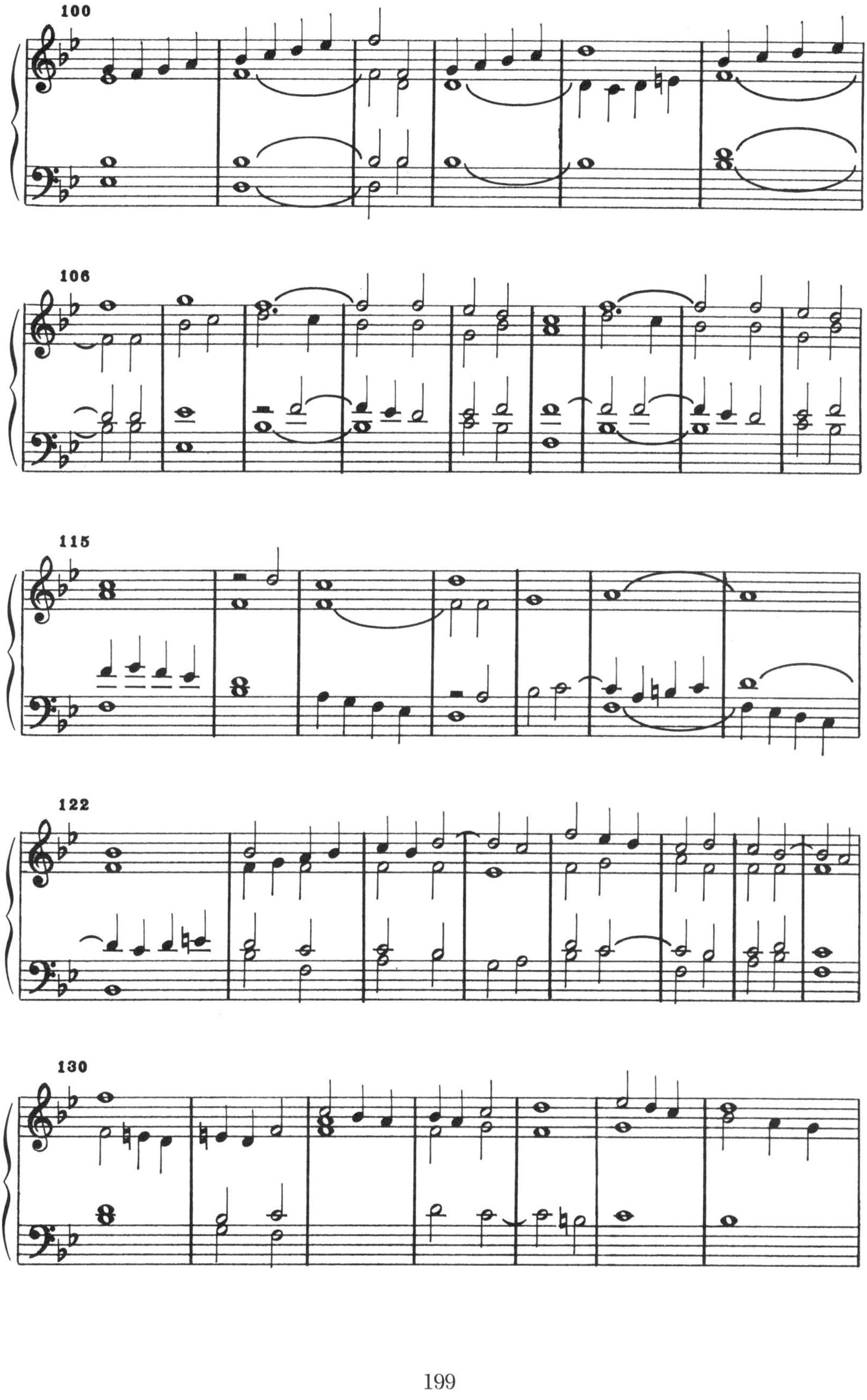
100
106
115
122
130

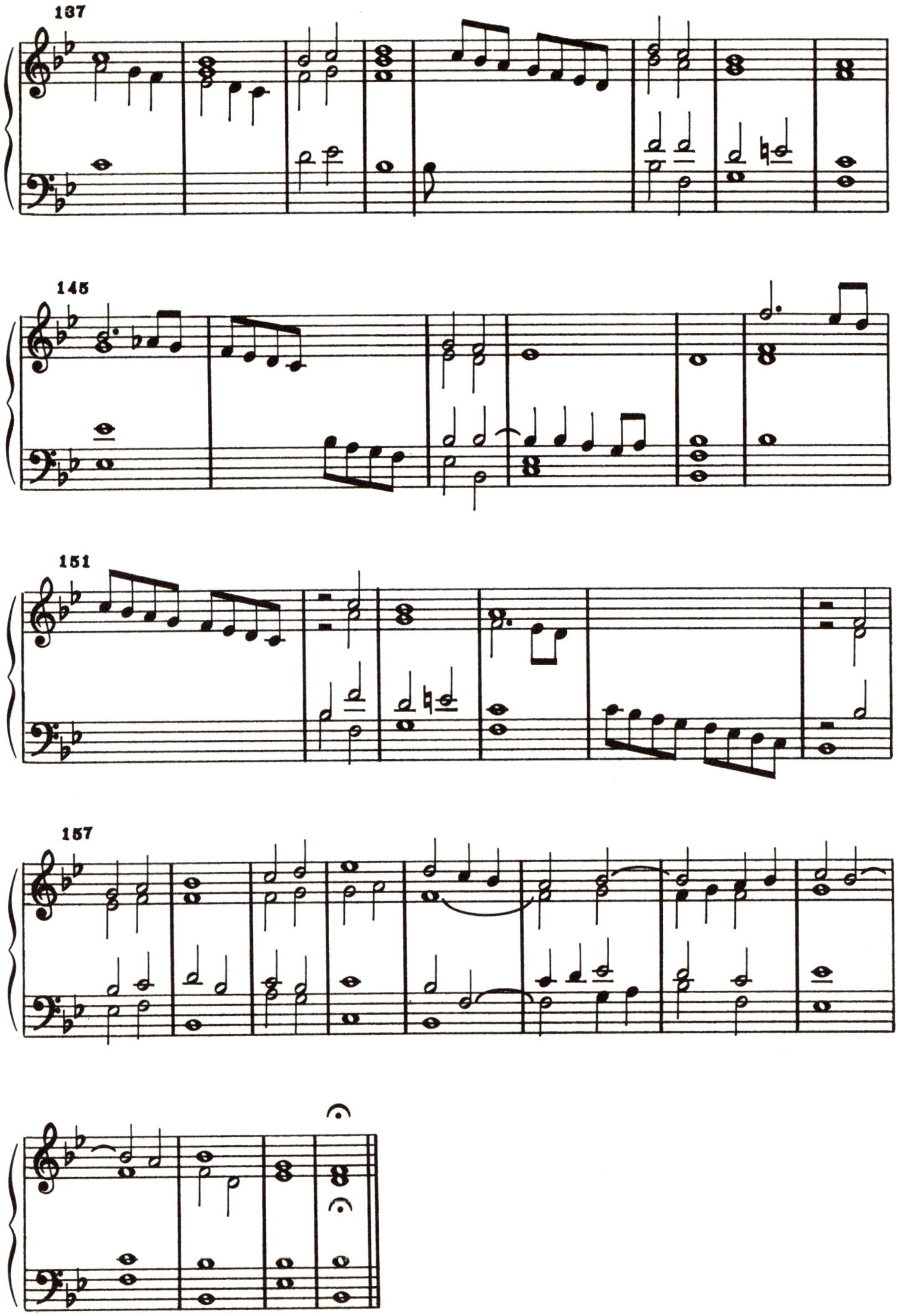
137
145
151
157

51. TENTO NO. 1 in Tones I and II (Fol. [M iv^v])

Moderato e Rubato

202

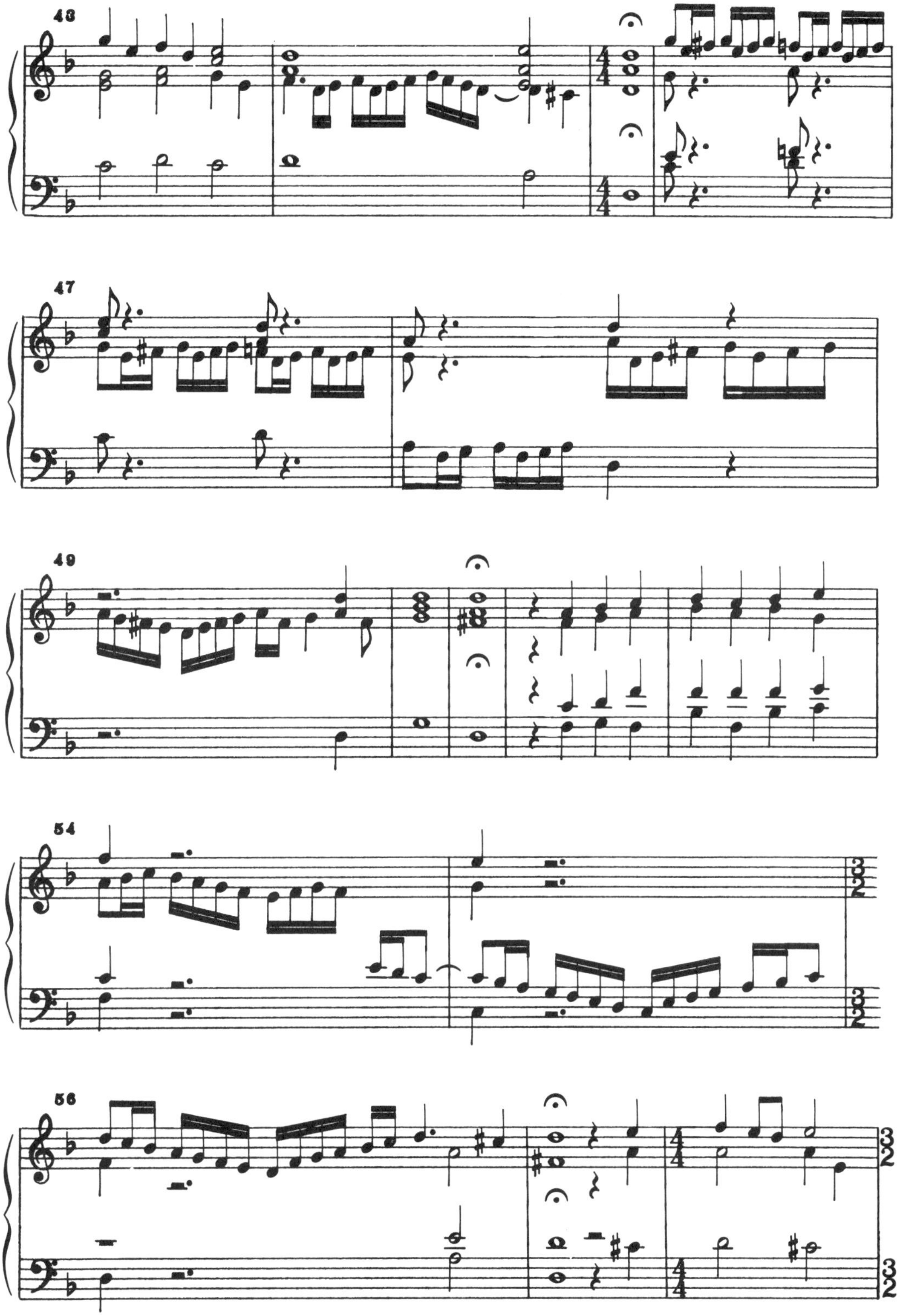
43
47
49
54
56

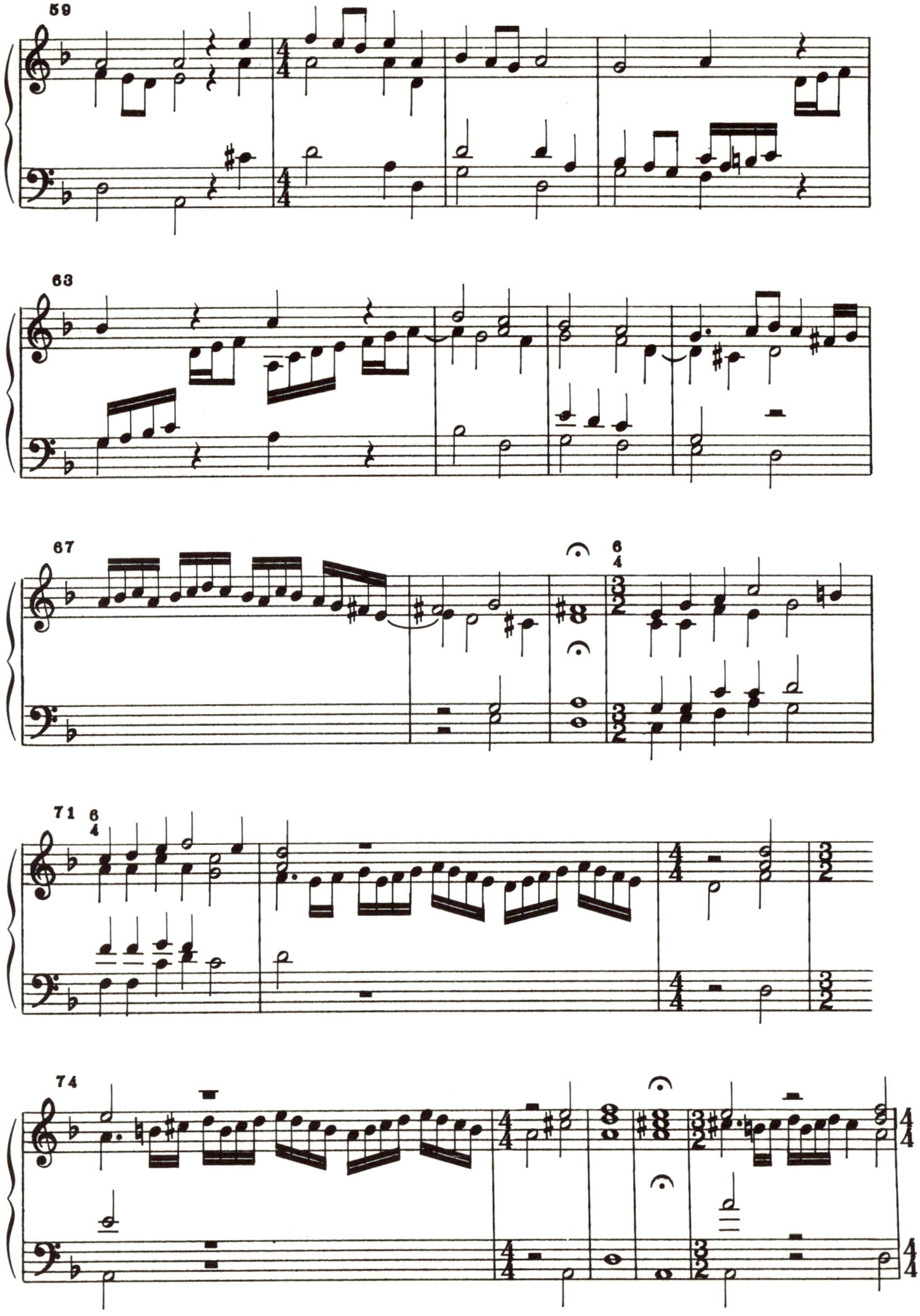
59
63
67
71
74

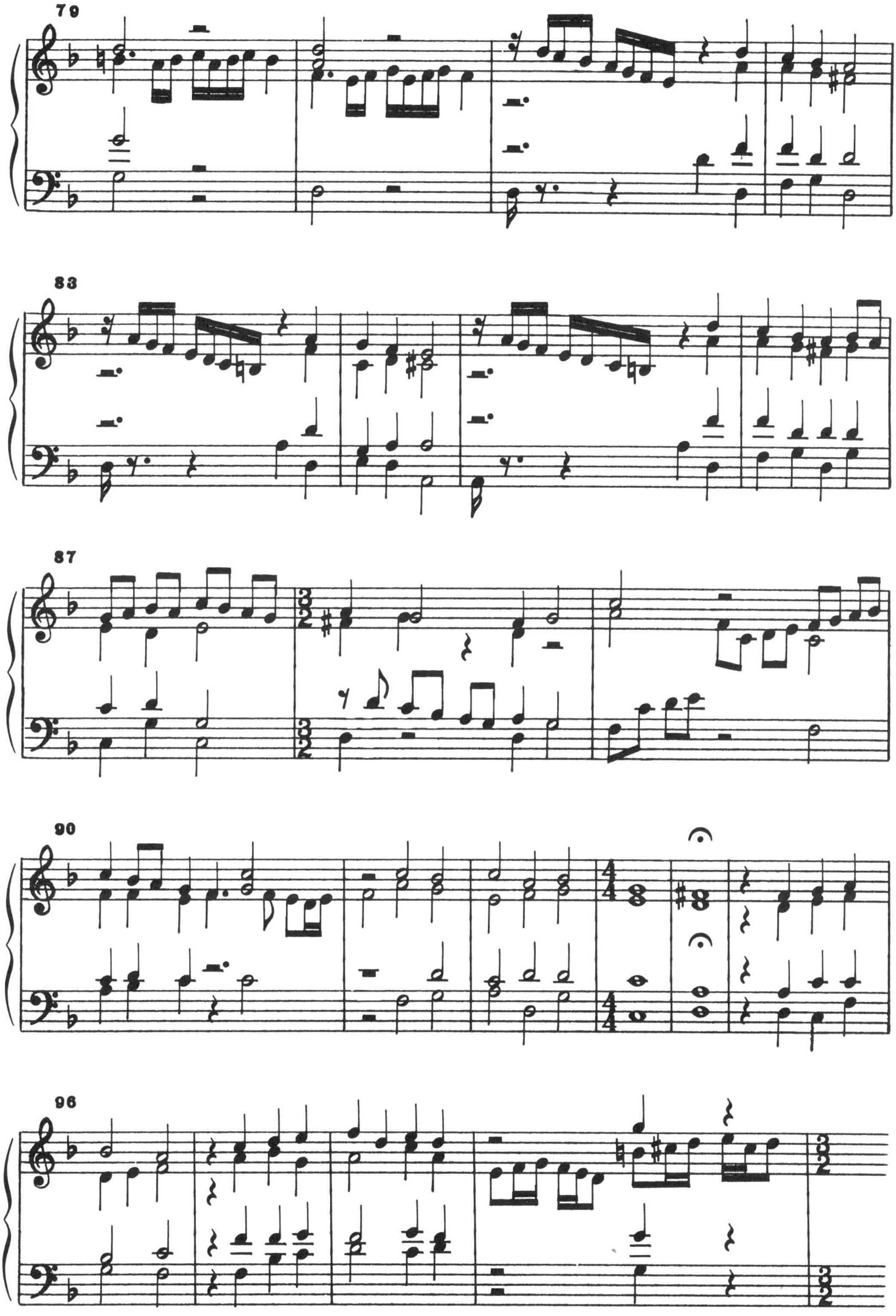
79
83
87
90
96

206

52. TENTO NO. 2 in Tones III and IV (Fol. Nr)

✻ To be played on Courses 4 and 5 (i.e., strings tuned to d and g).

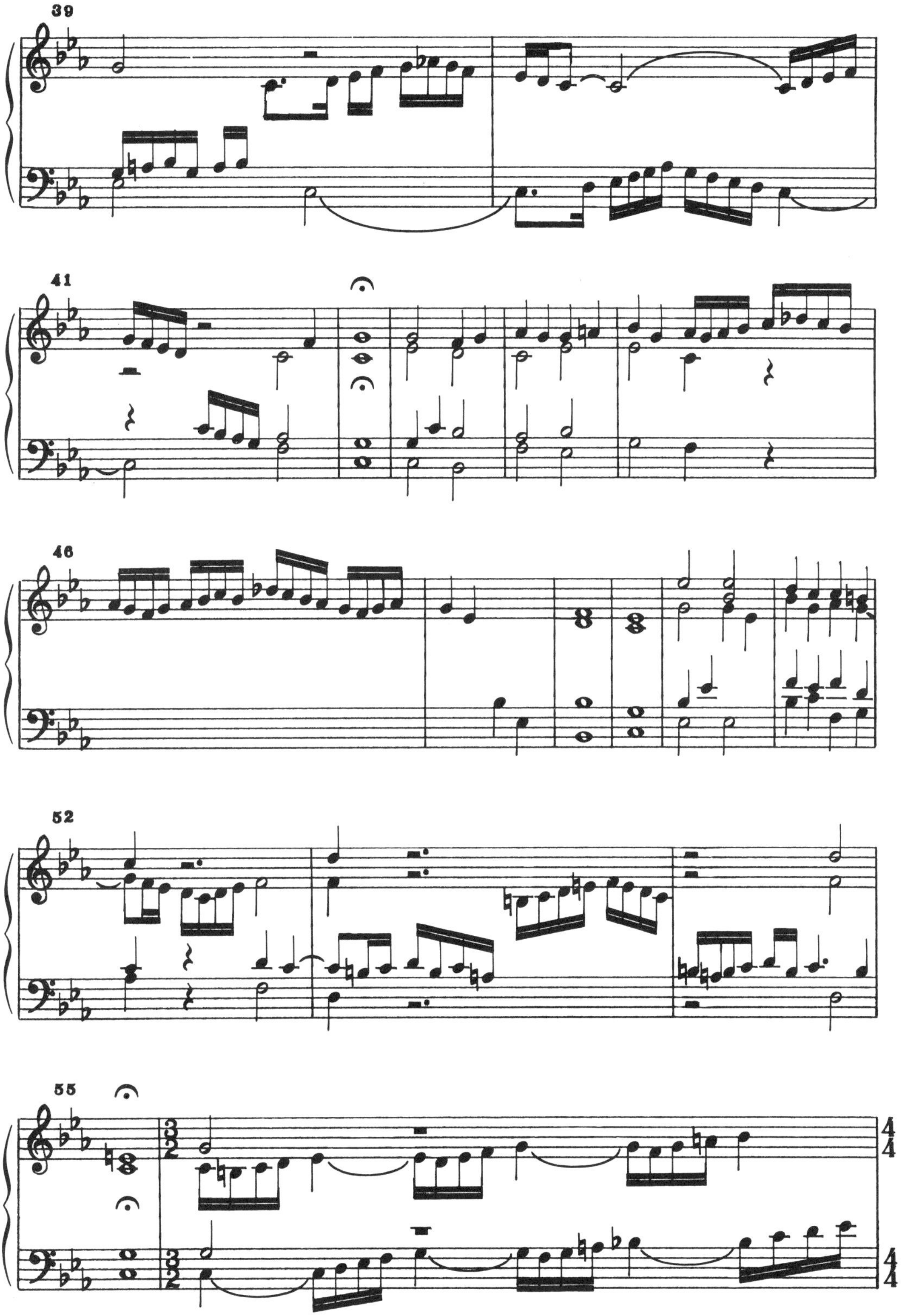
39
41
46
52
55

✱ To be played on Courses 4 and 5   (i.e., strings tuned to d and g).

211

53. TENTO NO. 3 in Tones V and VI (Fol. N iiiʳ)

Moderato e Rubato

213

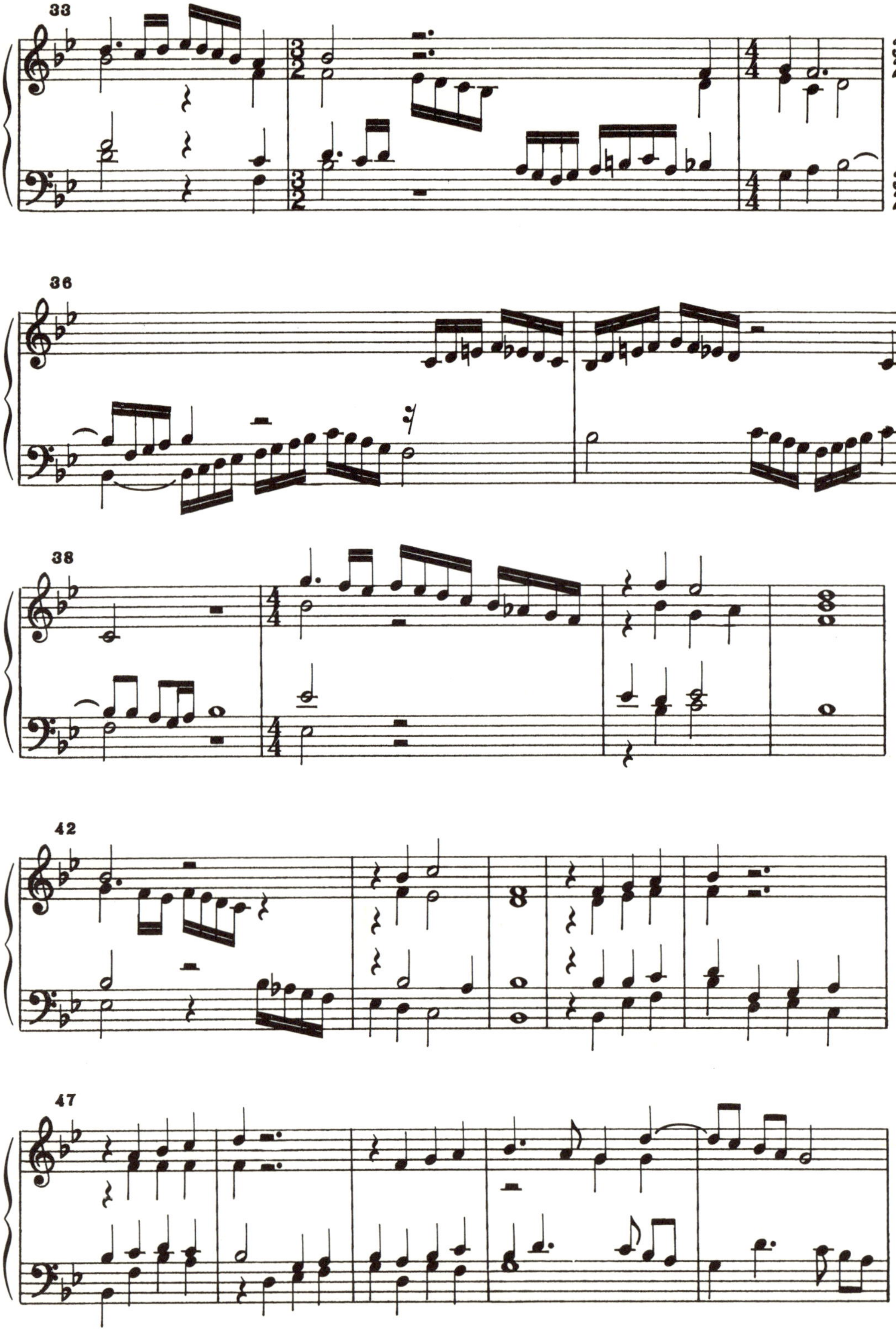
33
36
38
42
47

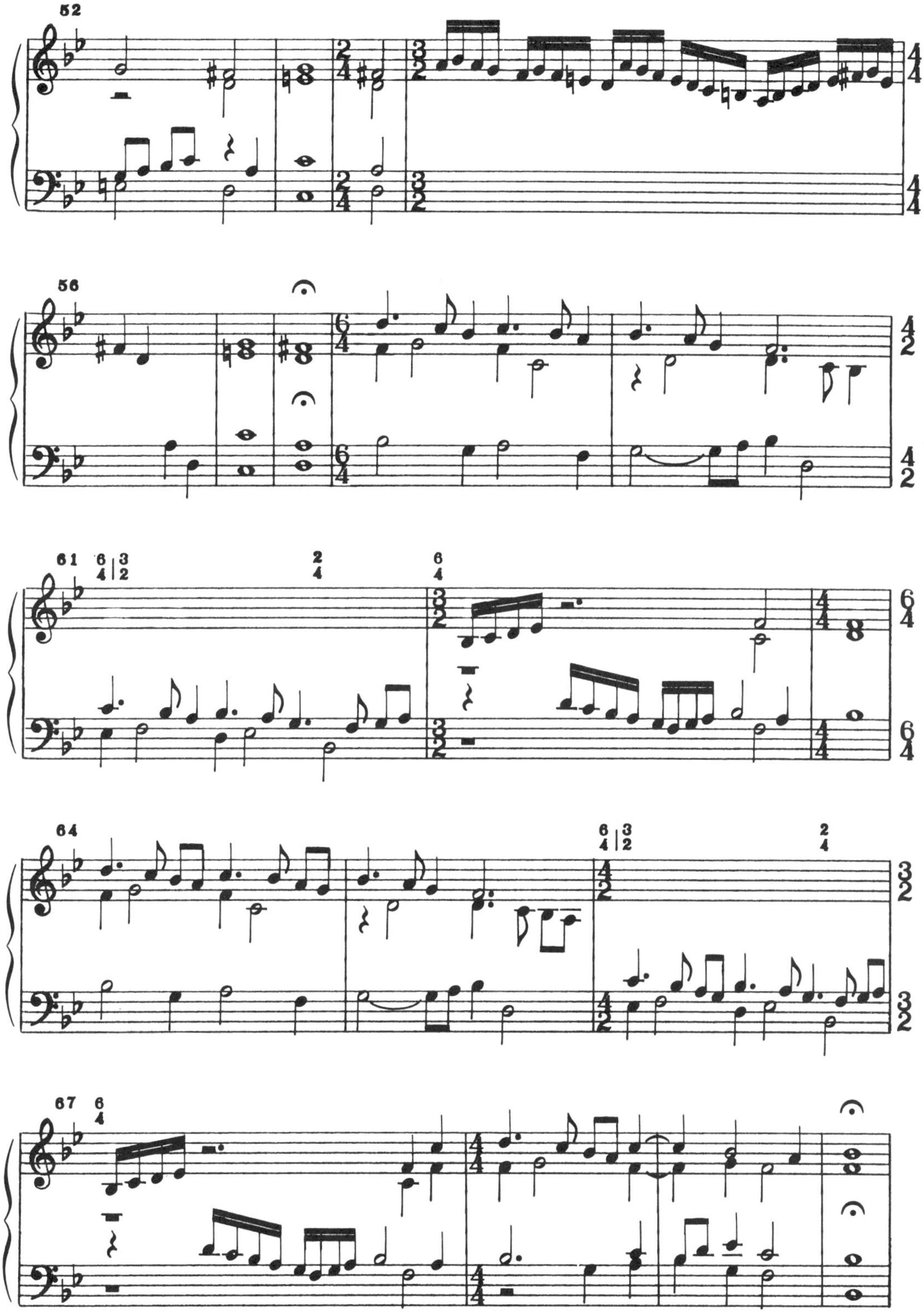
52
56
61
64
67

216

54. TENTO NO. 4 in Tones VII and VIII (Fol. [N vʳ])

Moderato e Rubato

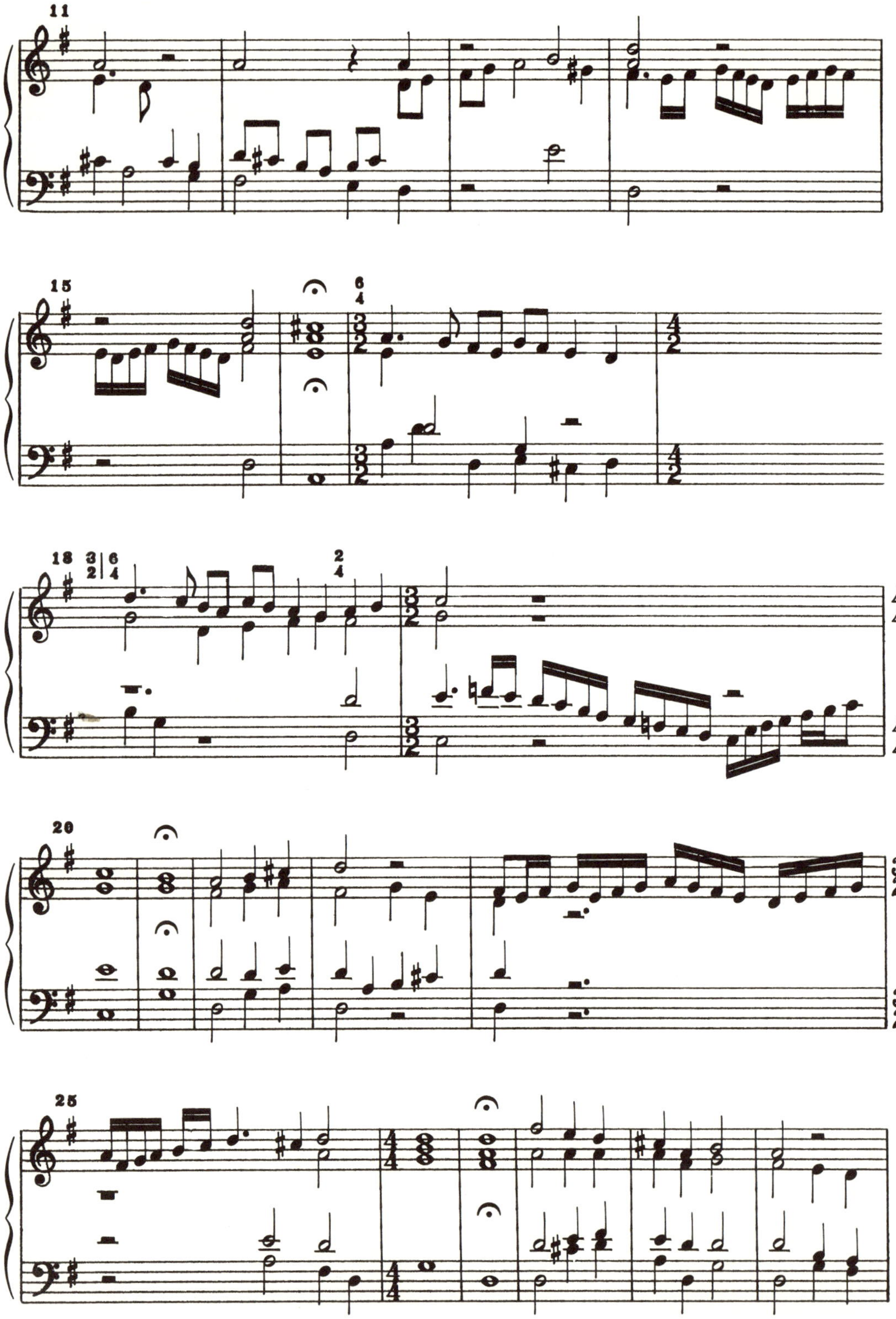
11
15
18
20
25

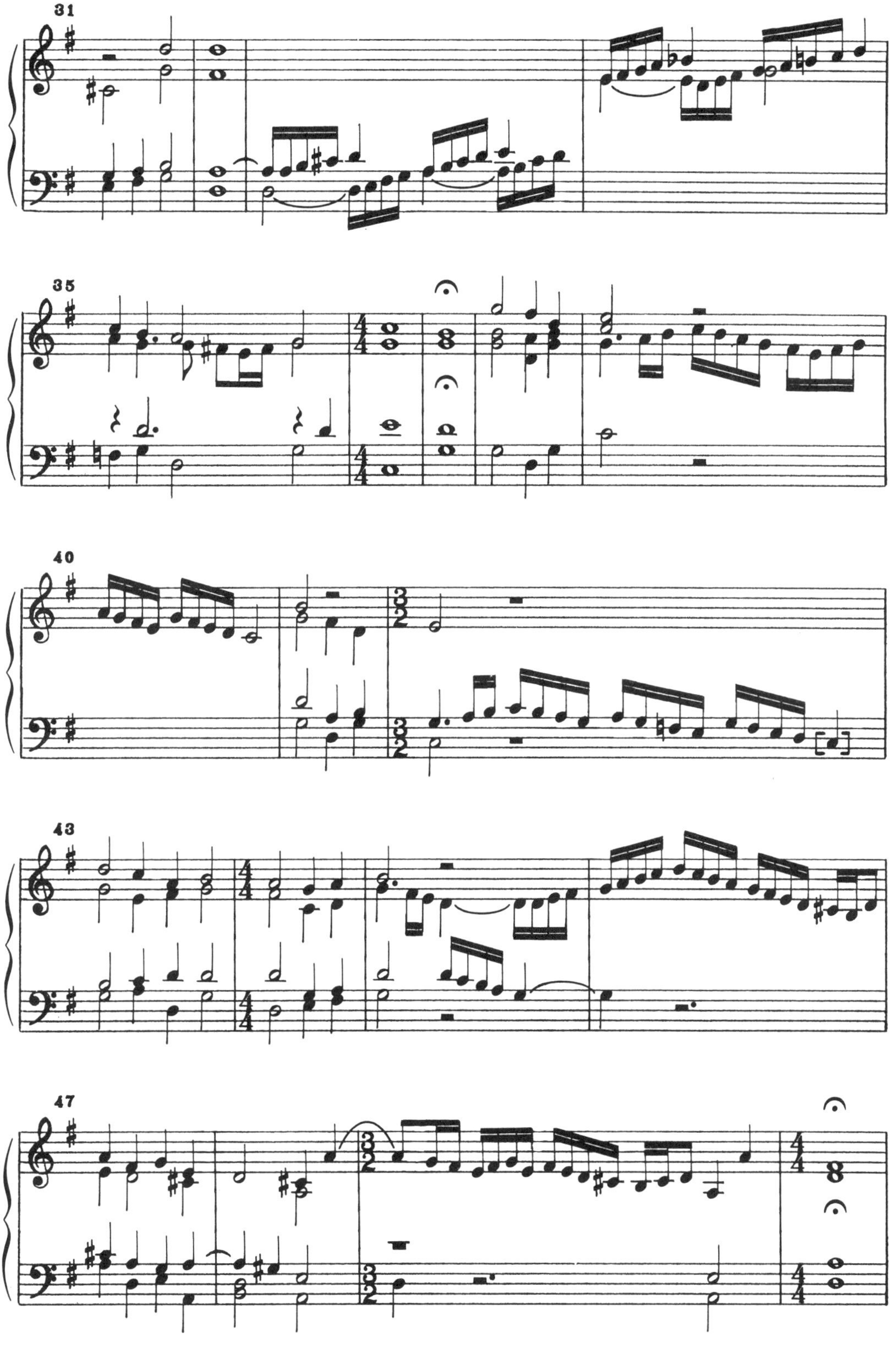
31
35
40
43
47

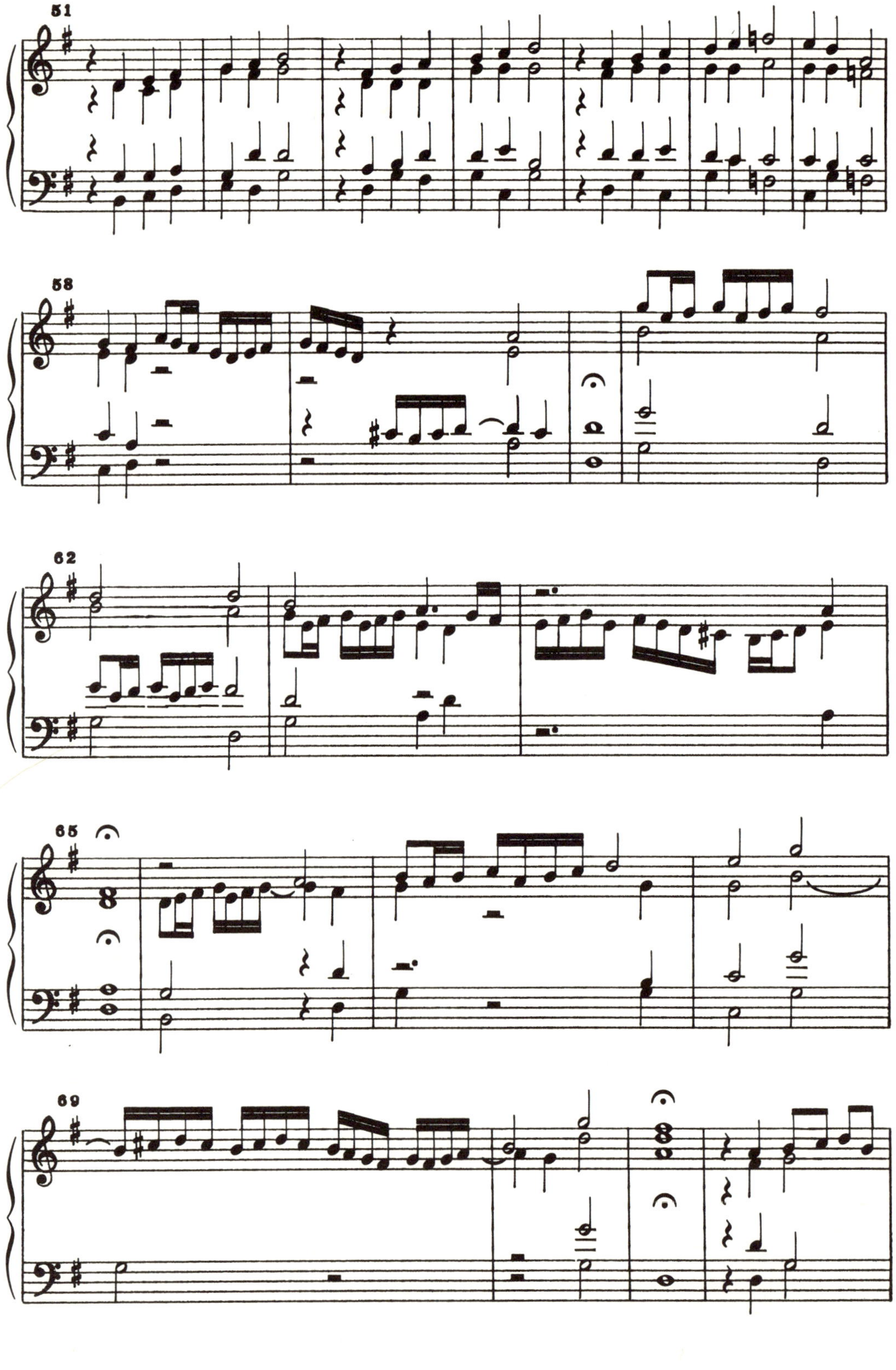
51
58
62
65
69

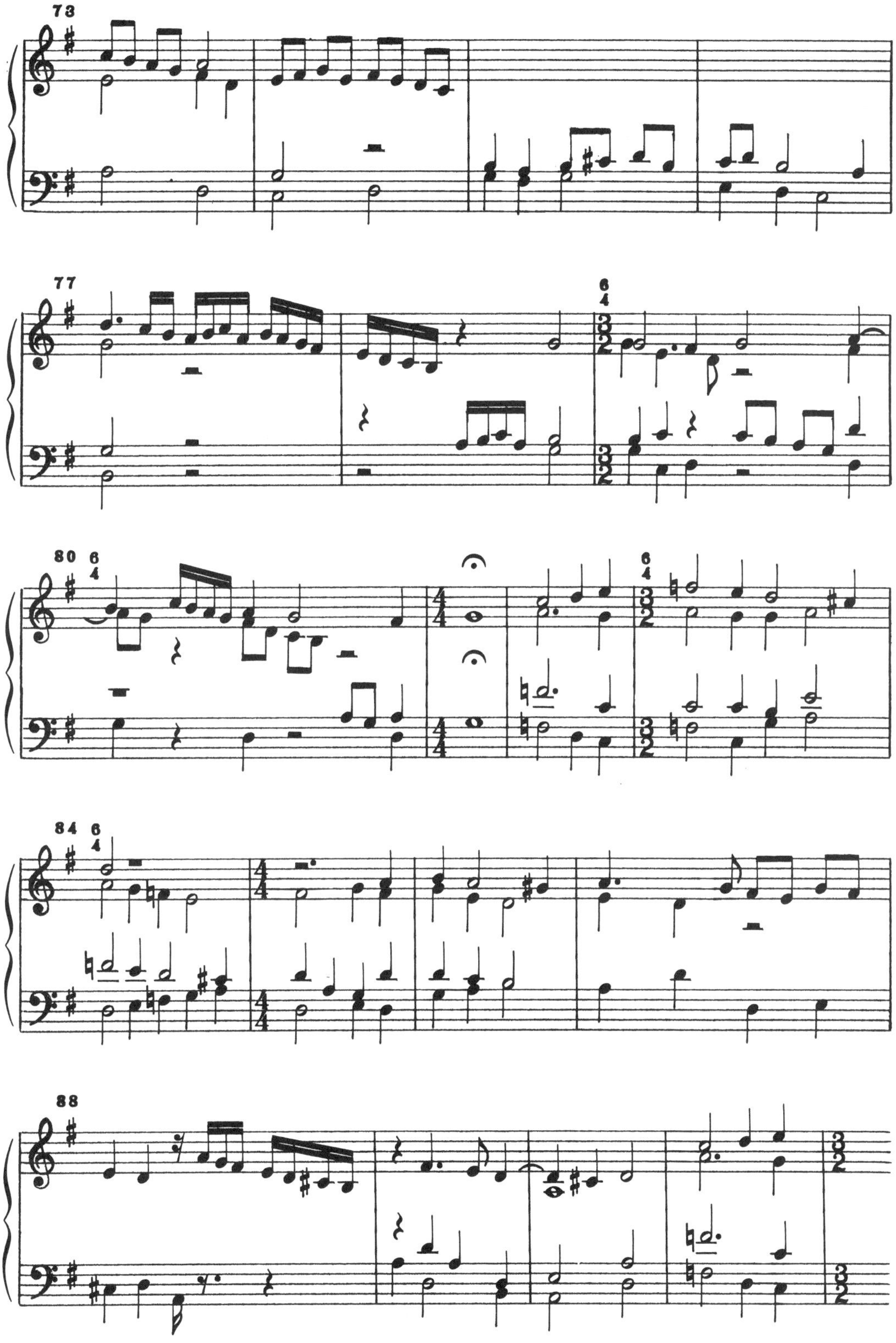
73
77
80
84
88

55. FANTASIA NO. 34 in Tone VII (Fol. O^r)

Allegro Moderato

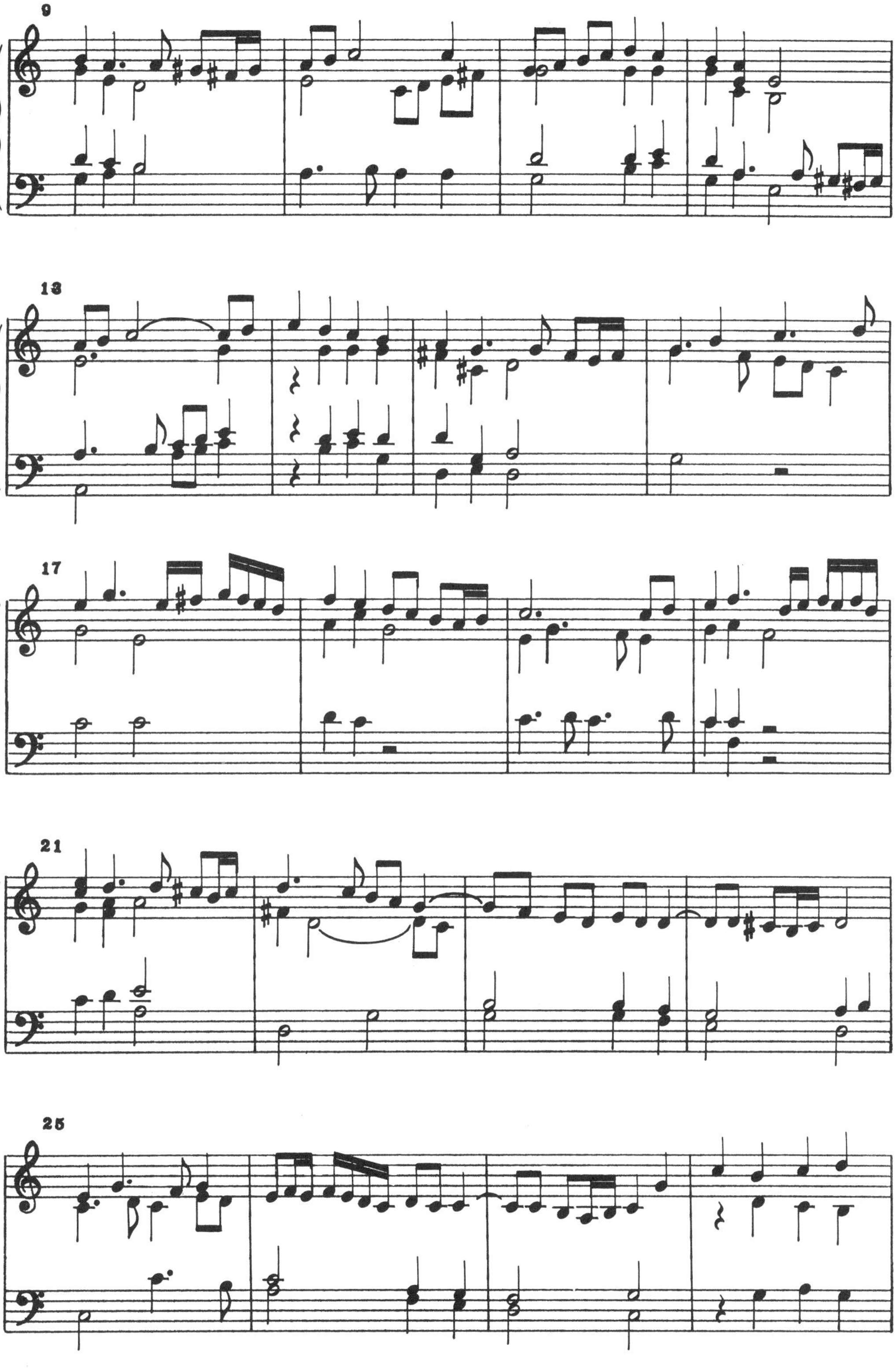
9
13
17
21
25

224

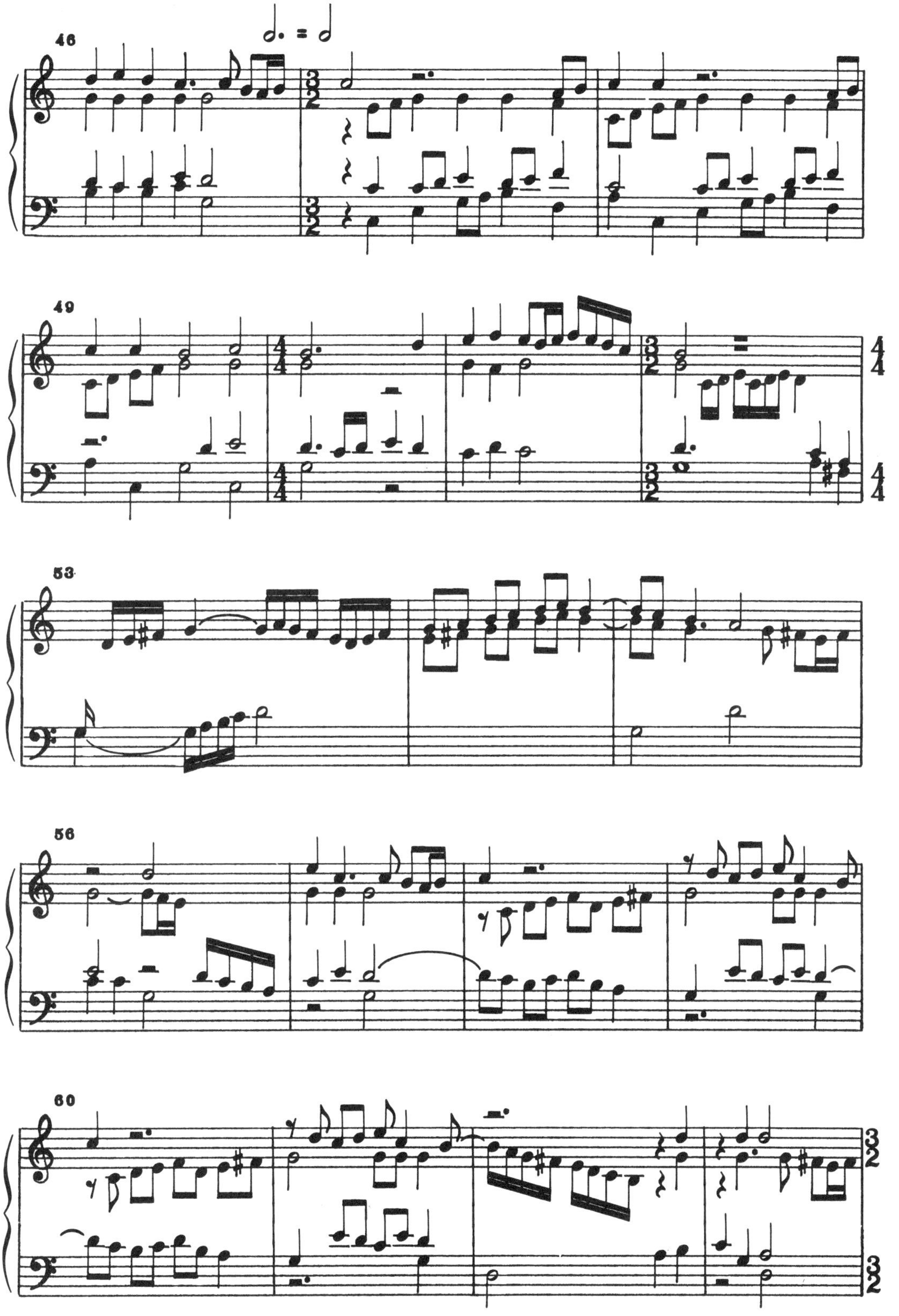
46
49
53
56
60

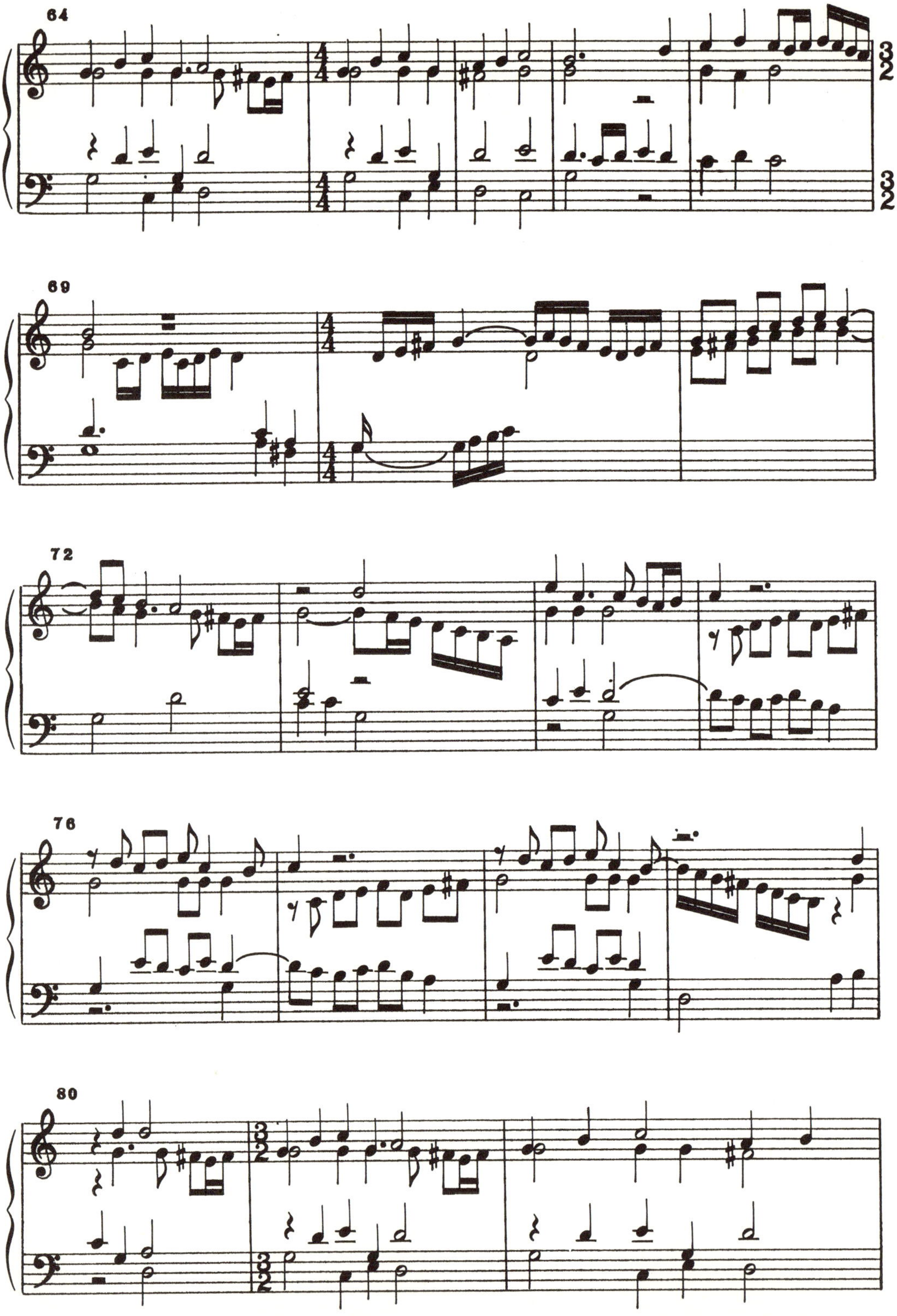
64
69
72
76
80

56. FANTASIA NO. 35 in Tone VIII (Fol. O ii^v)

Molto Allegro

228

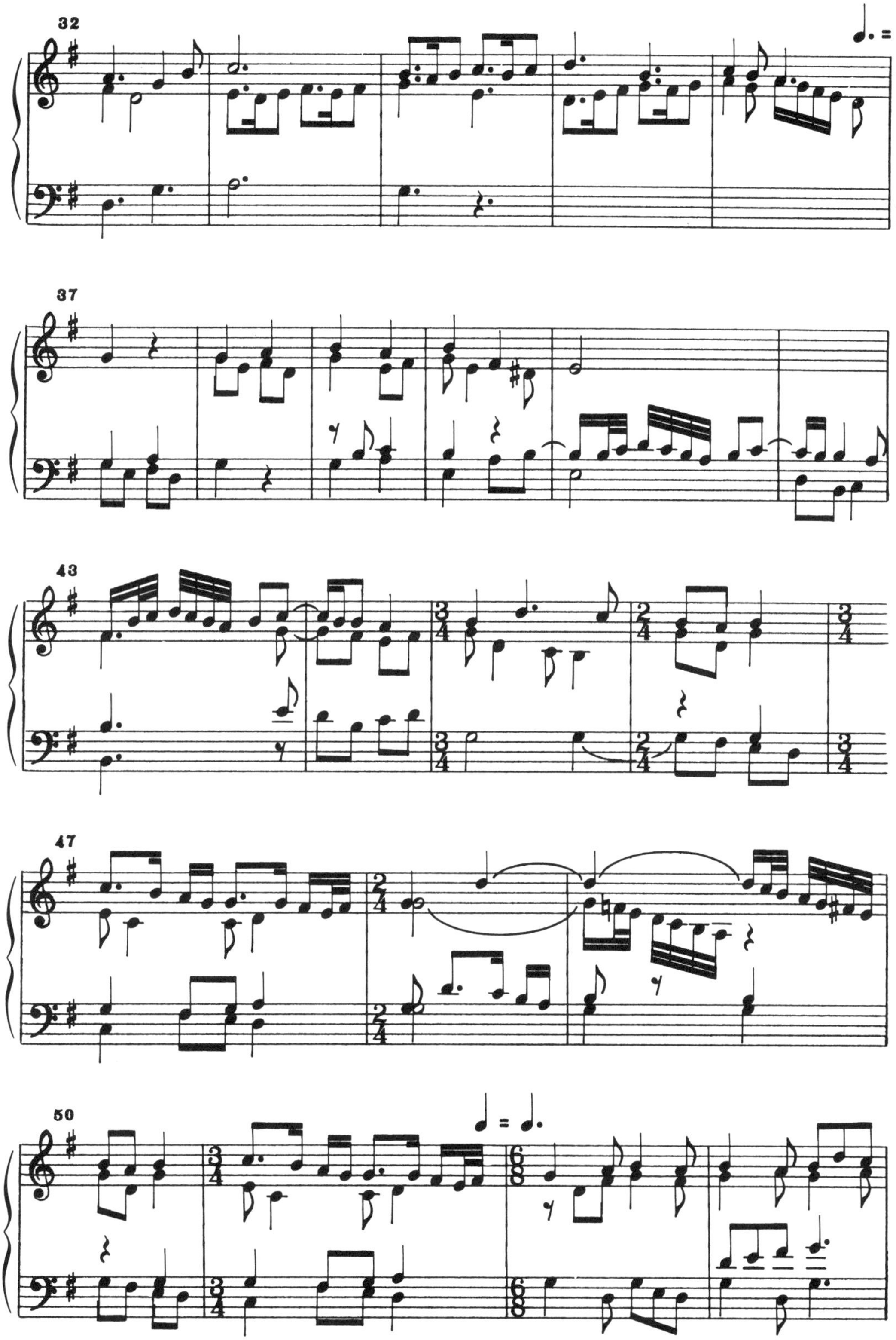
32
37
43
47
50

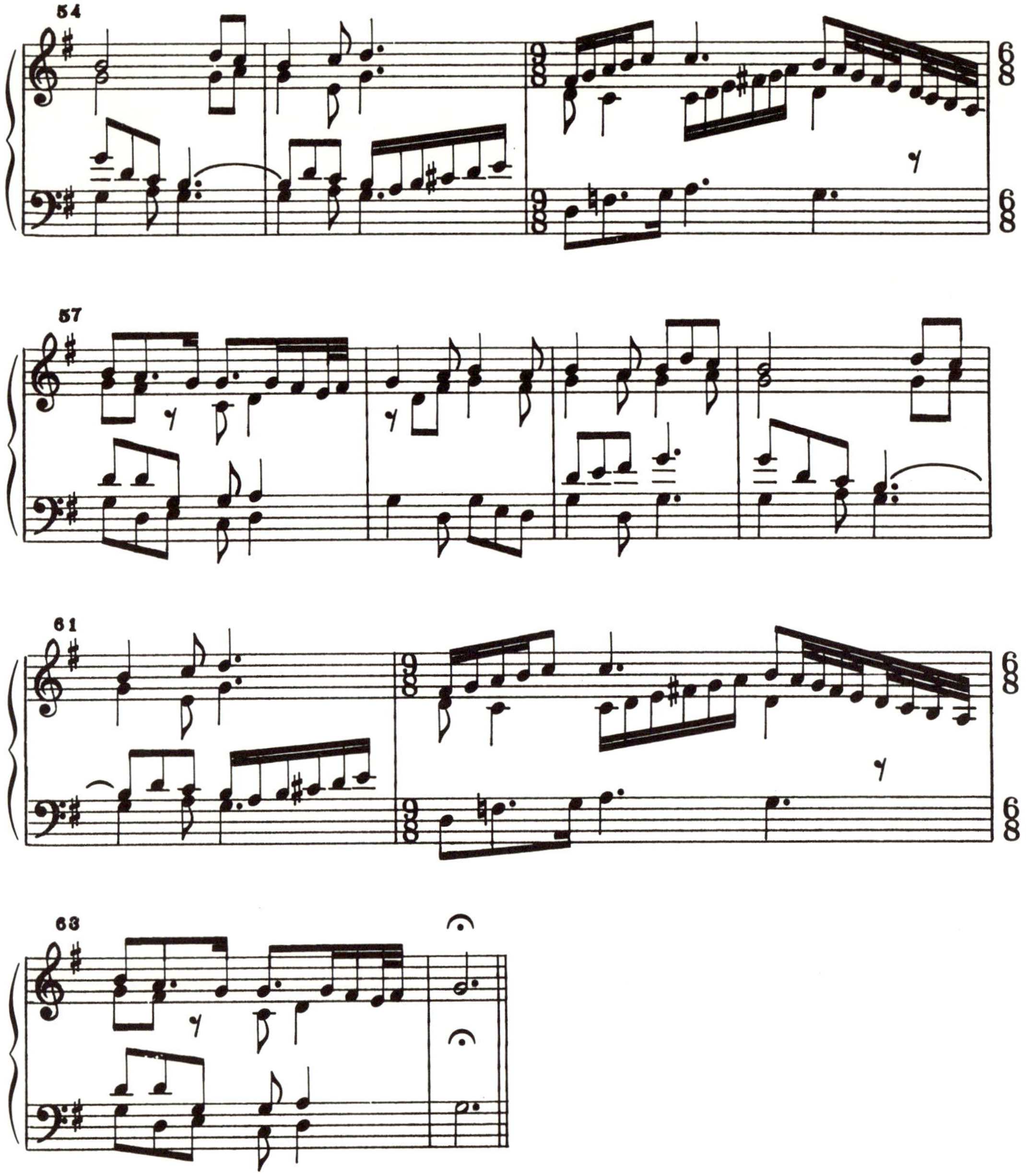
54
57
61
63

57. FANTASIA NO. 36 in Tones VII and VIII (Fol. [O iv^r])

Moderato

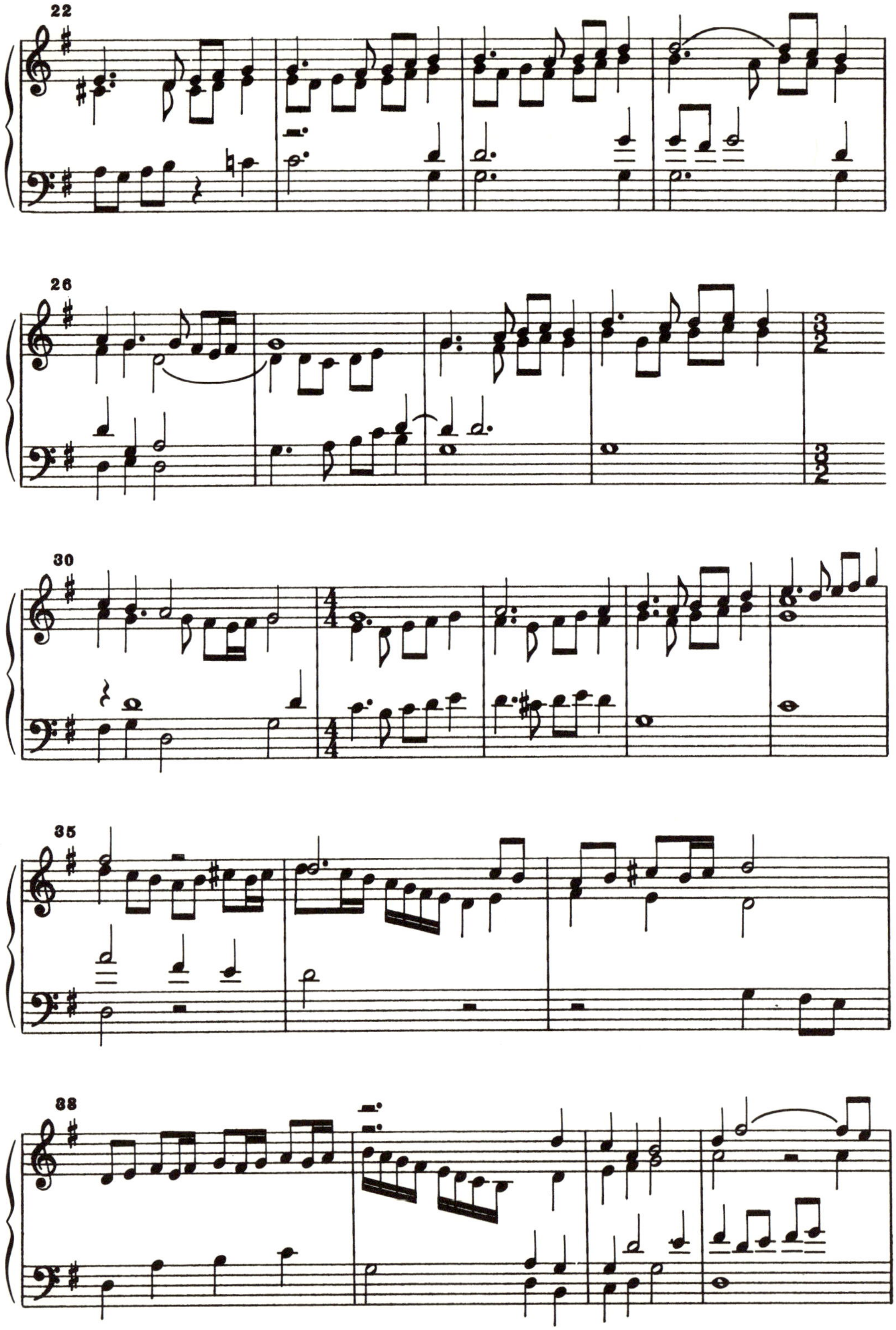
22
26
30
35
38

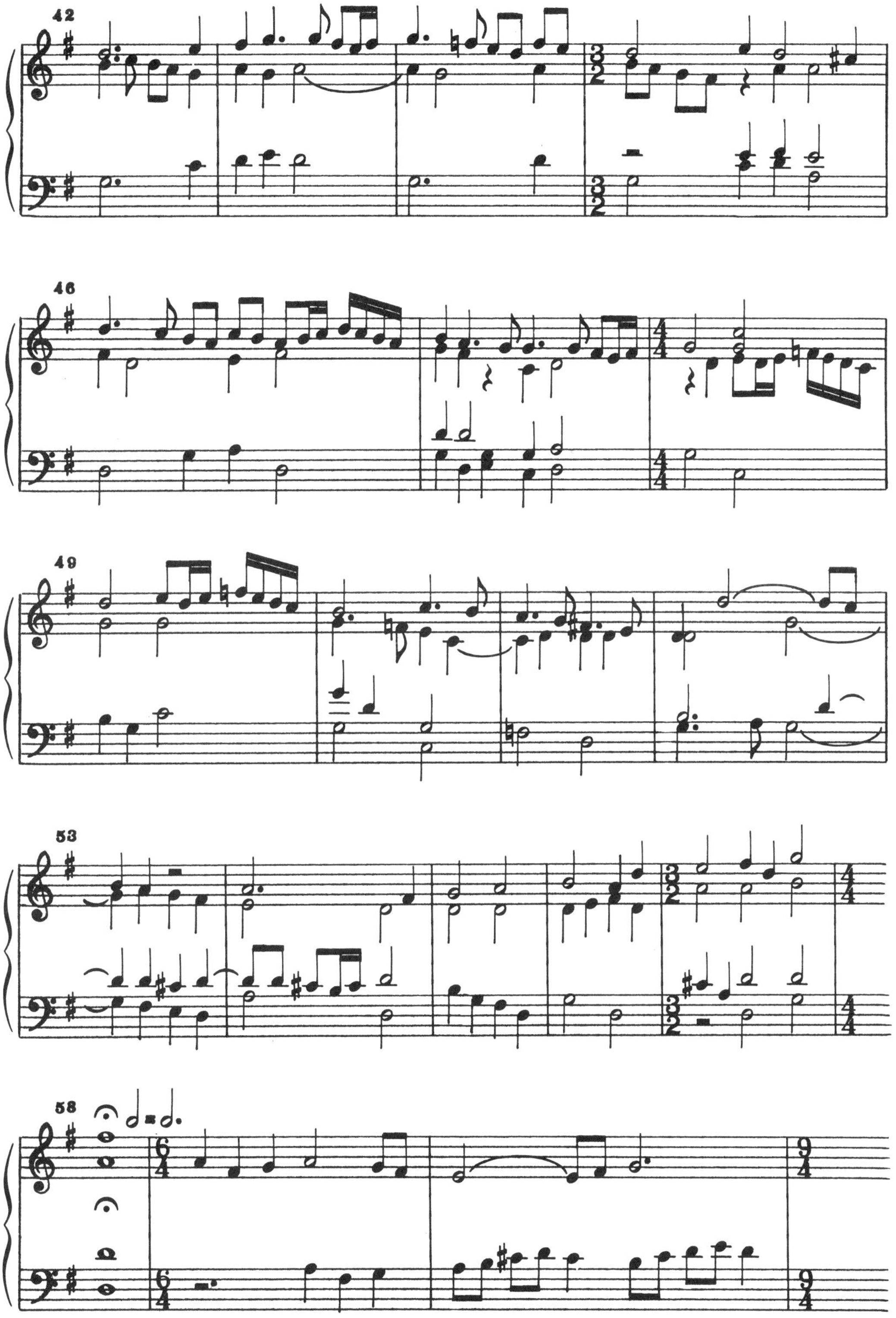
42
46
49
53
58

234

235

58. FANTASIA NO. 37 in Tones VII and VIII (Fol. [O vi^r])

Moderato

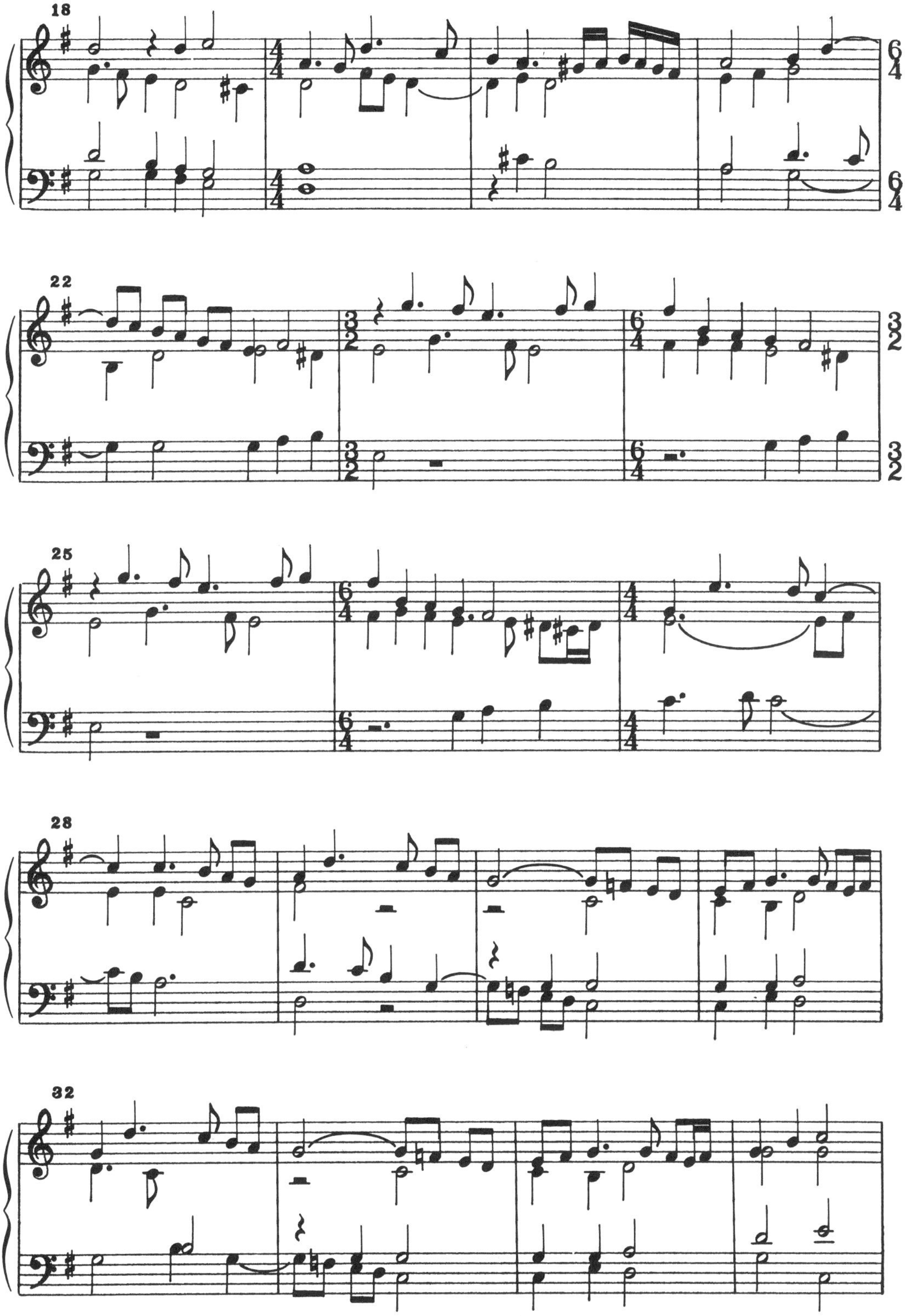
18
22
25
28
32

59. FANTASIA NO. 38 in Tone VI (Fol. Pr)

Allegro Moderato

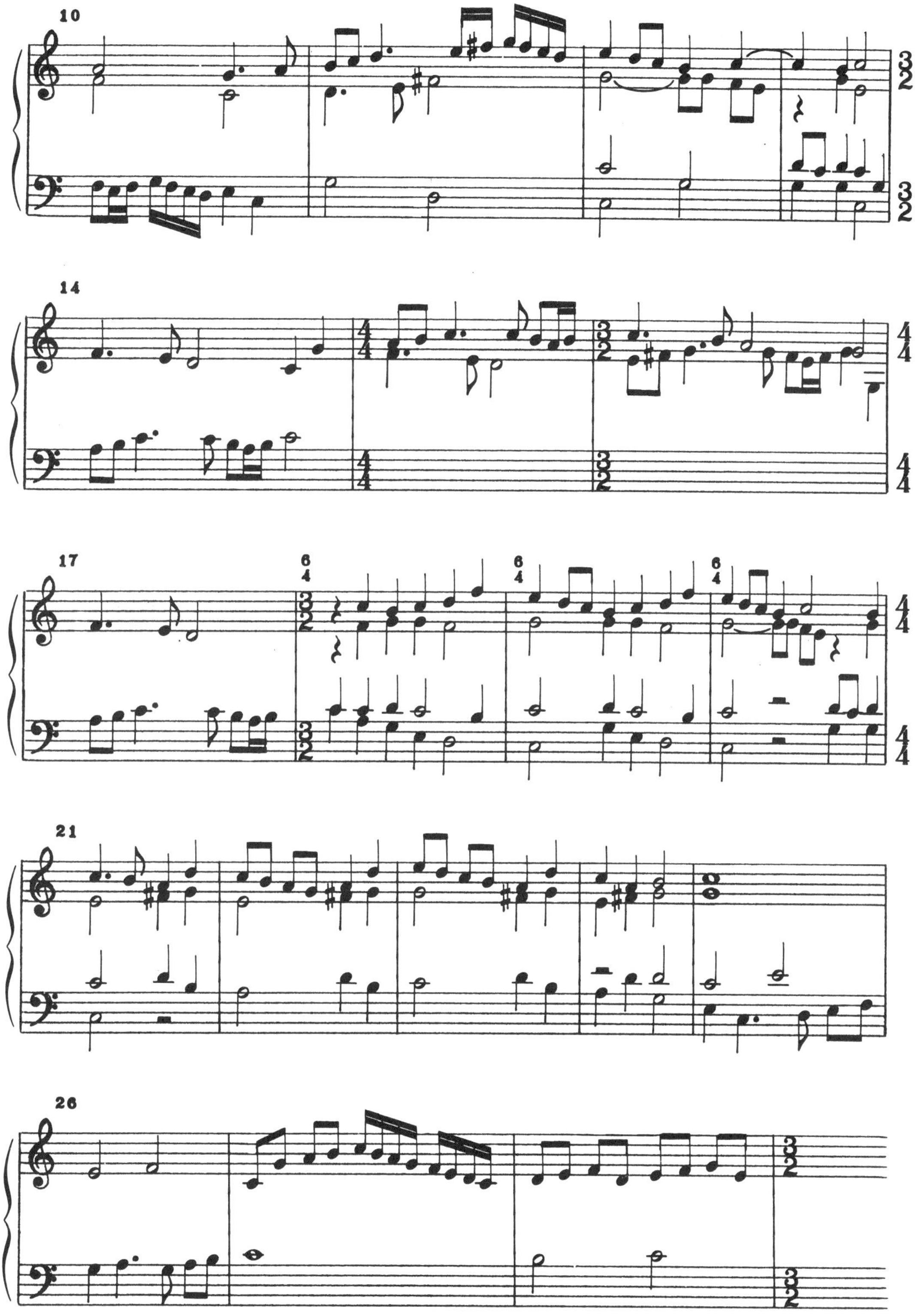
10
14
17
21
26

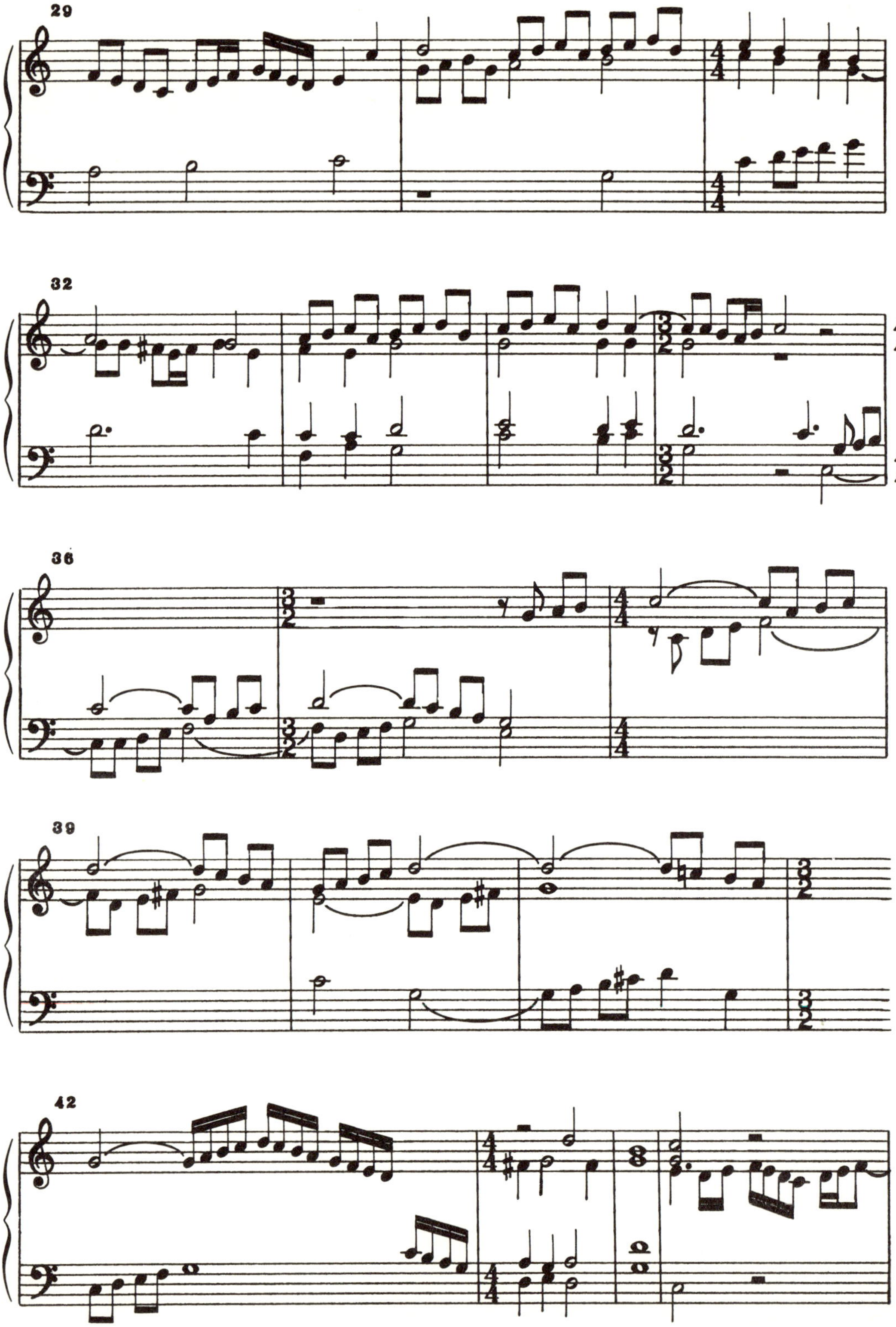
29
32
36
39
42

241

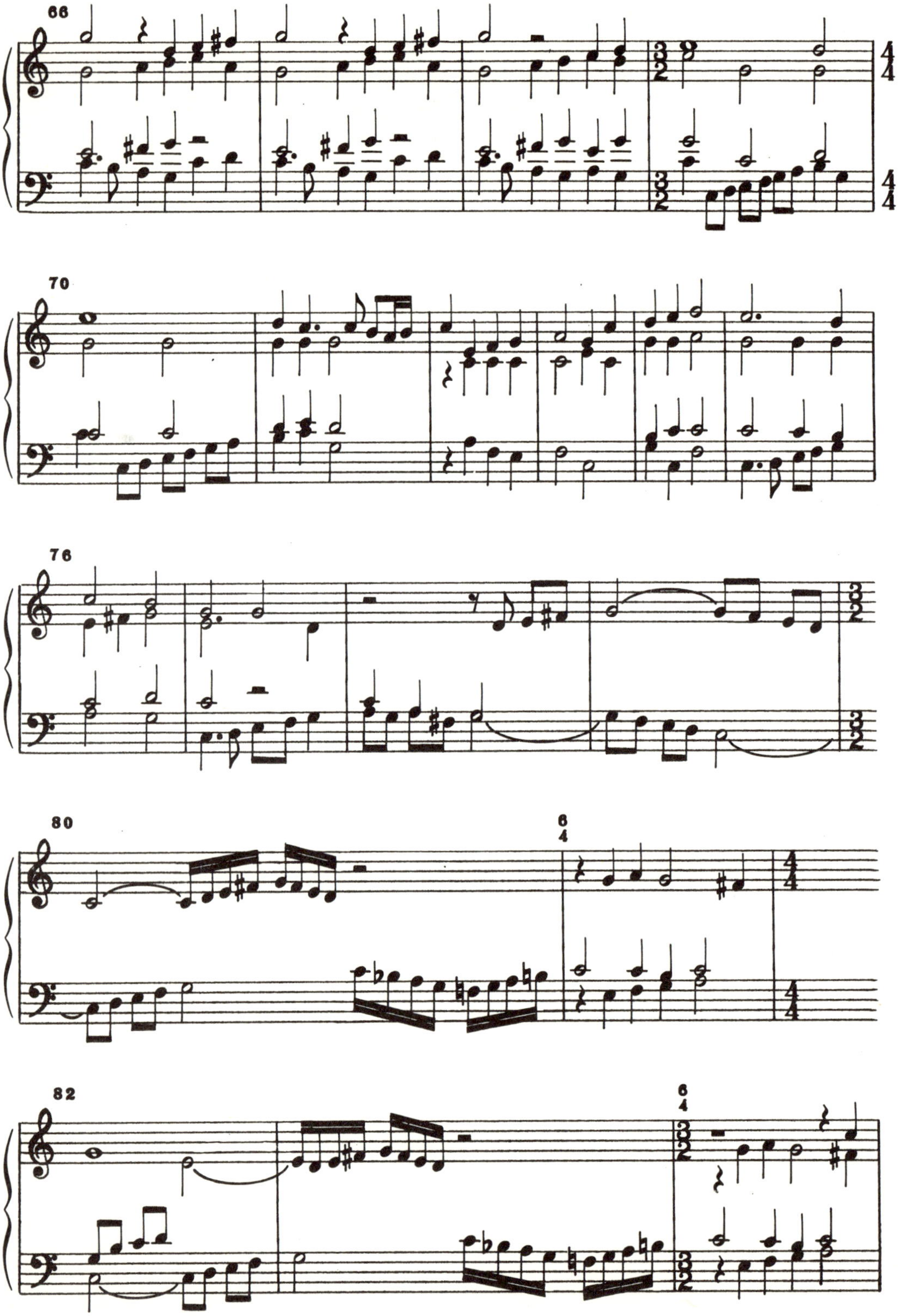
66
70
76
80
82

60. FANTASIA NO. 39 in Tones VII and VIII (Fol. P iii^r)
Allegro Moderato

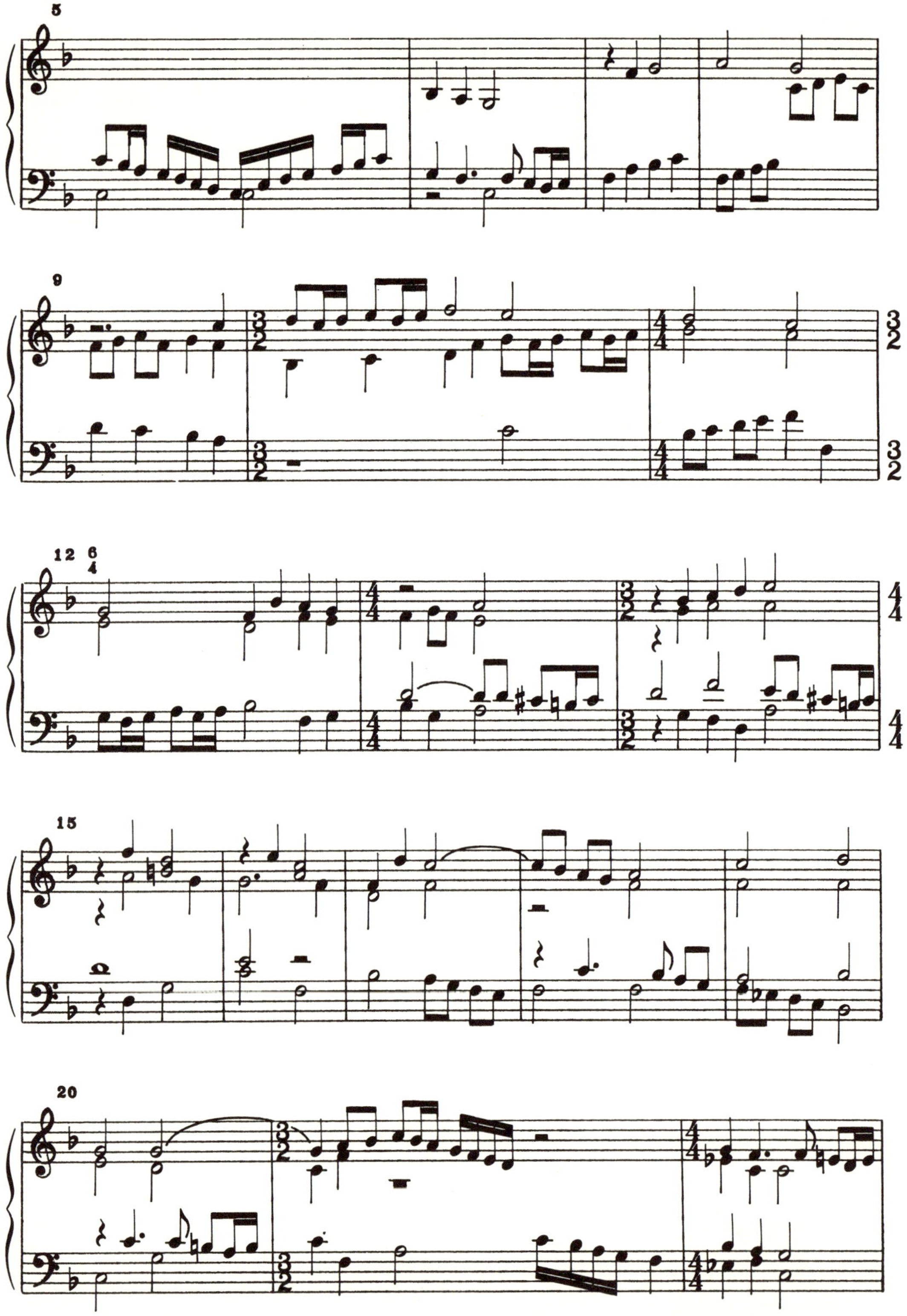

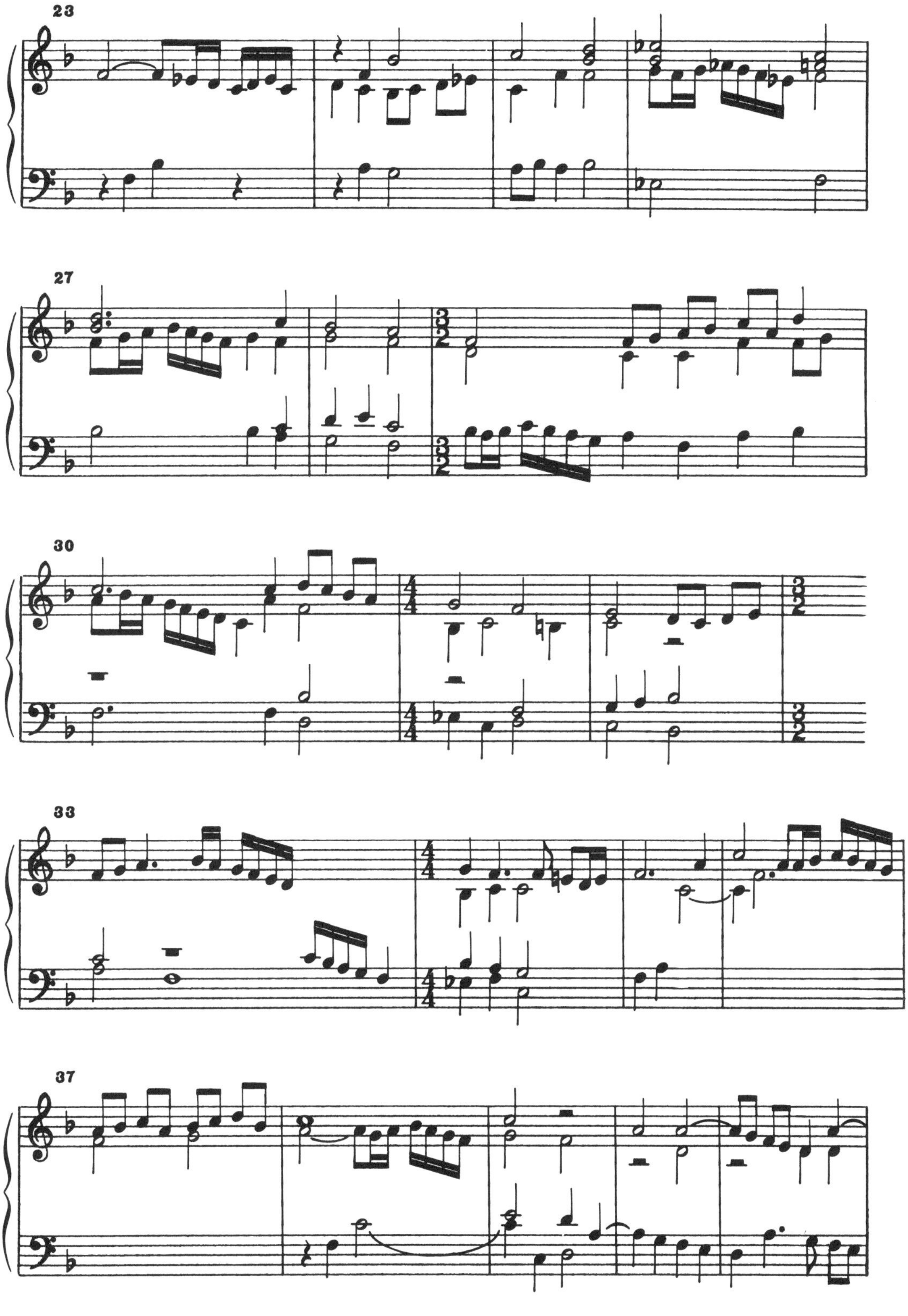
23
27
30
33
37

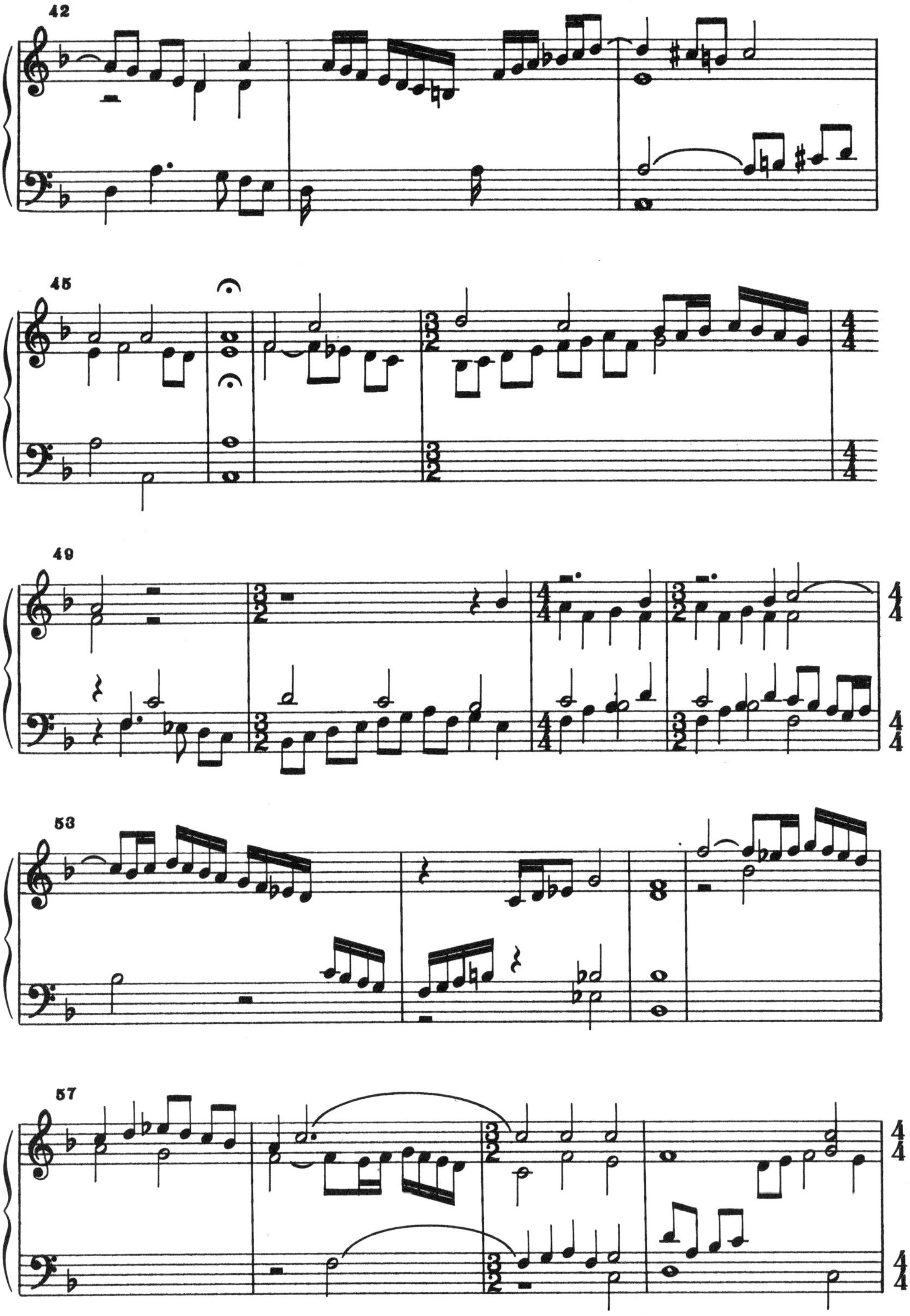
42
45
49
53
57

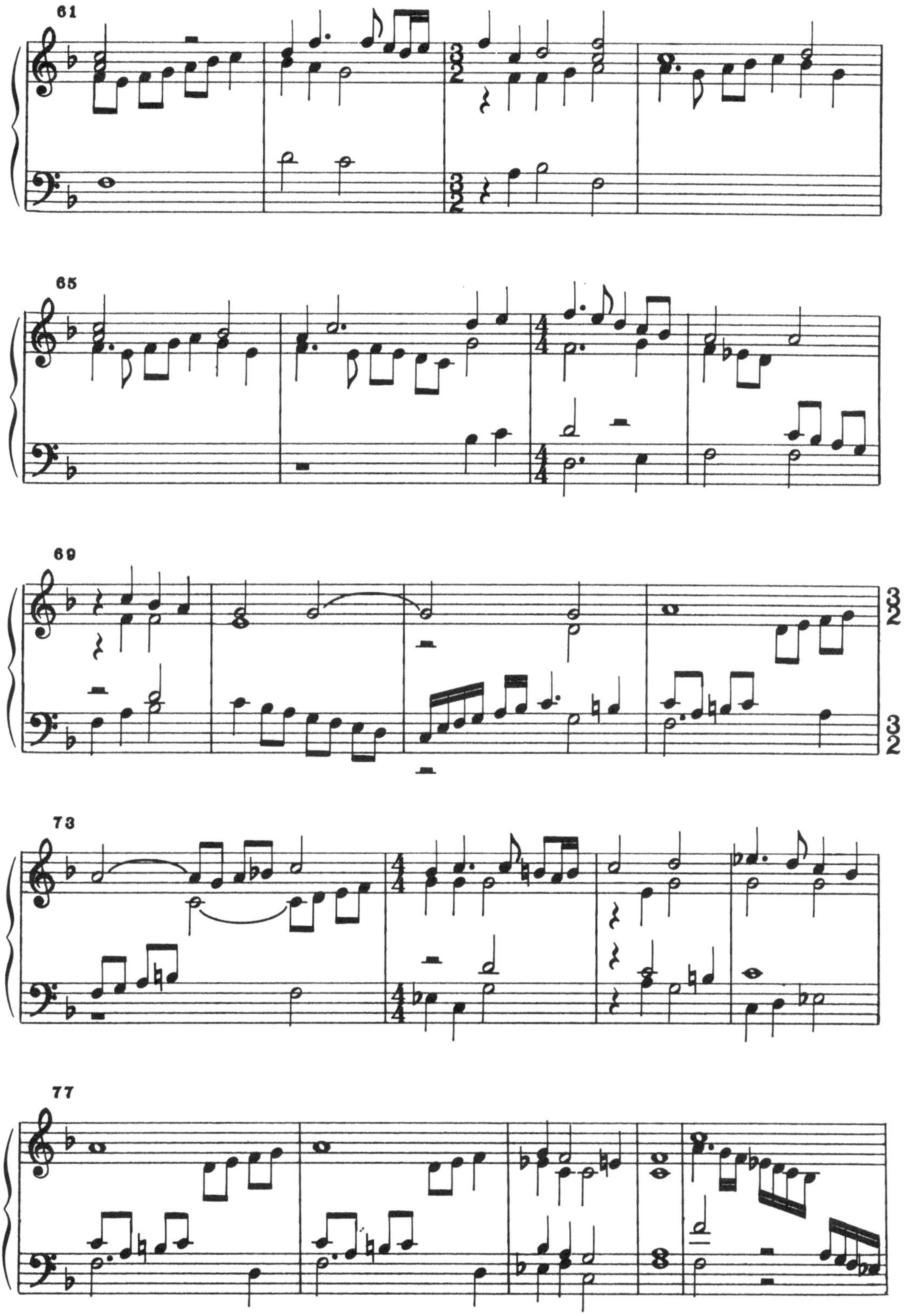
61
65
69
73
77

61. FANTASIA NO. 40 in Tones VII and VIII (Fol. [P v^r])

Allegro Moderato

✸ To be played on Courses 4 and 5   (i.e., strings tuned to d and g).

[sic]

✸ To be played on Courses 4 and 5 (i.e., strings tuned to d and g).

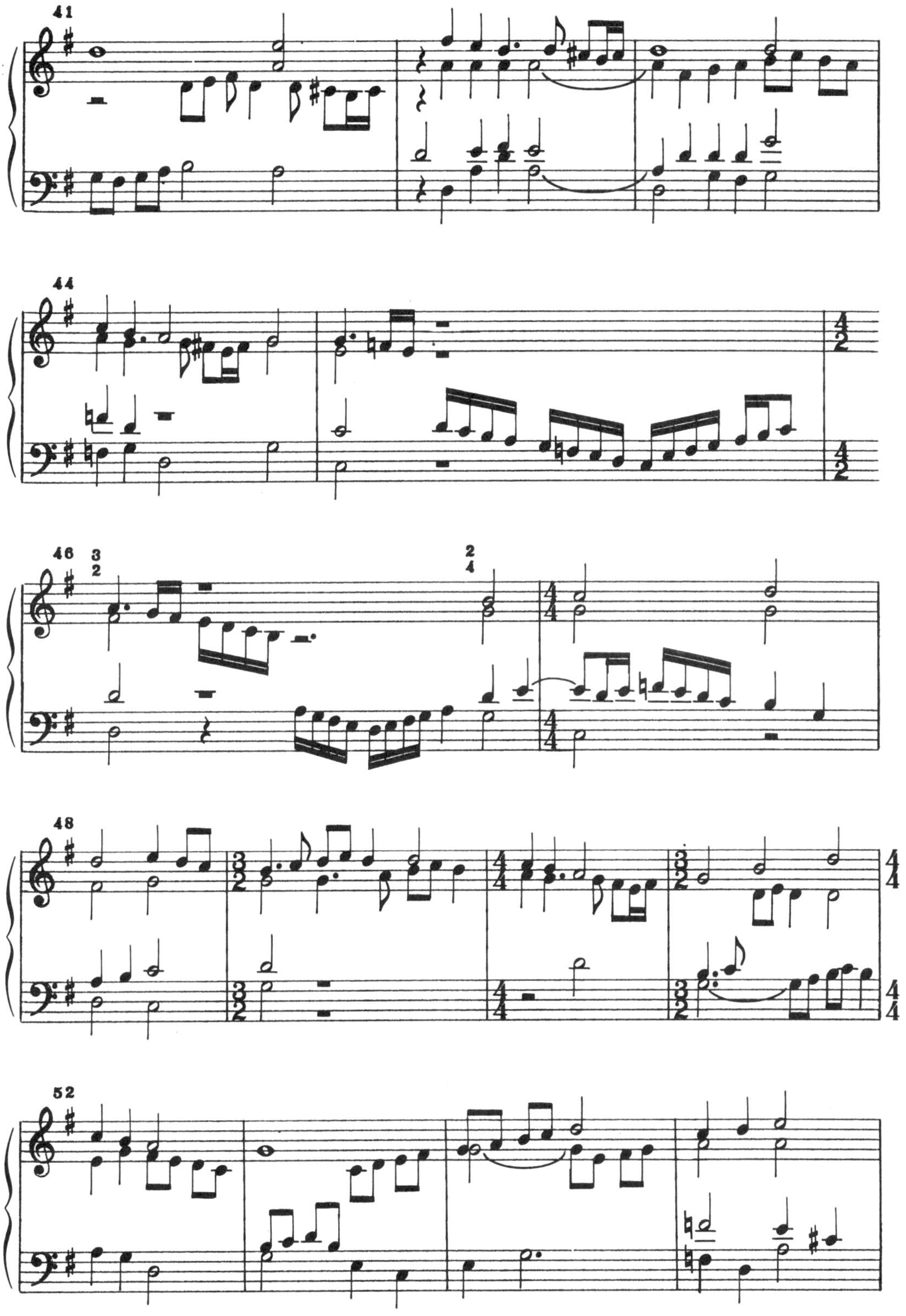
41
44
46
48
52

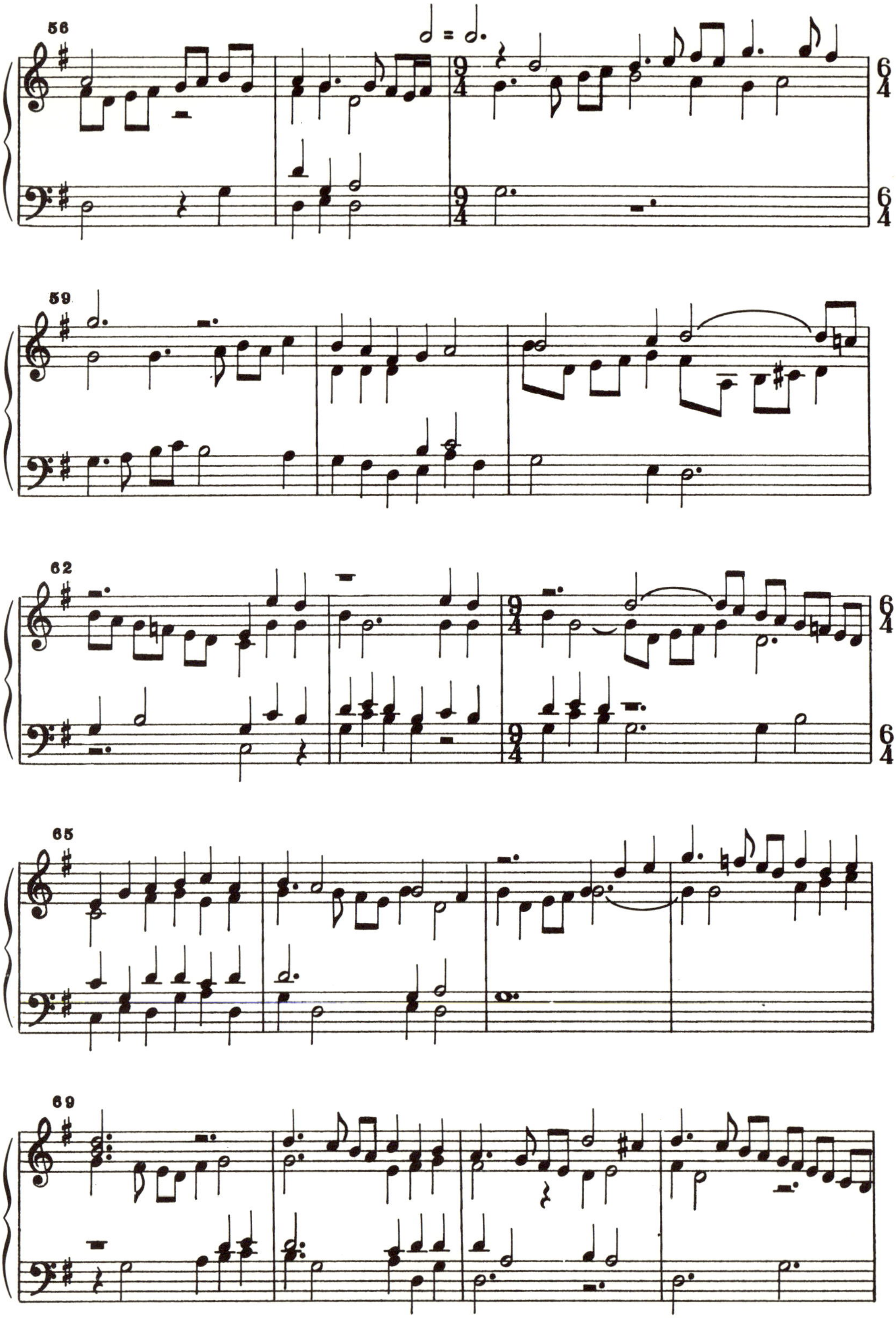
56
59
62
65
69

253

62. **VILLANCICO NO. 7,** *"Al amor quiero vencer"* (Fol.Q ii[r] [= Q[r]]) ✱

A. Molto Lento

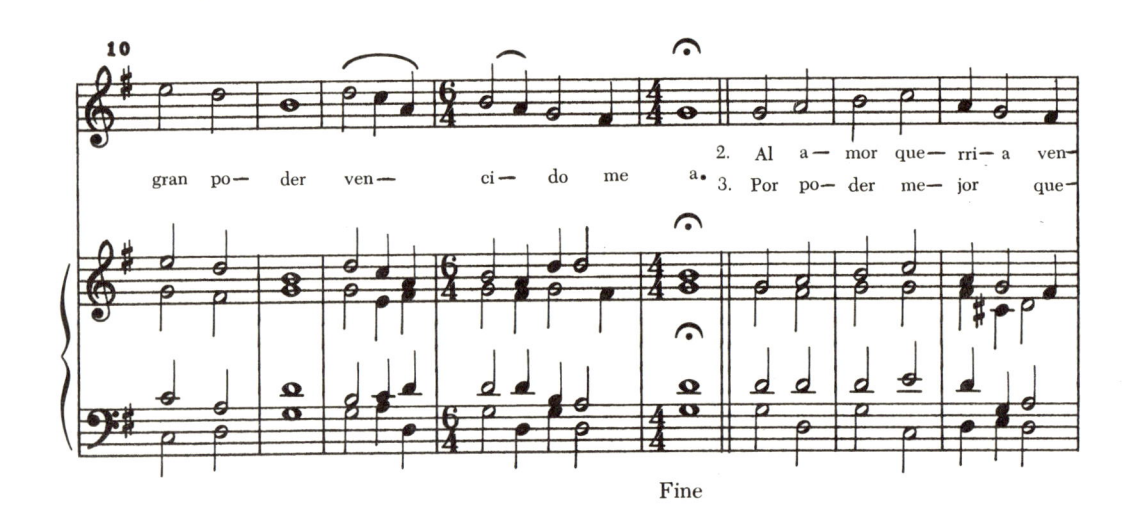

1. Al a—mor quie— ro ven—cer mas quien po— dra. Qu'e-lla con su
4. Quien tu—vies— se tal po— der mas quien po— dra.

gran po— der ven— ci— do me a. 2. Al a—mor que—rri—a ven-
3. Por po— der me— jor que-

Fine

cer y con bien ser del ven—ci— do.
rer pa—ra ser me— jor que—ri— do.

D.C. al Fine

✱ Two settings.

254

B. Allegro Moderato

1. Al amor quiero vencer mas quien podra.
4. Quien tuviesse tal poder mas quien podra.

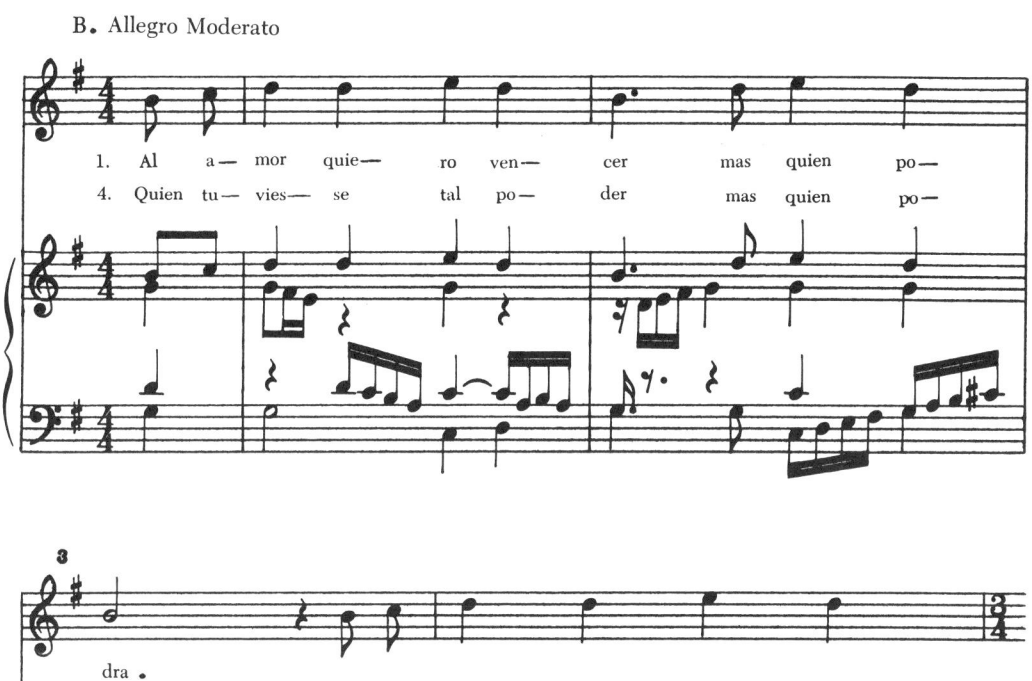

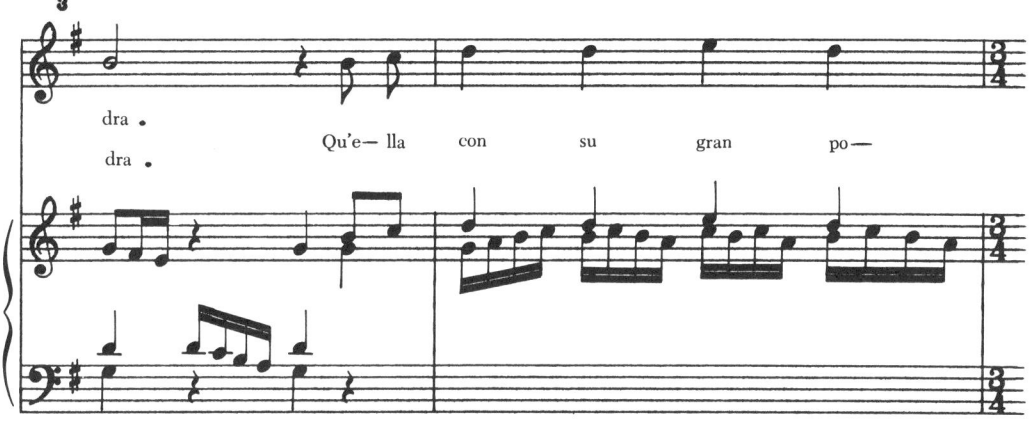

Qu'ella con su gran poder vencido me ha.

Fine

D.C. al Fine

63. VILLANCICO NO. 8, *"Aquel cavallero"* (Fol. Q ii^v [= Q^v]) ❋

A. Molto Lento

1. A-quel ca-va-lle-ro, ma-dre, que de mi se e-
4. Su a-mor tan ver-da-de-ro me-re-ce que

na-mo-ro. 2. Ma-
di-ga yo. Pe-na el y mu-e-ro yo. 3. Tam-

Fine

dre, a-quel ca-va-lle-ro que va he-ri-do d'a-mo-res.
bien sien-to sus do-lo-res por-que d'e-llas mis-mas mue-ro.

D.C. al Fine

❋ Two settings.

B. Allegro Moderato

1. A — quel ca — valle — ro, ma — dre, que de mi
4. Su a — mor tan ver — da — de — ro me — re — ce

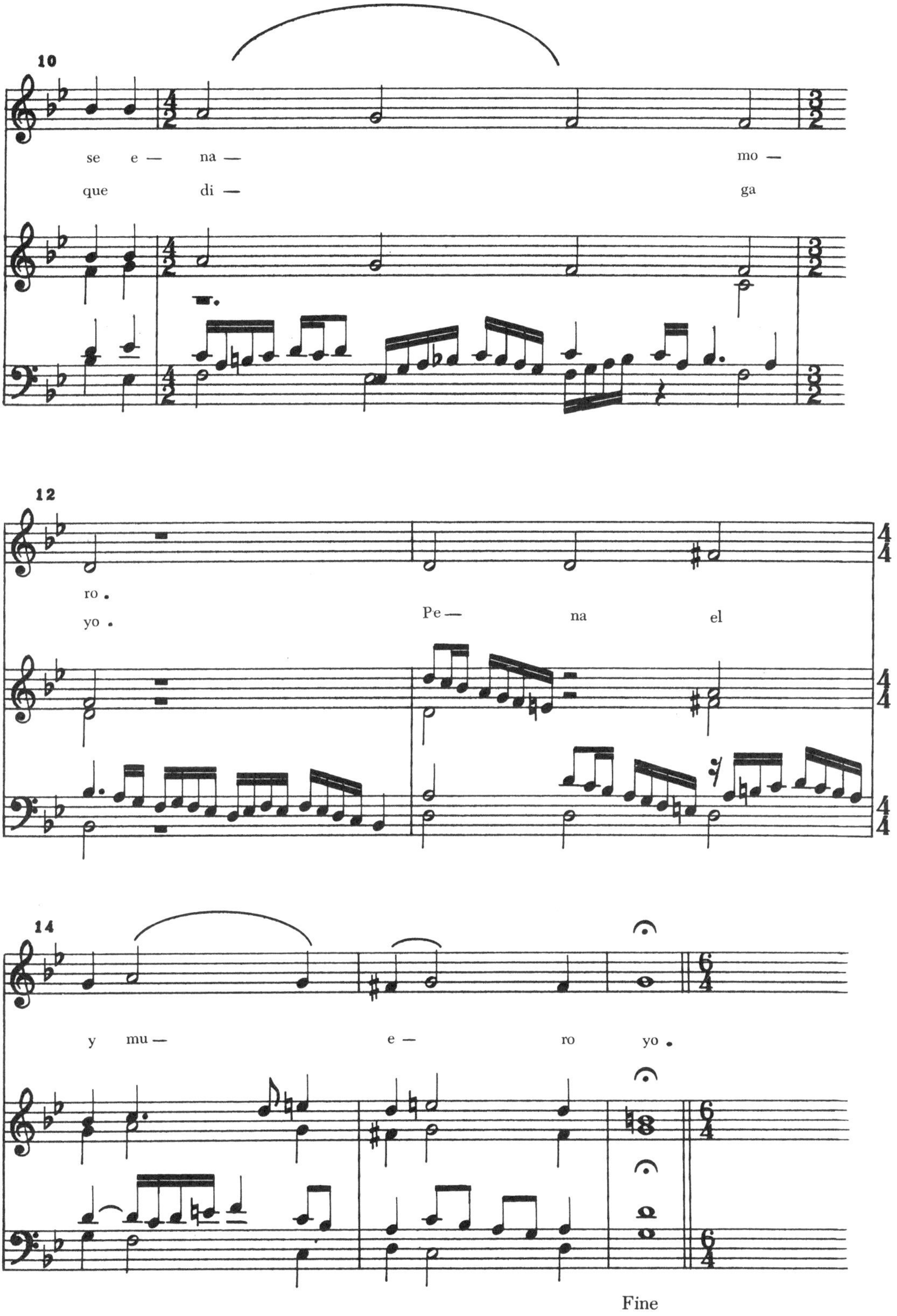
10
se e — na — mo —
que di — ga
12
ro .
yo .
Pe — na el
14
y mu — e — ro yo .
Fine

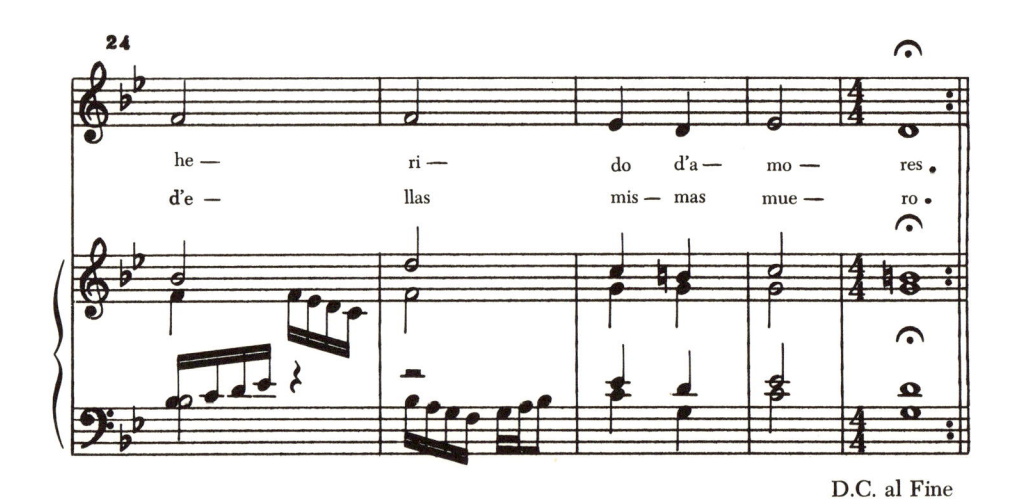

2. Ma — dre, a — quel ca — va — lle — ro que va he — ri — do d'a — mo — res.
3. Tam — bien sien — to sus do — lo — res por — que d'e — llas mis — mas mue — ro.

D.C. al Fine

64. VILLANCICO NO. 9, "*Amor que tan bien sirviendo*" (Fol. Q ii^v) ✱

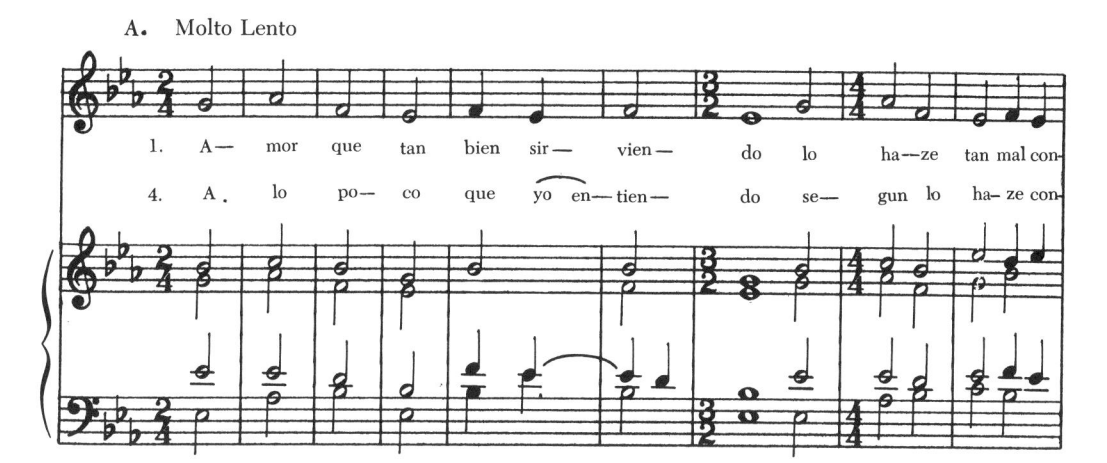

A. Molto Lento

1. A—mor que tan bien sir—vien—do lo ha—ze tan mal con—
4. A. lo po—co que yo en—tien—do se—gun lo ha—ze con—

mi—go. No es a—mor mas e—ne—mi—go. 2. No
mi—go. 3. Mas

· Fine

es a—mor quien as—si tra—ta que quien tra—ta de tal su—
ma—ta que no la mu—er—te quan—do con la vi—da

✱ Two settings.

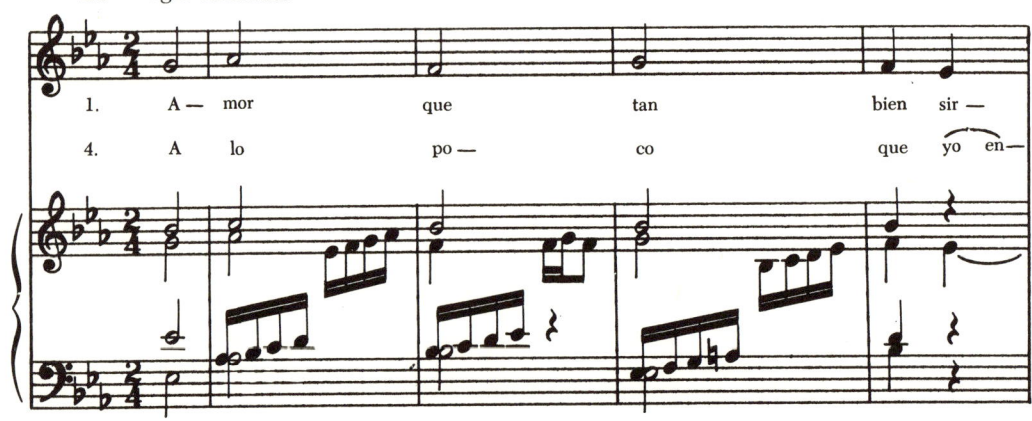

D.C. al Fine

B. Allegro Moderato

1. A— mor que tan bien sir—
4. A lo po— co que yo en—

6
vien — do lo
tien — do se —
9
ha — ze tan mal con — mi — go. No
gun lo ha — ze con — mi — go.
12
es a — mor mas e — ne — mi —

2. No es a—mor quien as—si tra—ta que quien tra-ta de tal su—er—te.

3. Mas ma—ta que no la mu—er—te quan-do con la vi—da ma—ta.

Fine

D.C. al Fine

65. VILLANCICO NO. 10, *"Levayme, Amor, da questa terra"* (Fol. [Q iii[r]]) ❋

A. Molto Lento

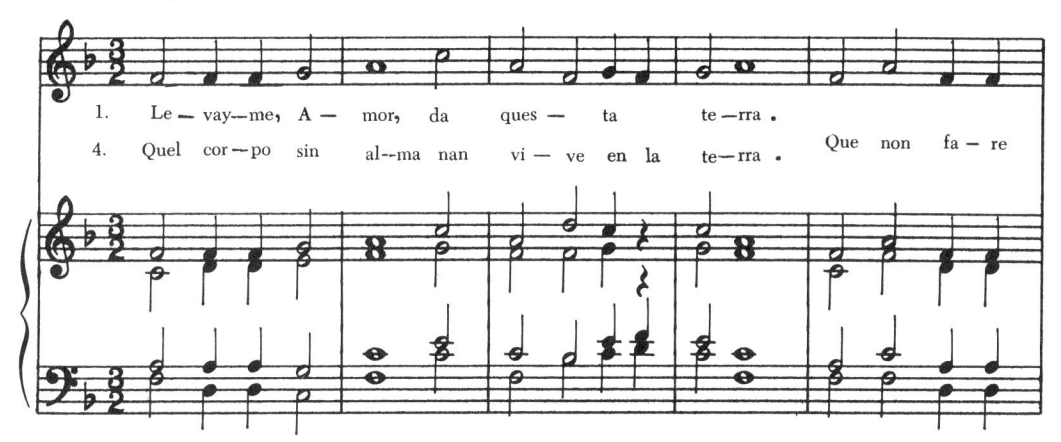

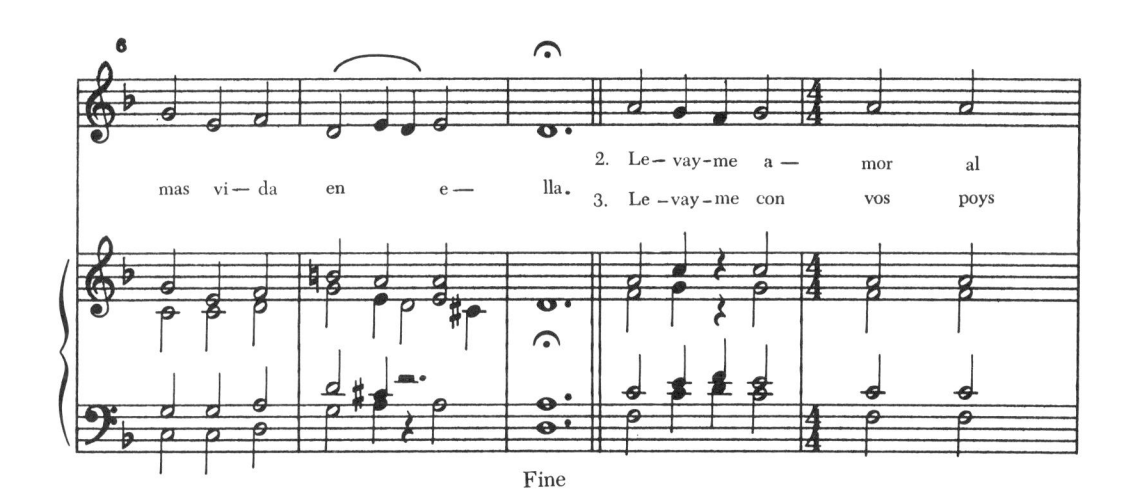

1. Le—vay—me, A— mor, da ques— ta te—rra. Que non fa—re
4. Quel cor—po sin al—ma nan vi—ve en la te—rra.

mas vi—da en e—lla. 2. Le—vay—me a— mor al
3. Le—vay—me con vos poys

Fine

ys— la per—di—da.
soys mi—ñya vi—da.

D.C. al Fine

❋ Two settings.

265

B. Allegro Moderato

1. Le — va — y — me, A — mor,
4. Quel cor — po sin al — ma

da ques — ta te — rra.
non vi — ve en la te — rra.

Que non fa — re mas

vi — da en e — lla.

Fine

2. Le—vay—me a— mor al ys— la per— di— da.
3. Le—vay—me con vos poys soys mi— ñya vi— da.

D.C. al Fine

66. **VILLANCICO NO. 11**, *"Un cuydado que mia vida ten"* (Fol. [Q iv^r]) ✽

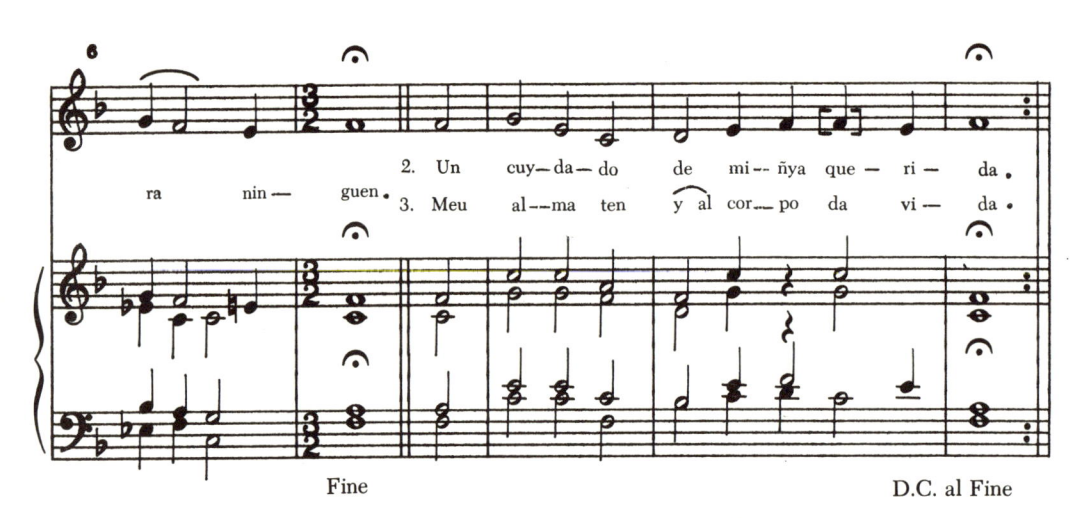

A. Molto Lento

1. Un cuy—da—do que mi—a vi— da ten. Que non lo sa—be—
4. Mi cor—po lo sen—te, mi al— ma lo ten.

ra nin— guen. 2. Un cuy—da—do de mi—ñya que—ri—da.
3. Meu al—ma ten y al cor—po da vi—da.

Fine   D.C. al Fine

✽ Two settings.

B. Allegro Moderato

1. Un cuy — da — do que
4. Mi cor — po lo

mi — a vi — da ten. Que
sen — te, mi al — ma lo ten.

non lo sa — be — ra nin—

2. Un cuy—da—do de mi—ñya que—ri—da.
3. Meu al—ma ten y al cor—po da vi—da.

Fine   D.C. al Fine

67. **VILLANCICO NO. 12**, *"Perdida teñyo la color"* (Fol. [Q iv^v]) ✻

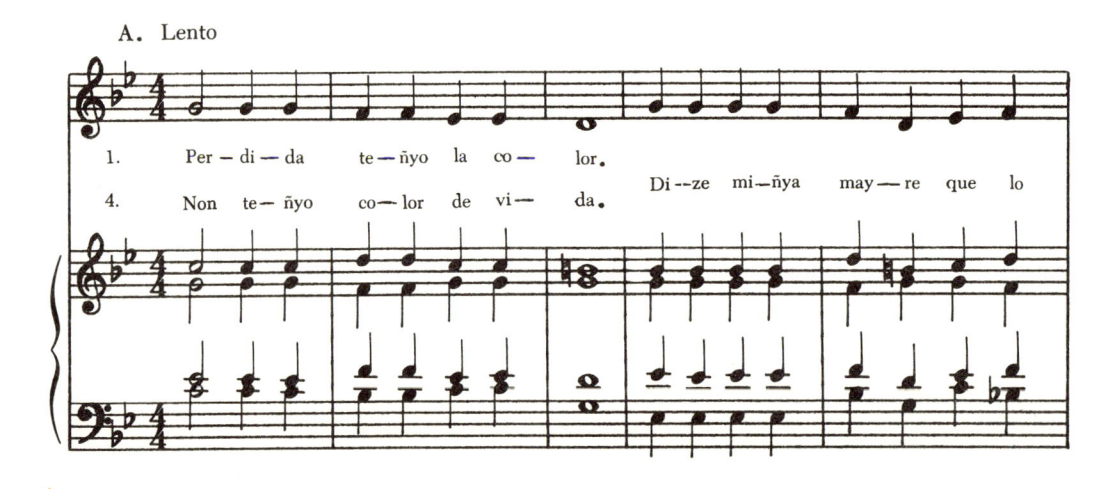

A. Lento

1. Per—di—da te—ñyo la co—lor. Di—ze mi—ñya may—re que lo
4. Non te—ñyo co—lor de vi—da.

✻ Two settings.

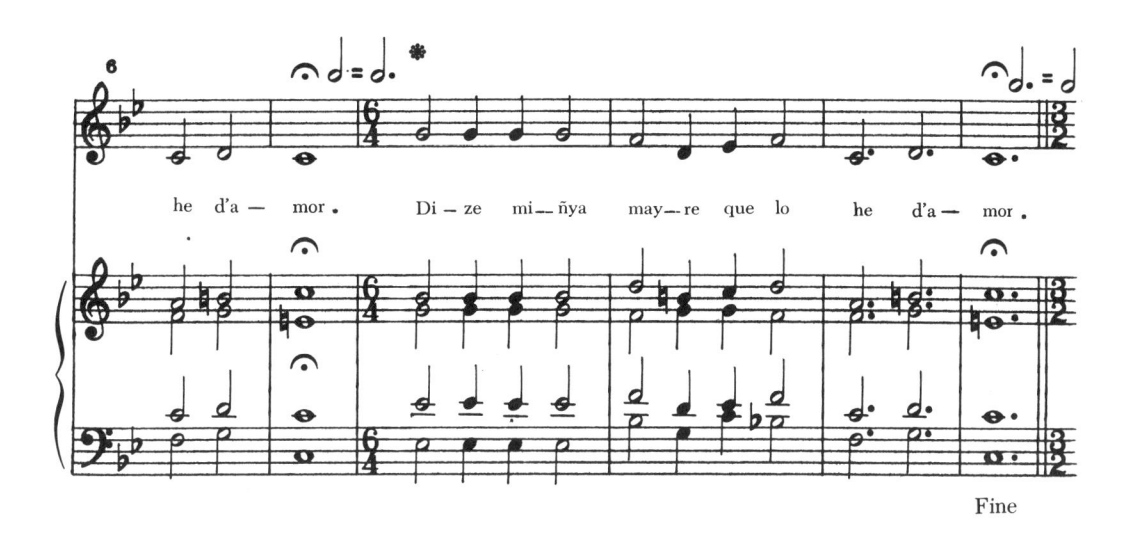

❋ Measures 8-11 may be omitted (cf. Critical Notes).

B. Allegro Moderato

1. Per—di—da te—ñyo la co—lor.
4. Non te—ñyo co—lor de vi—da.

Di—ze mi—ñya may—re que lo
he d'a—mor.
2. La co—lor te—ñyo per—di—da.
3. Por u—na des—co—ñyo—ci—da.

Fine D.C. al Fine

68. ROMANCE NO. 3, *"Con pavor recordo el moro"* (Fol. [Q iv^v])

Moderato e Rubato

1. 2. Con pa — vor re — cor — do el mo — ro
5. No de — xan — do co — sa a — vi — da

y em — pe — ço
de quan — to

de gri — tos
pue — do ma —

✻ To be played on Courses 4 and 5 (i.e., strings tuned to d and g).

✻✻ To be played on Courses 2 and 3 (i.e., strings tuned to b and e').

275

mi dor—mir siem—pre es ve—lar; mis ves—ti—dos son pe—sa—res

que no se pue — den ras — gar.

D.C. al Fine

69. ROMANCE NO. 4, *"Triste estava, muy quexosa, la triste reyna troyana"* (Fol. R. ii[r])

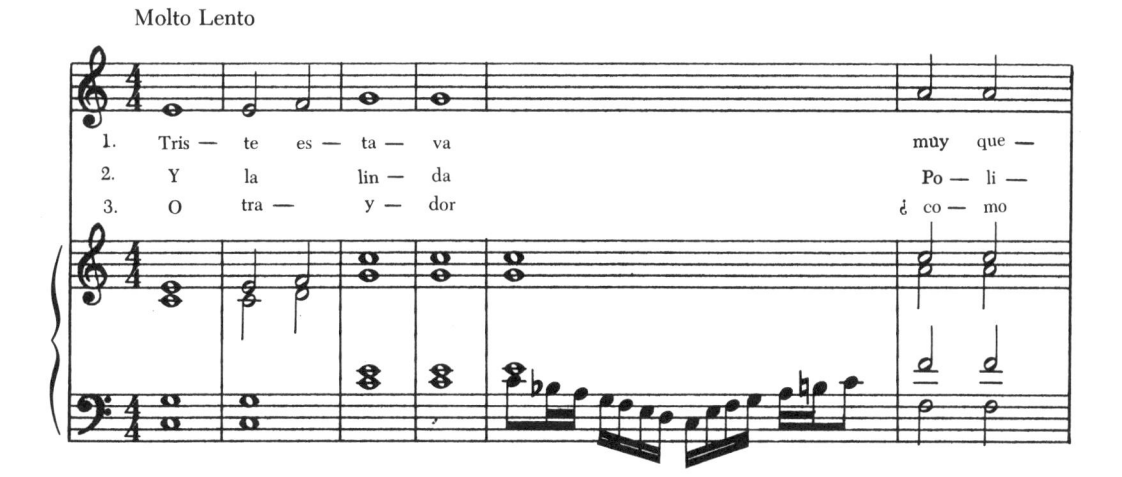

Molto Lento

1. Tris — te es — ta — va   muy que —
2. Y la   lin — da   Po — li —
3. O tra — y — dor   ¿ co — mo

xo —
ce —
pu — dis — te
sa
na

la tris — te rey — na tro — ya — na
en el tem — plo de — go — lla — da
[sic] en mu — ger ven — gar tu sa — ña?

en ver a sus hi — jos mu — er — tos
so br'el se — pul — cro de Ar — chi — les
No bas — to su her — mo — su — ra

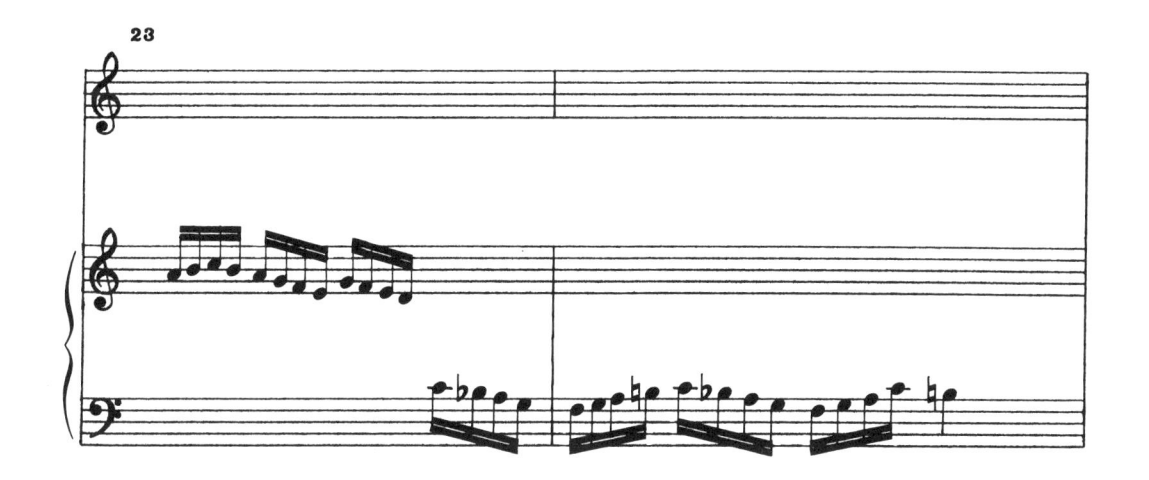

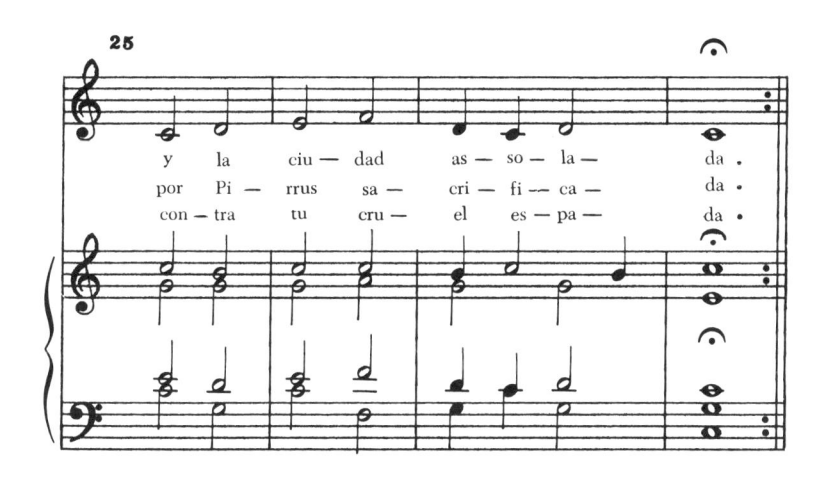

y la ciu - dad a - so - la - da.
por Pi - rrus sa - cri - fi - ca - da.
con - tra tu cru - el es - pa - da.

70. SONNET NO. 4, *"O gelosia d'amanti"* [Sannazaro] (Fol. R. ii^v)

mor — te, che con tu — a vi — sta tur — bi il ciel se — re — no; O ser — pen — te na — sco — sto in dol — ce se — no che i lie — ti fior de

mi e spe—ran—çe ai mor—te, tra pro-spe-ri suc-ces-si, ad—ver-sa sor—te, tra so—a—ve vi— van—de, a—spro ve—ne—no; Da qual — fu—ria in—fer—na—le al mon—do

35
u — ci — sti ?, o cru—del mon—stro, o pes—te dai mor— ta — li, che ai
39
fa— ti li gior—ni me— i a—ma— ri e tri— sti.
42
Tor—na— ti giu, non rra— dop — piar mie — i

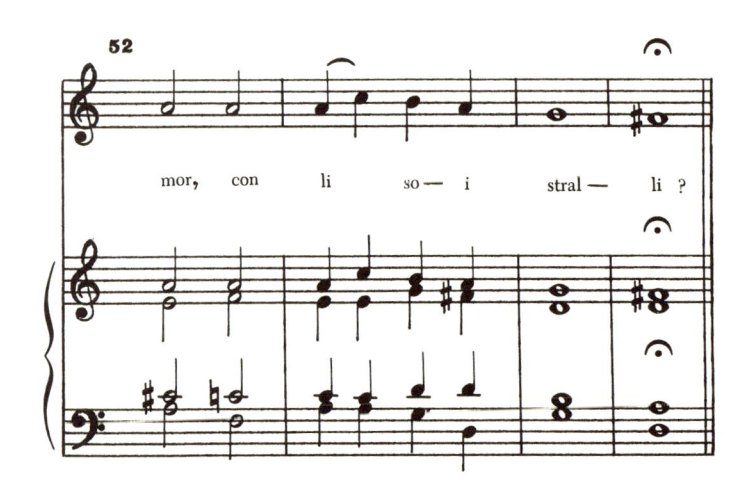

ma — li! In-fe- li- ce pa- u- ra, ad che ve- ni- sti? Hor non bas- sta- va A- mor, con li so- i stral- li?

71. SONNET NO. 5, *"Madonna per voi ardo"* (Fol. R iii^v) ❋

Molto Lento

Ma— don— na, per voi ar— do

et voi non lo cre— de— te.

Per—che non pi a quan—to bel—la se—

❋ The vihuela passagework in this *soneto* may be omitted, in which case, observe, for the length of the final note of each phrase, the bracketed rhythmic values above the staves (Cf. Critical Notes).

❋❋ To be played on Courses 1 and 2 (i.e., strings tuned to e' and a').

285

※ To be played on Courses 1 and 2 (i.e., strings tuned to e' and a').

22
ge — te che per voi mo—ro et ar — do
25
et per mi — rar vo— stra bel — ta in — fi — ni —
29
ta
et voi so — la ser —

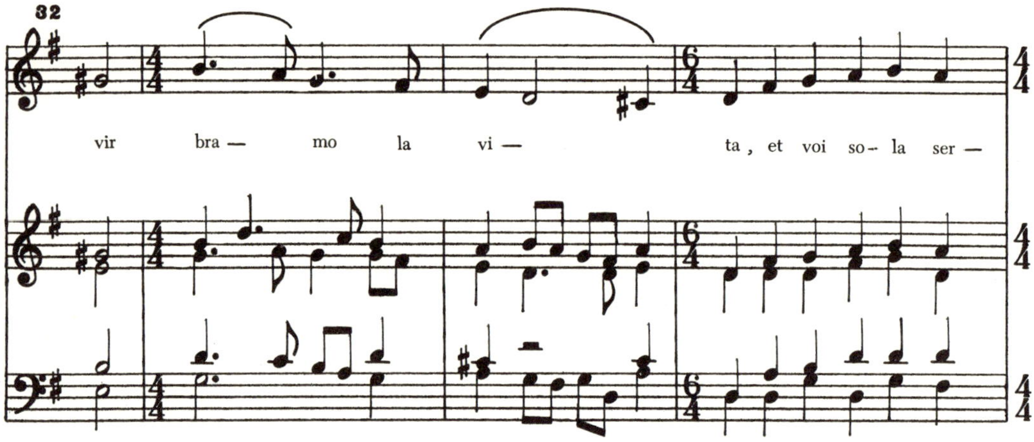
32
vir bra — mo la vi — ta , et voi so — la ser —

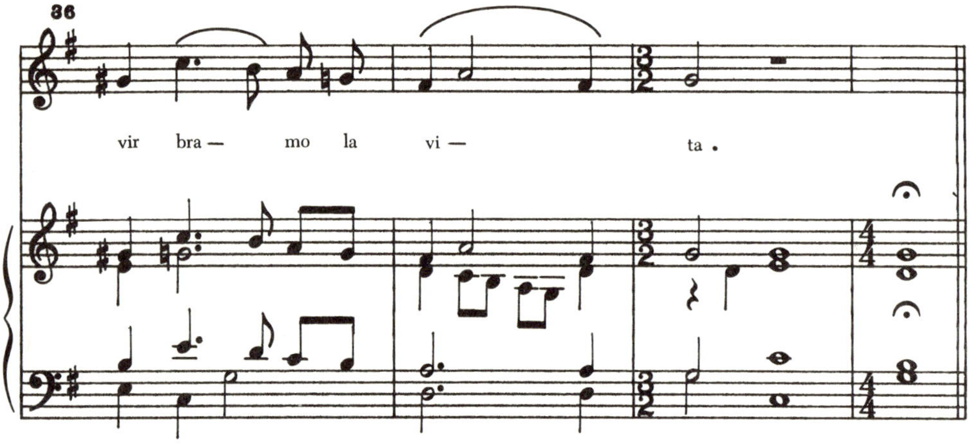
36
vir bra — mo la vi — ta .

72. SONNET NO. 6, *"Gentil mia donna"* [Petrarch] (Fol. [R iv^v])

Allegro Moderato

lu — me che mi mo — stra la vi — a ch'al ciel con — du —

ce; et per lun — go co — stu — me, den — tro la do — ve sol con a —

mor seg — gio, qua — si vi — si — bil —
men — te il cor tra — lu — ce, il cor tra —
lu — ce, il cor tra — lu — ce.

Postface

Critical Notes

Critical Notes

The POSTFACE to this edition contains all text from *El Maestro* not previously translated[1] and a list of source errors. The Errata List given by Milán at the end of his volume (on fol. [R vi^v]) has been incorporated into the list of source errors. The measure, beat, and rhythmic value are given in the list as they appear both in the original Milán print and, bracketed, in this edition.

The following abbreviations are used in the POSTFACE:

- S. — soprano
- Al. — alto
- T. — tenor
- Ba. — Bass
- V. — vocal line
- m. — measure(s)
- be. — beat(s)
- br. — breve
- sbr. — semibreve or whole note
- mi. — minim or half note
- smi. — semiminim or quarter note
- fu. — fusa or eighth note
- sfu. — semifusa or sixteenth note
- n. — note(s)

Fol. [A] vi^r:
This book, entitled *El Maestro*, is divided into two volumes [*libros*]. The first book is for beginners; and thus it contains music [which is] easy and suitable for hands a beginner may have. If there is one who has never played, the music given [will appear] difficult for him. He should not be surprised: all will [i.e., anything would] appear difficult to him. And giving him easy music at the beginning, he will have to content himself with what he is doing, and all will appear easy to him. And truly, most things are easy for man to grasp, if he does not make them difficult by not wanting to learn them. Years are lost in this [way]; and other [years] are lost because [beginners can]not find [any]one who knows how to teach them. And for this reason, this book follows the order [derived] from wishing to teach well. And thanks to this, the beginnings are easy, so that afterward the difficult [material] may be grasped easily.

What this first volume contains.

There are eight sections [*cuadernos*][2] in this volume. The first treats information and instructions for the said volume.

1. Cf. TEXTUAL MATTER, fn. 15.
2. Each *cuaderno* corresponds to a lettered "gathering" of folios in the book; since the folios are

El Maestro

The second and third sections give you easy music in divers tones suitable for the hands of a beginner.

The fourth and fifth sections present to you music with divers *redobles* to be played [by the] index finger [*dedillo*] and [by] two fingers [i.e., the thumb and index finger];[3] and [this music] has more in respect to *tañer de gala*[4] than much music or [than playing in strict] *compás*.

The sixth and seventh sections give you music somewhat more difficult, and [music] for more hands [*sic*; "fingers" is meant], with some *redobles*.

The eighth and last section provides you music for singing and playing *villancicos* and Italian things.

Fol. B^r:[5]
It is the purpose of this volume, as you have already heard, to form and compose music for vihuela de mano in the same way a teacher would do for a pupil who never had played; and for this reason, the music that now is for beginning is somewhat easy, because it forms a starting [point] for the beginner. It could be easier, but [then] it would lack substance; and because this music for getting started has to appear good, it will not suffer being easier than it is. Which music is written out as fantasias, as you will see below; by this means, any work of this book, in whichever tone it is, is entitled fantasia, in the sense that it only proceeds from the fantasy and industry of the author, who created it. Who very feelingly entreats all who pass through this book not to judge his works until they are played as each one would wish his works were. And played in their perfection, if they are not so perfect, they will be so in virtue and goodness, which excuse all faults.

Invocando dei auxilium: et gloriose virginis Marie matris sue: cuius immaculate conceptionis firmiter credendo incipit ad predictorum laudem primus liber presentis musice.

This first fantasia which is written here below is in the first tone; and the more it is played with the *compás* fast, the better it will appear. He who plays on the vihuela the endings [*terminos*] through which this fantasia moves will play in the first tone. Observe well the said fantasia, which cadences it forms, and what endings it has, and where it finishes, because in it will be seen all that the first mode legitimately may do.

Two things are to be considered in the following fantasias of the present volume. One, that they [the fantasias] are to be played with the *compás* fast or slow as the author wishes. The other, to observe well the tones which follow because they show how the tones are to be played on the vihuela. And for [a] more perfect knowledge of the said tones, they will be treated more lengthily at the end of this book.[6]

1. Fantasia No. 1 in Tone I (fol. B^v)
   A. Tempo: *Molto Allegro*. Reduction: 4:1.

Fol. B ii^v:
The fantasia written below is in the first tone, and it is also to be played with the *compás* fast. And it goes through the [same] endings as [where] the past fantasia moves, because through these endings music easier on the vihuela is provided than through other [end-

---

labeled "A" through "R" in *El Maestro*, it follows that there are seventeen *cuadernos* in the book (I = J). Most *cuadernos* in *El Maestro* consist of six folios. *Cuaderno* H, on the other hand, contains eight folios, while *cuaderno* Q comprises four.
3. Cf. Ward, "Vihuela de Mano," 90–91. The usual meaning of the term "*dedillo*" is "small finger"; modern Spanish for "index finger" is "*dedo índice*."
4. I.e., *tempo rubato*; see PREFACE.
5. Fol [A]vi^v is discussed in fn. 15 of the TEXTUAL MATTER.
6. Refer to TEXTUAL MATTER, where this material has been presented.

ings, in] which the music would have to ascend above the fifth fret. And so that they are not difficult for a beginner to play, they [i.e., these fantasias] move through these easy endings.

2. Fantasia No. 2 in Tone I (fol. B ii^v)
   A. Tempo: *Allegro*. Reduction: 4:1.

Fol. B iii^v:
The fantasia written below is in the first tone and also is to be played with the *compás* somewhat fast; it moves through the endings on the vihuela [through] which the two past fantasias move. I give you these three fantasias in the first tone and [which move] through the same ending [in] the book, because they move through easy parts, as I have already told you.

3. Fantasia No. 3 in Tone I (fol. B iii^v)
   A. Tempo: *Allegro Moderato*. Reduction: 4:1.

Fol. [B v^r]:
The fantasia written below is in the second tone and is to be played with the *compás* fast. And this second tone goes through the endings of the past fantasias. In order to know well the difference there is between the tones on the vihuela, at the end of this book what I have already said will be explained more lengthily.

4. Fantasia No. 4 in Tone II (fol. [B v^r])
   A. Tempo: *Allegro*. Reduction: 4:1.

Fol. [B vi^r]:
The fantasia written below is in the second tone and is also to be played with the *compás* whipped-up or fast. And it moves through the endings [through] which the past fantasia in the second tone moves.

5. Fantasia No. 5 in Tone II (fol. [B vi^r])
   A. Tempo: *Allegro*. Reduction: 4:1.
   B. Errors: *a*) m. 8, be. 3, Al.: c-sharp′ [m. 4, Al., third n.].
      b) m. 45: c-sharp′, f′, g′, a′ [m. 21, be. 1]; (corrected in Errata List).
      c) m. 46–c′, d′, e′, c′ [m. 21, be. 2]; (corrected in Errata List).

Fol. C^v:
This fantasia that follows is in the first tone and in the second, and because it uses the said two tones it will be said [to be in a] mixed tone, because if the said fantasia were only in the first tone, it could not form a cadence it does form on the second fret of the fourth [string] of the vihuela; and if it were only in the second tone, it could not form a cadence it does form on the fifth fret. And because it uses one tone and another, as is said above, it is said [to be in a] mixed tone.

6. Fantasia No. 6 in Tones I and II (fol. C^v)
   A. Tempo: [*Allegro*]; indication lacking. Reduction: 4:1.
   B. Errors: *a*) m. 91, be. 3–4, Al. and Ba.: b [m. 40, be. 1, second half].
      b) m. 122, be. 4, Al.: f′ [m. 53, Al., second n.].

Fol. C iii^r:
The fantasia written below is in the third tone, and the more it is played with the *compás* fast the better it will appear. Observe well through which endings it passes and the cadences it forms, and you will see all that the third tone can do legitimately.

7. Fantasia No. 7 in Tone III (fol. C iii^r)
   A. Tempo: *Molto Allegro*. Reduction: 4:1.
   B. Errors: *a*) m. 36, be. 3–4, S.: f-sharp' [m. 17, S., second n.]; (corrected in Errata List).

From Errata List:
This fantasia that follows is in the fourth tone and is to be played with the *compás* fast.

8. Fantasia No. 8 in Tone IV (fol. [C iv^v])
   A. Tempo: *Allegro*. Reduction: 4:1.

Fol. [C v^v]:
The fantasia written below is said [to be in a] mixed tone because it moves through the endings and cadences [through] which the third and fourth tones move; and because it takes from these said two tones and is mixed with them [*sic*], it is called "mixed"; and it is to be played with the *compás* fast.

9. Fantasia No. 9 in Tones III and IV (fol. [C v^v])
   A. Tempo: *Allegro*. Reduction: 4:1.
   B. Errors: *a*) m. 96, Al.: d' [m. 45, Al., first n.]; (corrected in Errata List).

Fol. D^r:
The fantasias of these present, fourth and fifth sections, [into] which we are now entering, demonstrate a [type of] music which is like [i.e., which consists of] a touching [*tentar*] [i.e., playing of] consonances mixed with *redobles* on the vihuela, which [*redobles*] commonly are spoken [of as] to be effected [by the] index finger [*dedillo*]. And in order to play it [this music] with its natural spirit, you must govern yourself in this way: play all that is [made up of] consonances with the *compás* slow and all that is [made up of] *redobles* with the *compás* fast, and pause a little in playing ["*parar de tañer*"] each high point [*coronado*]. This is the music of which I spoke in the table [of contents] of the present volume [saying] that you would find in the fourth and fifth sections [music] that has more in respect to *tañer de gala* than much music or [than playing in strict] *compás*. And these two following fantasias move through the endings of the first and second tones.

10. Fantasia No. 10 in Tones I and II (fol. D^v)
    A. Tempo: *Moderato e Rubato*. Reduction: 2:1.

11. Fantasia No. 11 in Tones I and II (fol. D ii^v)
    A. Tempo: *Moderato e Rubato*. Reduction: 2:1.

Fol. D iii^v:
The following fantasia moves through the endings of the third and fourth tones and is to be played with the above-mentioned *compás* and spirit of the past two fantasias; and the *redobles* of these three fantasias are best played with the index finger [*dedillo*], since they were composed to foster finger agility ["*soltura de dedo*"].

12. Fantasia No. 12 in Tones III and IV (fol. [D iv^r])
    A. Tempo: *Moderato e Rubato*. Reduction: 2:1.

Fol. [D v^r]:
The following fantasia is to be played with the spirit and *compás* of the past three fantasias. And it was composed to foster agility of two fingers [the thumb and index finger]. Play the *redobles* that are in it with two fingers, since it [the fantasia] was made solely for this; and it moves through the endings of the first tone.

Critical Notes

13. Fantasia No. 13 in Tone I (fol. [D v^r])
    A. Tempo: *Moderato e Rubato*. Reduction: 2:1.

Fol. [D vi^r]:
The following fantasia also is for playing *redobles* with two fingers [i.e., thumb and index finger]. And whenever you play the fourth and third tones through these endings [through] which this fantasia moves, raise the fourth fret of the vihuela a little so that the notes of the said fret are strong and not weak.

14. Fantasia No. 14 in Tones III and IV (fol. [D vi^r])
    A. Tempo: *Moderato e Rubato*. Reduction: 2:1.

Fol. E^r:
You have already seen with what sort of music the fourth section is filled. Here, the fifth section begins; and it is [made up of] the same sort of music. And so that you govern yourself better with it, so that it appears what it [truly] is, I already [have] told you that [in] all that is [made up of] *redobles*, play them[i.e., the *redobles*] quickly and the consonance slowly. So that in the same fantasia, you have to effect a change of *compás*. And for this [reason], I said to you that this music does not much depend on [a strict] *compás* to give it its natural spirit; and this fantasia moves through the endings of the fifth and sixth tones.

15. Fantasia No. 15 in Tones V and VI (fol. E^r)
    A. Tempo: *Moderato e Rubato*. Reduction: 2:1.
    B. Fol. E ii^r: "₵ ; this is the proportion of three minims in a *compás* which I described to you in the first section of instructions." (m. 93 [47]). Fol. E ii^v: ₵ (m. 114 [56]).

Fol. E ii^v:
In the past fantasia, you have seen through what endings on the vihuela you can play the fifth and sixth tones. In the following fantasia you [will] play these said tones through other endings. And because playing the fifth and sixth tones through these endings on the vihuela [through] which this fantasia moves is more usual, I have made this change of ending which you see.

16. Fantasia No. 16 in Tones V and VI (fol. E ii^v)
    A. Tempo: *Moderato e Rubato*. Reduction: 2:1.

Fol. [E iv^r]:
The present fantasia moves through the same endings on the vihuela [through] which the past fantasia moves; and it descends to the tenth fret of the vihuela, which said fret is indicated by this letter: ✶. And it is also in the fifth and sixth tones.

17. Fantasia No. 17 in Tones V and VI (fol. [E iv^r])
    A. Tempo: *Moderato e Rubato*. Reduction: 2:1.
    B. Errors: *a*) m. 3, last n.: e' [m. 1, last n.].
        b) m. 18, be. 3–4, Al.: d-flat' [m. 9, be. 2].
        c) m. 70, be. 1, Ba.: e [m. 33, be. 1].

Fol. [E v^v]:
The present fantasia is in the seventh and eighth tones. The reason why a certain fantasia is named [as being] in two tones in this type of music is because in this style of *tañer de gala* with these long *redobles*, it appears well that [in] the fantasias, [the strict tones] are ignored [by] passing through the endings of [both] their authentic and plagal [forms].

El Maestro

18. Fantasia No. 18 in Tones VII and VIII (fol. [E v^v])
    A. Tempo: *Moderato e Rubato*. Reduction: 2:1.
    B. Errors: *a*) m. 5, be. 3–4, S.: c′ [m. 2, be. 4].
    b) m. 22, Al.: d′ [m. 10, be. 5–6].
    c) m. 41, be. 1–2, Al.: a′; Ba.: b-flat [m. 18, be. 3, first half].
    d) m. 82, S., second n.: a′ [m. 38, S., seventh n.].

Fol. F^r:
Here finish the fourth and fifth sections. And to play the music in them with its natural spirit, as I have already told you another time, it has to be [done] in this way: [by] playing the consonances slow and the *redobles* fast. And I told you that, with this change of *compás*, you are not to play as you will play this music that follows hereinafter, which is like that [music] at the beginning [of the book], which you have to play entirely with an equal *compás*, without making [any] change. And the fantasia which follows now is in the fifth tone.

19. Fantasia No. 19 in Tone V (fol. F^v)
    A. Tempo: [*Moderato*]; indication lacking. Reduction: 2:1 (m. 1–151 [m. 1–71]); 4:1 (m. 152–end [m. 72–end]).
    B. Fol. F ii^v: ₵ (m. 108, 126 [m. 51, second half, and 60]), ₵ (m. 115, 132 [m. 55, 62]). Fol. F iii^r: ₵3 (m. 152 [m. 72]).
    C. Errors: *a*) m. 96, be. 3–4, S.: g′ [m. 44, be. 2].
    b) m. 129, S., second n.: a′ [m. 61].
    c) m. 144, Ba.: g [m. 68].
    d) m. 179, be. 1–2, Ba.: e-flat [m. 99]; (corrected in Errata List).
    e) m. 190, be. 3, S.: g′ [m. 110].

Fol. F iii^v:
In this past fantasia, you have seen where you may play the fifth tone on the vihuela, and through these same endings, the sixth tone too may be played. This fantasia that now follows is in the sixth tone, which I have transposed ["*he mudado por otra parte*"] on the vihuela, so that you may know that the sixth and fifth tones may also be played through the endings [through] which the present fantasia moves.

20. Fantasia No. 20 in Tone VI (fol. [F iv^r])
    A. Tempo: [*Moderato*]; indication lacking. Reduction: 2:1 (m. 1–111 [m. 1–44], 132–end [m. 65–end]); 4:1 (m. 112–131 [m. 45–64]).
    B. Fol. [F v^r]: ₵3 (m. 112 [m. 45]). Fol. [F v^v]: ₵ (m. 132 [m. 65]. Fol. [F vi^r]: ₵ (m. 174 [m. 85]), ₵ (m. 196 [96]).
    C. Errors: *a*) m. 6, Al., last n.: b-flat′ [m. 3, Al., fourth n.]; (corrected in Errata List).
    b) m. 8, last n. missing [m. 4, eighth n.]; (corrected in Errata List).
    c) m. 38, be. 3, Al.: e′ [m. 17, Al., eighth n.].
    d) m. 49, S., second n.: a′ [m. 22, S., third n.].
    e) m. 190–95: initial rhythmic value for each m. lacks dot [m. 93–95: relevant to be. 1 and 4 of each m.]; (corrected in Errata List).
    f) m. 194, Ba.: f-sharp [m. 95, Ba., first n.].

Fol. [F vi^v]:
The following fantasia is in the seventh tone and in it will be seen all that can be done legitimately, in endings as in cadences, [in] the seventh tone.

Critical Notes

21. Fantasia No. 21 in Tone VII (fol. [F vi^v])
    A. Tempo: [*Moderato*]; indication lacking. Reduction: 2:1 (m. 1–131 [m. 1–59]);
       4:1 (m. 132–end [m. 60–end]).
    B. Fol. G^v: ¢3 (m. 132 [m. 60]).

Fol. G ii^r:
The following fantasia is in the eighth tone and is to be played neither very slow nor very fast but with a well-measured *compás*. Its spirit copies the spirit of the pavans [*pavanas*] that they play in Italy. And since [they are] so pleasant, you will find then, after this fantasia, six fantasias that will seem to you, in their spirit and composition [*compostura*], [the same] as the very pavans that are played in Italy.

22. Fantasia No. 22 in Tone VIII (fol. G ii^r)
    A. Tempo: *Moderato*. Reduction: 2:1.
    B. Errors: *a*) m. 9, be. 4, Ba.: b-flat [m. 5, Ba., second n.].
       b) m. 11, be. 1, Al.: c-sharp' [m. 6].
       c) m. 97, be. 1, T.: d [m. 45].

Fol. G iii^v:
These six fantasias that follow, as I told you above, are similar in their spirit and composition to the very pavans that are played in Italy; and since they [the fantasias] copy them [the pavans] in everything, we call them [the fantasias] pavans. The first four were [newly] composed [*inventadas*] by me. The sound [*sonada*] of the two that follow afterward was created in Italy, and [i.e., but] the elaboration [*compostura*] on their sound is mine. They should be played with the *compás* somewhat fast and must be played two or three times [in succession]. And this pavan that initially follows moves through the endings of the first and second tones.

23. Pavan No. 1 in Tones I and II (fol. G iii^v)
    A. Tempo: *Allegro Moderato*. Reduction: 2:1.
    B. Errors: *a*) m. 13, be. 3–4, S. and Al.: c' [m. 13, be. 2].

Fol. [G iv^r]:
The following pavan moves through the endings of the third and fourth tones and, as I have already said, these pavans are to be played with the *compás* somewhat fast.

24. Pavan No. 2 in Tones III and IV (fol. [G iv^r])
    A. Tempo: *Allegro Moderato*. Reduction: 4:1.

Fol. [G v^r]:
The following pavan moves through the endings of the fifth and sixth tones and, as I have already said, [these pavans] must be played two or three times, in order for them to appear what they [truly] are.

25. Pavan No. 3 in Tones V and VI (fol. [G v^r])
    A. Tempo: *Allegro Moderato*. Reduction: 4:1.
    B. Errors: *a*) m. 9, Al.: c' [m. 5, be. 1].
       b) m. 38, be. 3–4, Ba.: b-flat [m. 19, be. 2, second half]; (corrected in Errata List).
       c) m. 39, be. 1–2, T.: c-sharp' [m. 20, be. 1].

Fol. [G v^v]:
The following pavan moves through the endings of the seventh and eighth tones.

El Maestro

26. Pavan No. 4 in Tones VII and VIII (fol. [G v^v])
    A. *Allegro Moderato*. Reduction: 4:1.
    B. Errors: *a*) m. 16, be. 1–2, S.: b' [m. 8, be. 2, first half].

Fol. [G vi^r]:
The sound [*sonada*] of the pavan that follows was created in Italy and they sing with it lyrics that read [as follows:] "*Qua la bella franceschina.*" The elaboration [*compostura*] that goes on it is mine, and it is in the eighth tone.

27. Pavan No. 5 in Tone VIII, "*La bella franceschina*" (fol. [G. vi^r])
    A. Tempo: *Allegro Moderato*. Reduction: 4:1.
    B. Errors: *a*) m. 11: barline in middle of measure [m. 5, second half].
              b) m. 34, second n.: a' [m. 15].

Fol. [G vi^v]:
This pavan is in [the] proportion of three semibreves [to a] *compás* and moves through the endings of the past pavan; and all the breves you find alone [in it] are now worth an [entire] *compás*.

28. Pavan No. 6 in Tone VIII (fol. [G vi^v])
    A. Tempo: *Allegro Moderato*. Reduction: 4:1.

Fol. [G vi^v]:
This which now follows is the eighth section, of music for singing and playing, which in the table [of contents] of the present volume I said you would find [here]. In which you will find *villancicos* and *sonadas* in Castilian, and in Portuguese, and in Italian. The colored ciphers form the voice [part], which is to be sung. Study first the villancico as it is on the vihuela; and [when you] know [how] to play it well, follow the colored ciphers, observing [on] which string of the vihuela they [are] play[ed] and that [cipher] you sing.

29. Villancico No. 1, "*Toda mi vida hos amé*" (fol. H^r)

    Lyrics: "All my life I [have] loved you.
            If you love me, I do not know it.
            Well do I know that you love disaffection
                and forgetfulness.
            I know that I am abhorrent, since I [have
                come] to know disfavor.
            And, forever shall I love you.
            If you love me, I do not know it."

    First Setting (A)—(fol. H^r)
    A. Tempo: [*Lento*]; indication lacking. Reduction: 2:1.

Fol. H^r:
This villancico that follows is the same one as is above; and in the way [in] which it now is arranged [*sonado*], the singer is to sing [in an] unadorned [fashion] [*llano*] and the vihuela [is played] somewhat quickly.

(29.) Second Setting (B)—(fol. H^r)
    A. Tempo: *Allegro Moderato*. Reduction: 2:1.

Fol. H^v:
In the way [in] which this villancico that follows is arranged here, the singer may add vocal ornamentation ["*hacer garganta*"] and the vihuela is to [be] play[ed] very slowly.

Critical Notes

30. Villancico No. 2, "*Sospiró una señora que yo ví*" (fol. H^v)

    Lyrics: "A lady I saw sighed.
    Would that it were for me.
    A lady sighed and has given me to understand.
    That she sighs from having great sadness,
    from [him for] whom she weeps.
    I already know that she is a scoffer and
    even though [it is] thus.
    Would that it were for me."[7]

    First Setting (A)–(fol. H^v)
    A. Tempo: *Molto Lento*. Reduction: 2:1.
    B. Errors: *a*) m. 27: superfluous syllable, "lo" (omitted).

Fol. H^v:
The following villancico is the same, and in the way [in] which it is arranged now, the singer is to sing [in an] unadorned [fashion] and the vihuela is to [be] play[ed] fast.

(30.) *Second Setting (B)*–(fol. H^v)
   A. Tempo: *Allegro*. Reduction: 4:1.
   B. Errors: *a*) m. 24–25: barline missing [m. 9, be. 2–3].

Fol. H ii^r:
In the way [in] which this villancico that follows is here arranged, the singer is to sing [in an] unadorned [fashion] and the vihuela [is] play[ed] somewhat fast.

31. Villancico No. 3, "*Agora viniesse un viento*" (fol. H ii^r)

    Lyrics: "[If] now there should come a wind.
    That would hurl me yonder, inside.
    [If] now there should come such a good wind
    as I would wish.
    That would hurl me yonder, within, into my
    lady's skirts.
    And it would make me so content.
    That would hurl me yonder, inside."

    A. Tempo: *Allegro Moderato*. Reduction: 2:1.

Fol. H ii^r:
Here, the Portuguese villancicos begin. And in the way [in] which this first one that follows is arranged, the singer may add vocal ornamentation and the vihuela [is] play[ed] slowly.

32. Villancico No. 4, "*Quien amores ten*" (fol. H ii^r)

    Lyrics: "Whoever has loves, as the aim of what
    is good.
    [So] that there is no wind that comes and goes.
    Whoever has loves there in Castile.
    And has as his love a noble maiden.
    The aim of what is good is not to
    leave her.
    [So] that there is no wind that comes and goes."

---

7. The lyrics of this villancico were apparently written by Juan Fernández de Heredia; see Trend, *Luis de Milán*, 48; Ward, "Vihuela de Mano," 440.

El Maestro

First Setting (A)—(fol. H ii^r)
A. Tempo: *Lento*. Reduction: 2:1.
B. Errors: *a)* m. 6–7: barline missing [m. 4].

Fol. H ii^v:
The following villancico is [the same as] the above-mentioned one, and in the way [in] which it is arranged now, the singer is to sing [in an] unadorned [fashion] and the vihuela [is] play[ed] quickly. [At bottom of page:] The *buelta*[8] of the *sonada* above serves for this one below.

(32.) *Second Setting (B)*—(fol. H ii^v)
A. Tempo: *Allegro*. Reduction: 4:1.

Fol. H iii^r:
In the way [in] which the following villancico is arranged, the singer is to sing [in an] unadorned [fashion], because the vihuela goes [along] descanting; and it is to be played somewhat quickly.

33. Villancico No. 5, "*Falai miña amor*" (fol. H iii^r)

    Lyrics: "Speak, my love, speak to me.
    If you do not speak to me, kill me, kill me.
    Speak to me, my love, [so] that I [can] make
    you know.
    That, if you do not speak to me, I have no
    being.
    Since you have [the] power, speak to me.
    If you do not speak to me, kill me, kill me."

    A. Tempo: *Allegro Moderato*. Reduction: 4:1.
    B. Errors: *a)* m. 7, be. 3–4, S.: second and third n. missing [m. 3]; (corrected in Errata List).

Fol. H iii^r:
In the way [in] which the following villancico is arranged, the singer may add vocal ornamentation.

34. Villancico No. 6, "*Poys dezeys que me quereys ben*" (fol. H iii^r)

    Lyrics: "Since you say that you love me well, because
    you make conversation with nobody.
    You say that you love me.
    I see that you are teasing.
    If you converse with nobody, I will not
    [i.e., cannot] love you better [than I do]."

    First Setting (A)—(fol. H iii^r).
    A. Tempo: [*Lento*]; indication lacking. Reduction: 2:1
    B. Errors: *a)* m. 15, T. n. missing [m. 7]; (corrected in Errata List).

Fol. H iii^r:
In the way [in] which this same villancico is arranged [below], the singer is to sing [in an] unadorned [fashion].

8. The *buelta* (i.e., *vuelta*) in *El Maestro* comprises the third and fourth lines of the lyrics, which are set to the same phrase of music. In No. 34, the *buelta* comprises lines two and three of the lyrics. For discussion of villancico form, see Reese, *Music in the Renaissance* (rev. ed., 1959), 581–82; Ward, "Vihuela de Mano," 149, 155, etc.

Critical Notes

(34.) *Second Setting (B)*–(fol. H iii[r])

A. Tempo: [*Allegro*]; indication lacking. Reduction: 4:1.

Fol. H iii[v]:

In the way [in] which this *romance* that follows is arranged, the singer is to sing [in an] unadorned [fashion] and the vihuela is to move neither very quickly nor very slowly. Play the first part twice, as the text of the *romance* indicates to you, and the second part similarly.

35. Romance No. 1, *"Durandarte, Durandarte"* (fol. H iii[v])

Lyrics: "Durandarte,[9] Durandarte, good proved knight,
you ought to remember that good time past,
when in finery and graceful actions, you
proclaimed your interest;
Now ignored [by you], tell me, why have you
forgotten me?"
"[Such] words are flattering, Madam, [from one]
of your station, but if I have changed, you
have caused me to do so; for you loved Gayferos
when I was banished, and so as not to suffer
insult, I shall die despairingly."

A. Tempo: *Moderato*. Reduction: 2:1.

Fol. H iv[r]:

In the way [in] which this *romance* that follows is arranged here, the singer is to sing [in an] unadorned [fashion] and the vihuela is to move [along] played with the *compás* neither very slow nor very fast. The music that follows after the cadences [*finales*] is only to be played [by the vihuela]; and the voice is to be silent there, [that is,] where the colored cipher terminates. And all is governed as in the *romance* past.

---

[9]. I.e., Roland. "Durandarte," also known as "Durindana," "Durendal," "Durandal," "Durendart," was Roland's sword. It was not unusual for a knight to be known by the name of his sword. For a more complete reading of the text of this *romance*, refer to A. Durán (ed.), *Colección de Romances Castellanos anteriores al Siglo XVIII*, IV (= *Romancero de Romances Caballerescos e Históricos*, 1832), 131.

Gayferos, a strong adversary of the northern Franks led by Charlemagne's father, Pippin the Short, was transformed by epic poetry into a companion of Charlemagne's who died at Roncevalles. *Romances* concerning both Gayferos and Durandarte or Roland (or "Roldan") are contained in: *Colección de los Mejores Autores*, XVI (= *Romancero Caballeresco*, Madrid, 1874).

The Gayferos of epic poetry married Melisendra (also Melisandra, Melisenda), Charlemagne's daughter; an incident from their life together is treated in the episode of Master Peter's Puppet Show in Cervantes' *Don Quixote* (Part II, Book iii, Chapter 26), set to music by Manuel de Falla.

A four-part "Durandarte" by a certain *Millán* may be found in the Cancionero de Palacio, No. 445; see H. Anglés (ed.), *La Música en la Corte de los Reyes Católicos, III: Polifonía Profana–Cancionero Musical de Palacio, II* (series *Monumentos de la Música Española*, X, 1951), 193; A. T. Davison and W. Apel (eds.), *Historical Anthology of Music* (rev. edit., Cambridge, 1966), I, 100. No. 113 of the Cancionero is an anonymous setting of a *romance* in which Gayferos is mentioned; refer to Anglés, II: *Polifonía Profana–CMP, I* (series *MME, V*, 1947), 138. See also M. Querol Gavaldá, *La Musica en las Obras de Cervantes* (1948), 57–63.

El Maestro

36. Romance No. 2, "*Sospirastes Baldovinos*" (fol. H iv^v)

Lyrics: "You sighed, Baldovinos, [about] the things
that I most wanted, or you fear the Moors,
or you have a lady-friend in France."
"I do not fear the Moors, nor do I have a
lady-friend in France; but, you a Moor and I
Christian, we are leading an unsatisfactory
life.
If you come with me to France, all will be
happiness for us;
I shall enter jousts and tournaments to
serve you every day.
And you will see the flower of [the] best chivalry
of the world;
I will be your knight [and] you will be my
lovely lady."[10]

A. Tempo: *Moderato*. Reduction: 2:1.

Fol. [H v^v]:
Here begin the works in Italian; and in the following *soneto* the singer is to sing with some vocal *quiebro* and the vihuela is to move neither rapidly nor slowly.

37. Sonnet No. 1, "*Amor che nel mio pensier vive*" (fol. [H v^v])

Lyrics: "Love, which lives and reigns in my
thoughts [and] holds the most important
place in my heart, sometimes comes armed
to the forefront, there to stay and there
to establish its sign.
She, who teaches us to love and suffer
and wants to restrain that great desire
[and] inflamed hope [with] reason, modesty,
and reverence, herself disdains our ardor.
Whereupon Love, fearful, flees to the heart,
abandoning all its enterprises, and weeps
and trembles, there hiding itself
and appearing no more.
What can I do, fearing my master
[i.e. Love], if unfulfilled at
the final hour?
He who dies loving well dies well."

PETRARCH[11]

10. The complete text of this *romance* about Baldovinos (also Valdovinos, Balduinus, Baudouin, Baldwin), surely one of the sweetest lovers in history and literature, may be found in: F. J. Wolf and C. Hofmann (eds.), *Romances Viejos Castellanos*, second edit., rev. by M. Menéndez y Pelayo, II (series *Antología de Poetas Líricos Castellanos*, IX, 1899–1900), 247; see also Wolf and Hofmann, p. 55. The text given by Wolf and Hofmann follows the *Nueve romances ... compuestos por Juan de Ribera* (1605). See also Querol Gavaldá, *La Musica*, 49.
11. The original poem may be found in: F. Petrarca, *Rime, Trionfi, e Poesie Latine* (ed. F. Neri, G. Martellotti, E. Bianchi, and N. Sapegno, 1951), 205; *Parnaso Italiano*, III (ed. C. Muscetta and D. Ponchiroli, 1958), 197. Rhyming translations of this poem may be found in: T. Campbell (ed.), et al., *The Sonnets, Triumphs, and Other Poems of Petrarch* (1890), 138–39; J. Auslander (ed.), *The Sonnets of Petrarch* (1931), 109.

Critical Notes

    A. Tempo: *Moderato*. Reduction: 2:1.
    B. Errors: *a*) m. 12, be. 1–2, V. n. not indicated [m. 12, be. 1]; (corrected in Errata List).
        b) m. 84, text reads *"piagne"* [m. 84].

Fol. [H vi^v]:
This sonnet that follows is to be played neither very quickly nor slowly. And the singer should gloss [*glose*] with his voice wherever there is place [for glossing] and wherever he does not sing [in an] unadorned [fashion].

38. Sonnet No. 2, *"Porta chiascun nela fronte signato"* (fol. [H vi^v])

    Lyrics: "Everyone carries his destiny, with which he
        was born into the world, indicated in his
        face.
    Some [are] bitter and sad, some cheerful
        and happy.
    And this is why it happens that he,
        [although] not in a state of virtue,
        flies in glory with the favor and help
        of heaven, while the other [person] sinks
        sadly to the depths, although born of
        good blood.
    Some enjoy being pilgrims; some serve
        gentlemen, some lords;
    some fall in battle; some die on the sea;
    some desire treasure, some fame and honor.
    My destiny is to love and to die at last,
        from having loved too much."

    A. Tempo: *Moderato*. Reduction: 2:1.
    B. Errors: *a*) m. 3, be. 2, T. n. lacking [m. 2, be. 1, second half].

Fol. [H vii^v]:
The following sonnet is to be played somewhat gaily. And the singer is to sing [in an] unadorned [fashion]; and wherever it will fit, [the singer should] gloss with his voice, be it [a] *quiebro* or, as they say, to trill [*trinar*].

39. Sonnet No. 3, *"Nova Angeleta"* (fol. [H vii^v])

    Lyrics: "[An] ingenious angel, on agile wing,
        came down from the sky to the fresh shores
        where I, by chance, wandered alone.
    Because it saw me without companion and
        without guide,
        it fashioned a snare of woven silk in
        the green grass of the path.
    Then, I was captured and was not regretful,
    such a sweet light came from its eyes,
        such a sweet light came from its eyes."

                                                                             Petrarch[12]

    A. Tempo: *Piuttosto Gioioso*. Reduction: 2:1.

12. The original poem may be found in: Petrarca, *Rime*, 148; *Parnaso*, III, 144. Rhyming translations may be found in the following works: Campbell, *Sonnets, Triumphs*, 101; W. D. Foulke, *Some Love Songs of Petrarch* (1915), 133; H. L. Peabody, *Madrigals and Odes from Petrarch* (1940), 13.

El Maestro

Fol. [H viii^v]:
This book, as I have already told you, is divided into two volumes. And it was necessary that this be so, because its purpose is to develop a vihuelist. And in order to demonstrate beginnings [*principios*], it was necessary that one part—which is that which you have seen up to here—of the book be for providing beginnings. Wherein you have found at the beginning easy music, to allow some development of the hands. And after the latter, you have found a type of music which has more respecting *tañer de gala* than the serving [of a strict] *compás*, for the reason that I told you there: playing the vihuela in consonances mixed with *redobles*, to foster agility of the index finger [here, *didillo*] and of two fingers [i.e., thumb and index finger]. After this, you have found music [in] which there was a clear need for manual dexterity and [agility of the] index finger, as you did in the past music. Finally, you have found music to sing and to play, in Castilian, and in Portuguese, and in Italian, as I promised you in the table [of contents] of the first volume, which is this one that finishes here.

From here on, the second volume begins, with the same order as possessed by the past volume. In giving you the music for [the] fantasias, with their rules and commentary, [I have] given you in this second volume an arrangement of music as I offered you in the table [of contents] of the past volume. Except that the earlier music is easier and this that follows more difficult, because what you have seen up to here has presented [music of] beginning and medium [difficulty], and this [music that follows] brings [the book] to an end. For this [reason] it is much more difficult, as you will see. But it will not be so difficult to whomever can play easily any [composition] he reached in the book until here; because there is nothing difficult that is not easy to him to whom nothing is difficult.

The fantasia that follows is in the first tone, transposed [*por otra parte*], which I described to you in the first volume. And so, you will see the tones transposed on the vihuela in this second volume, as you have seen in this past volume. And, [this fantasia] is to be played with a *compás* neither very fast nor very slow.

40. Fantasia No. 23 in Tone I (fol. J^r)
    A. Tempo: *Moderato*. Reduction: 2:1.[13]

13. The transcription of the beginning of Fantasia No. 23 was problematical. Measures 1–8 of the transcription provided, rebarred in $\frac{4}{4}$, could instead have been transcribed as indicated above the staff in the signatures in small characters, i.e., in four groups each consisting of a pair of $\frac{3}{4}$ measures followed by a $\frac{2}{4}$ measure.

    I chose the former version—with its syncopations—as the one I believe to be more correct, because in the notation of this fantasia, Milán has provided the unique instances in *El Maestro* of the division of a semibreve by a barline, illustrated in the second musical example of his Introduction, measures 13–14. The semibreve treated this way is used in measures 1–2, 47, and 50 of Fantasia No. 23 (measures 2–3, 107–08, and 113–114 of the original tablature version) and always seems to imply syncopation. The dotted note (semibreve or minim) followed by a tie over the barline of the tablature, illustrated in the same example of the Introduction, measures 17–18, is used occasionally in *El Maestro* (cf. Nos. 3, 6, 40, 49, and 56) and also seems to imply or bring about evasion of a strong beat. Proof positive for the preferred interpretation of the rhythmic character of the beginning of Fantasia No. 23 would seem to come from No. 56, Fantasia No. 35, measures 3–4 (original tablature: measures 6–7), where a dotted minim tied over the barline forms the vehicle for an unequivocal indication of syncopation. Evidently, in *El Maestro*, therefore, there are some of the earliest uses of the barline to represent a downbeat, rather than as a mere notational convenience.

    One cannot rule out entirely, however, as a possible meaning for this passage, the groups of $\frac{3}{4}$ and $\frac{2}{4}$ measures mentioned above; consequently, this interpretation has been provided as well.

Critical Notes

    B. Errors: *a*) m. 107, be. 1–2, S.: f-sharp' [m. 59, be. 1].

Fol. J iii^r:

The following fantasia is in the second tone and is to be played with a well-measured *compás* that is neither very slow nor very fast.[14]

41. Fantasia No. 24 in Tone II (fol. J iii^r)
    A. Tempo: *Moderato*. Reduction: 2:1.
    B. Errors: *a*) m. 104, be. 3–4, Ba.: b-flat [m. 50, be. 2].
              b) m. 115: divided into halves by barline [m. 55, be. 1–2].
              c) m. 173, be. 4, Ba.: b-flat [m. 79, Ba., last n.].
              d) m. 189, be. 1–2, S.: b' [m. 86, S., penultimate n.]; (corrected in old ink in Biblioteca Nacional, Madrid, copy of *El Maestro*).

Fol. [J v^r]:

The following fantasia moves through the endings of the first and second tones; because it partakes of the two [tones] and is mixed with them, it is said [to be in a] mixed tone. And it is to be played with the *compás* as [in] the past fantasia.

42. Fantasia No. 25 in Tones I and II (fol. [J v^r])
    A. Tempo: *Moderato*. Reduction: 2:1.
    B. Errors: *a*) m. 25, S.: g' [m. 11, be. 3–4]; (corrected in Errata List).
              b) m. 117, T.: fifth n. missing [m. 54]; (corrected in Errata List).
              c) m. 132, be. 3–4: final rhythmic value of m. is smi. [m. 61, be. 4]; (corrected in Errata List).
              d) m. 146, be. 4, Al.: a' [m. 67, Al., last n.]; (corrected in Errata List).

Fol. K^v:

The following fantasia is in the third and fourth tones, and because it moves through the endings of the said two tones, it is called "mixed." It is to be played neither very quickly nor very slowly, but with a well-measured *compás*.

43. Fantasia No. 26 in Tones III and IV (fol. K^v)
    A. Tempo: *Moderato*. Reduction: 2:1.
    B. Errors: *a*) m. 31, be. 4, Al.: d' [m. 15, Al., second n.]; (corrected in Errata List).
              b) m. 41, be. 1–2, T. n. missing [m. 20, be. 1]; (corrected in Errata List).

Fol. K ii^v:

This fantasia is in the third tone, which I have transposed for you because the third and fourth tones appear better on the vihuela where this fantasia moves than where the past fantasia moves; it is to be played with the *compás* slow.

44. Fantasia No. 27 in Tone III (fol. K iii^r)
    A. Tempo: *Lento*. Reduction: 2:1.
    B. Errors: *a*) m. 57, be. 1–3, initial chord reads: c, c-sharp', e', c'' [m. 27, initial 1½ be. of m.]; (corrected in Errata List).
              b) m. 59, Ba.: f [m. 28, be. 1–2].
              c) m. 160, Ba.: f [m. 71, be. 1].
              d) m. 168, Ba.: f [m. 74, be. 2].
              e) m. 175, be. 1–2, T.: b-flat [m. 77, T., first n.].
              f) m. 222, be. 2, S.: c'' [m. 93, S., third n.].

14. Another transcription of this fantasia may be found in my *Tempo Notation*, 53.

El Maestro

Fol. [K v^r]:
The following fantasia is in the fourth tone and moves through the same places on the vihuela as the past fantasia, because, as I have already said, the third and fourth tones appear better where they move now; and [this fantasia] is to be played with the *compás* slow.

45. Fantasia No. 28 in Tone IV (fol. [K v^r])
    A. Tempo: *Lento*. Reduction: 2:1 (m. 1–137 [m. 1–61]); 4:1 (m. 138–47 [m. 62–65]); 2:1 (m. 148–98 [m. 66–88]); 4:1 (m. 199–end [m. 89–end]).
    B. Fol. [K vi^v]: ₵3 (m. 138 [m. 62]), ₵ (m. 148 [m. 66]). Fol. L^r: ₵3 (m. 199 [m. 89]).
    C. Errors: *a*) m. 85, Al.: e-flat′ [m. 38, be. 1–3].
        b) m. 109, T.: e-flat′, d′ [m. 49, be. 3–4].
        c) m. 135: rhythm unclear [m. 60, be. 3–4].
        d) m. 142, be. 1, second half, Al.: e′ [m. 64, Al., second n.].
        e) m. 220, be. 1–2, Al.: e′ [m. 97, be. 7–8]; be. 2, second half, Ba.: e-flat [m. 97, be. 8, second half].

Fol. L^r:
The following fantasia moves through the endings of the third and fourth tones, and because it partakes of the two and mixes itself with them, it is called "mixed"; it is to be played neither very quickly nor very slowly.

46. Fantasia No. 29 in Tones III and IV (fol. L^r)
    A. Tempo: *Moderato*. Reduction: 2:1.
    B. Errors: *a*) m. 11, bc. 4, S.: d′ [m. 6, S., seventh n.].
        b) m. 57, be. 1–2, Ba.: e-flat′ [m. 27, be. 3].
        c) m. 73, two n. in Ba. printed as be. 3 and 4 [m. 35, be. 1–2].
        d) m. 154, be. 4, T.: c′ [m. 72, T., sixth n.].
        e) m. 178, be. 3, T.: e-flat′ [m. 80, T., penultimate n.].
        f) m. 205, last n.: e′ [m. 91].

Fol. L iii^v:
The following fantasia moves through the endings of the third and fourth tones and is called "mixed," like the past fantasia; it is to be played with the *compás* somewhat fast.

47. Fantasia No. 30 in Tones III and IV (fol. L iii^v)
    A. Tempo: *Allegro Moderato*. Reduction: 4:1 (m. 1–156 [m. 1–70]); 8:1 (m. 157–85 [m. 71–84]); 4:1 (m. 186–end [m. 85–end]).
    B. Fol. [L iv^r]: ₡ (m. 76 [m. 38]), ₵ (m. 106 [m. 50]). Fol. [L iv^v]: ₵3 (m. 157 [m. 71]). Fol. [L v^r]: ₵ (m. 186 [m. 85]).
    C. Errors: *a*) m. 68, be. 3–4, T.: e-flat′ [m. 33, T., sixth n.].
        b) m. 94, on the initial dotted mi., Ba. and S. read: g, b [m. 44, initial dotted fu.]; (corrected in Errata List).
        c) m. 146, be. 4, Ba.: b-flat [m. 67, Ba., fourth n.].

Fol. [L v^r]:
The following fantasia is in the sixth tone and is to be played with the *compás* whipped-up, which means fast; the sixth, rather than the fifth tone, can be played more properly here, because it [i.e., the fifth tone] lacks [an] ending [here].[15]

---

15. For another transcription of Fantasia No. 31, refer to my *Tempo Notation*, 64.

Critical Notes

48. Fantasia No. 31 in Tone VI (fol. [L v^r])
    A. Tempo: *Allegro*. Reduction: 4:1 (m. 1–96 [m. 1–42]); 8:1 (m. 97–129 [m. 43–53]); 4:1 (m. 130–end [m. 54–end]).
    B. Fol. [L v^v]: ₵3 (m. 97 [m. 43]). Fol. [L vi^r]: ₵ (m. 130 [m. 54]). Fol. [L vi^v]: ₡ (m. 184 [m. 80]).
    C. Errors: *a*) m. 48, be. 1–2, T.: a [m. 20, be. 3].
        b) m. 106, be. 1, Al.: c-sharp″ [m. 46, Al., initial n.]; (corrected in old ink in Biblioteca Nacional copy).
        c) m. 141: rhythm ambiguous [m. 59, second half].

Fol. M^r:
The following fantasia is in the sixth tone and is to be played with the *compás* somewhat fast. I have already told you that only the sixth [tone] can be formed perfectly here, because the legitimate ending for the fifth tone is lacking.

49. Fantasia No. 32 in Tone VI (fol. M^r)
    A. Tempo: *Allegro Moderato*. Reduction: 4:1.
    B. Errors: *a*) m. 84, be. 3–4, Ba.: f [m. 40, Ba., last n.]; (corrected in Errata List).
        b) m. 174, Ba.: b [m. 85, be. 1].

Fol. M ii^v:
The following fantasia is in the sixth tone and is to be played at [i.e., from] the beginning with the *compás* slow. Until here, I have figured the *compás* for you with a semibreve, commonly called "*al compassillo*." In the present fantasia I figure the *compás* for you with a breve. This I have done because, if it is difficult for you to understand counting [the rhythmic value of] the notes [*el canto*] in *compasillo* due to the *corcheas* [i.e., *fusae*] found there, it will be easier to understand this *compás mayor* if the figures with it [are] as you now see.[16]

50. Fantasia No. 33 in Tone VI (fol. M ii^v)
    A. Tempo: *Lento*. Reduction: 2:1.
    B. Errors: *a*) m. 5, Ba., last n.: b-flat [m. 5].
        b) m. 52, Ba.: b-flat [m. 52].
        c) m. 108, Ba.: c′ [m. 108].
        d) m. 109, be. 3–4, S.: n. lacking [m. 109].

Fol. [M iv^v]:
The kind of music that now follows is similar to the music of the fourth and fifth sections of the first volume. There I explained to you the spirit and *compás* with which you are to play. Its art consists of touching [*tentar*] the vihuela in consonances mixed with *redobles*. And [the initial *tento*] moves through the endings of the first and second tones.

51. Tento No. 1 in Tones I and II (fol. [M iv^v])
    A. Tempo: *Moderato e Rubato*. Reduction: 2:1.
    B. Errors: *a*) m. 135, be. 1–2, T.: d′ [m. 65, be. 1].
        b) m. 147, be. 2–3, Ba.: c [m. 71, Ba., second n.].
        c) m. 183, be. 4, T.: d′ [m. 88, T., fourth n.].

Fol. N^r:
The following fantasia is of the same type as the past fantasia, [consisting of] playing [*tentando*] the vihuela with *redobles* and consonances. I have already told you with what

---

16. Refer to my *Tempo Notation*, 16–17; for another transcription of Fantasia No. 33, see p. 59 in *Tempo Notation*.

El Maestro

style and *compás* you are to play these fantasias, so that, more appropriately, they may be spoken [of as] *tentos*. And these [*sic*] that follow move through the endings of the third and fourth tones.

52. Tento No. 2 in Tones III and IV (fol. N^r)
    A. Tempo: *Moderato e Rubato*. Reduction: 2:1.
    B. Errors: *a*) m. 157, be. 2, Al.: g′ [m. 83, Al., second n.].

Fol. N iii^r:
The following *tentos* go through the endings of the fifth and sixth tones; they are to be played neither very slow nor very fast, but with the *compás* that I already described to you in music of this type.

53. Tento No. 3 in Tones V and VI (fol. N iii^r)
    A. Tempo: *Moderato e Rubato*. Reduction: 2:1.

Fol. [N v^r]:
The following *tentos* move through the endings of the seventh and eighth tones; the consonances are to be played slowly and the *redobles* quickly, as I have already told you.

54. Tento No. 4 in Tones VII and VIII (fol. [N v^r])
    A. Tempo: *Moderato e Rubato*. Reduction: 2:1.
    B. Errors: *a*) m. 40: rhythmic symbol for fifth n. lacking [m. 19, T., eighth n.].
             b) m. 83: last n. lacking [m. 42].
             c) m. 139, T.: g′; Al.: c″ [m. 71].

Fol. O^r:
Here the four *tento*-fantasias [*fantasias de tentos*], which have passed through all eight tones, are finished. And from here on we return, following the order of the book, to the fantasias played with a strict [*ygual*] *compás*. The fantasia that follows is in the seventh tone and is to be played with the *compás* somewhat fast.

55. Fantasia No. 34 in Tone VII (fol. O^r)
    A. Tempo: *Allegro Moderato*. Reduction: 2:1 (m. 1–61 [m. 1–31, first half]); 4:1 (m. 62–91 [m. 31, second half–46]); 2:1 (m. 92–end [m. 47–end]).
    B. Fol. O^v: ₵3 (m. 62 [m. 31, second half]). Fol. O ii^r: ₵ (m. 92 [m. 47]).
    C. Errors: *a*) m. 24, T., penultimate n.: g [m. 12].
             b) m. 29, be. 1–2, Al.: g′; be. 3–4, S.: f-sharp′ [m. 15, be. 1, Al.; S., second n.]; (corrected in Errata List).
             c) m. 34, Al.: e-flat′; Ba.: b [m. 17, be. 2–3].
             d) m. 87 [m. 44]: same as at *a*).

Fol. O ii^v:
The following fantasia is in the eighth tone and the more it is played with the *compás* fast, the better it will appear.

56. Fantasia No. 35 in Tone VIII (fol. O ii^v)
    A. Tempo: *Molto Allegro*. Reduction: 4:1 (m. 1–111 [m. 1–51]); 8:1 (m. 112–end [m. 52–end]).
    B. Fol. O iii^r: ₢ (m. 59 [m. 27]). Fol. O iii^v: ₵ (m. 79 [m. 37]), ₵3 (m. 112 [m. 52]).

Fol. [O iv^r]:
The following fantasia moves through the endings of the seventh and eighth tones; because it employs the ending of the two, it is said [to be in a] mixed tone. It is to be played neither very fast nor very slow.

Critical Notes

57. Fantasia No. 36 in Tones VII and VIII (fol. [O iv^r])
    A. Tempo: *Moderato*. Reduction: 2:1 (m. 1–124 [m. 1–58]); 4:1 (m. 125–50 [m. 59–70]); 2:1 (m. 151–end [m. 71–end]).
    B. Fol. [O v^r]: ₡3 (m. 125 [m. 59]). Fol. [O v^v]: ₡ (m. 151 [m. 71]).
    C. Errors: *a*) m. 18, be. 3–4, S.: b'; T.: b [m. 8, be. 4].
        b) m. 37, T., fourth n.: g [m. 17, T., fifth n.].
        c) m. 149, be. 1, Ba.: g [m. 70, be. 1].

Fol. [O vi^r]:
The following fantasia moves through the endings of the past fantasia, is in the same tone, and is to be played in the same way.

58. Fantasia No. 37 in Tones VII and VIII (fol. [O vi^r])
    A. Tempo: *Moderato*. Reduction: 2:1.
    B. Errors: *a*) m. 1, sixth n.: d' [m. 1]; (corrected in Errata List).
        b) m. 85, be. 2–3, Ba.: b [m. 38, Ba., fourth n.]; (corrected in old ink in Biblioteca Nacional copy).

Fol. P^r:
The following fantasia is in the sixth tone and is to be played with the *compás* somewhat fast. Through these same parts, the eighth [tone] can be provided; the difference is that [with] the two [tones] cadencing on the same note, if it is the sixth [tone], one will say "F-fa-ut", and [if] the eighth [tone], "G-sol-re-ut".[17]

59. Fantasia No. 38 in Tone VI (fol. P^r)
    A. Tempo: *Allegro Moderato*. Reduction: 2:1.
    B. Errors: *a*) m. 22, Al.: f [m. 11, be. 3–4].
        b) m. 80, be. 3, T.: g [m. 36, T., third n.].

Fol. P. iii^r:
The following fantasia is in the seventh and eighth tones and is to be played somewhat fast. One can also play the fifth and sixth tones here, as you saw in the past fantasias [*sic*].[18]

60. Fantasia No. 39 in Tones VII and VIII (fol. P iii^r)
    A. Tempo: *Allegro Moderato*. Reduction: 2:1.
    B. Errors: *a*) m. 87, be. 3–4, Ba.: b [m. 40, be. 2].
        b) m. 161 and 162 [m. 73, be. 2 and be. 3]: order reversed (corrected in Errata List).
        c) m. 193, Ba. and T.: e [m. 89, be. 3–4].

Fol. [P v^r]:
The following fantasia moves through the endings of the seventh and eighth tones and is to be played with the *compás* somewhat fast.

61. Fantasia No. 40 in Tones VII and VIII (fol. [P v^r])
    A. Tempo: *Allegro Moderato*. Reduction: 2:1 (m. 1–134 [m. 1–57]); 4:1 (m. 135–79 [m. 58–78]); 2:1 (m. 180–end [m. 79–end]).
    B. Fol. [P. vi^r]: ₡3 (m. 135 [m. 58]). Fol. [P vi^v]: ₡ (m. 180 [m. 79]).
    C. Errors: *a*) m. 18, T.: c-sharp' [m. 8, be. 3].
        b) m. 143, S., last n.: b' [m. 61].

17. The fairly frequent use of F-sharp in Fantasia No. 38 may account for Milán's statement. Indeed, large sections of Fantasia No. 38 seem to be in Modes VII and VIII.
18. Fantasias Nos. 38 and 39, both of which may be *catholica*, will be studied in greater detail in a forthcoming article by myself.

El Maestro

Fol. [P. vi^v]:
The music that now follows consists of villancicos in Castilian and Portuguese and sonnets in Italian. I already told you how you have to govern yourselves in the music for singing and playing which I provided in the first volume. And there is nothing more to tell you, except that [when the music is] set [on] the vihuela, the voice that you are to sing is [found on] the string that plays the colored cipher; so that all the colored ciphers that are played on the strings of the vihuela, you are to sing.

You are to perform [*leer*] the lyrics [*letra*] in this way: you will perform the first verse until the end of the villancico; and after this comes the *buelta*, and you will perform its two verses; and you will return to the beginning and will finish with the verse that remained for performance.

Fol. Q ii^r [= Q^r]:
In the way [in] which this villancico that follows is arranged here, the singer may add vocal ornamentation and the vihuela is to be played very slowly.

62. Villancico No. 7, "*Al Amor quiero vencer*" (fol. Q ii^r [=Q^r])

    Lyrics: "I want to conquer Love, but who is capable.
        When she, with her great power, has
          vanquished me.
        I wanted to conquer Love and [then] to
          belong truly to the vanquished.
        So as to be able to love better in order
          to be better cherished.
        Whoever would have such power, but who
          will be capable.
        When she, with her great power, has
          vanquished me."

    First Setting (A)–fol. Q ii^r [= Q^r])
    A. Tempo: *Molto Lento*. Reduction: 2:1.

Fol. Q ii^r [= Q^r]:
In the way [in] which this same villancico is arranged here, the singer is to sing [in an] unadorned [fashion] and the vihuela moves somewhat quickly.

(62). *Second Setting (B)*–(fol. Q ii^r [= Q^r])
    A. Tempo: *Allegro Moderato*. Reduction: 4:1.
    B. Errors: *a*) m. 15, T., last n.: c-sharp' [m. 1].

Fol. Q ii^v [= Q^v]:
In the way [in] which the following villancico is arranged here, the singer may add vocal ornamentation and the vihuela is to move very slowly.

63. Villancico No. 8, "*Aquel cavallero*" (fol. Q ii^v [= Q^v])

    Lyrics: "That gentleman [knight?], mother, who fell
          in love with me.
        He is suffering and I am dying.
        Mother, that gentleman who is wounded by love.
        I too feel his pain, because I am dying from
          the very same.
        His so true love merits that I say.
        He is suffering and I am dying."

Critical Notes

First Setting (A)–fol. Q ii^v [= Q^v])
    A. Tempo: *Molto Lento*. Reduction: 2:1.

Fol. Q ii^v [= Q^v]:
In the way [in] which this same villancico is now arranged, the singer is to sing [in an] unadorned [fashion] and the vihuela is to move somewhat quickly.

(63.) *Second Setting (B)*–(fol. Q ii^r)
    A. Tempo: *Allegro Moderato*. Reduction: 2:1.

Fol. Q ii^v:
In the way [in] which the following villancico is arranged here, the singer may add vocal ornamentation and the vihuela is to move along, played very slowly.

64. Villancico No. 9, "*Amor que tan bien sirviendo*" (fol. Q ii^v)
    Lyrics: "Love, which [I have] so well [been]
        serving, treats me so poorly.
    It is not Love, but an enemy.
    Love is not whoever so behaves; indeed,
        whoever behaves in such a way.
    Kills more than death, when, with life,
        he kills.
    According to what little I understand, [from] the
        way it treats me.
    It is not love, but an enemy."

First Setting (A)–(fol. Q ii^v)
    A. Tempo: *Molto Lento*. Reduction: 2:1.

Fol. [Q iii^r]:
The following villancico is the same one, and the singer is to sing [in an] unadorned [fashion] and the vihuela moves somewhat quickly; the *buelta* serves both [settings].

(64.) *Second Setting (B)*–(fol. [Q iii^r])
    A. Tempo: *Allegro Moderato*. Reduction: 2:1.

Fol. [Q iii^r]:
Here begin the villancicos in Portuguese. And according to [the way in which] the following one is arranged, the singer may add vocal ornamentation and the vihuela is to move very slowly.

65. Villancico No. 10, "*Levayme, Amor, da questa terra*" (fol. [Q iii^r])
    Lyrics: "Take me, Love, away from this Earth.
    I don't want to live on it anymore.
    Take me, Love, to the lost island.
    Since you are my life, take me with you.
    That soulless body doesn't live on the Earth.
    I don't want to live on it anymore."

First Setting (A)–(fol. [Q iii^r])
    A. Tempo: *Molto Lento*. Reduction: 2:1.

Fol. [Q iii^v]:
The following villancico is the same one; and in the way [in] which it is arranged, the singer is to sing [in an] unadorned [fashion] and the vihuela moves somewhat quickly; the *buelta* serves both [settings].

El Maestro

(65.) *Second Setting (B)*—(fol. [Q iii^v])
    A. Tempo: *Allegro Moderato*. Reduction: 2:1.

Fol. [Q iv^r]:
In the way [in] which the following villancico is arranged the singer may add vocal ornamentation and the vihuela is to move very slowly.

66. Villancico No. 11, "*Un cuydado que mia vida ten*" (fol. [Q iv^r])

    Lyrics: "My life has a concern.
        Of which no one will ever know.
        A concern for my beloved.
        My soul has, and it gives vigor to my body.
        My soul has it, my body feels it.
        Of which no one will ever know."[19]

    First Setting (A)—(fol. [Q iv^r])
    A. Tempo: *Molto Lento*. Reduction: 2:1.
    B. Errors: *a*) m. 3, Ba.: c [m. 1, be. 2].

Fol. [Q iv^r]:
The following villancico is the same one; and according to [the way in which] it is arranged now, the singer is to sing [in an] unadorned [fashion] and the vihuela moves somewhat quickly; the *buelta* serves both [settings].

(66.) *Second Setting (B)*—(fol. [Q iv^r])
    A. Tempo: *Allegro Moderato*. Reduction: 2:1.

Fol. [Q iv^v]:
The following villancico is arranged so that the singer may add vocal ornamentation and the vihuela is to move slowly. If you wish to, do not perform the proportion [i.e., m. 13–19 (m. 8–11 of the transcription contained in this edition)] which is at the end of the villancico.

67. Villancico No. 12, "*Perdida teñyo la color*" (fol. [Q iv^v])

    Lyrics: "I have lost my color.
        My mother says that it is from love.
            (*My mother says that it is from love.*)
        I have lost my color.
        Over someone whom I do not know.
        I do not have the color of life.
        My mother says that it is from love."

    First Setting (A)—(fol. [Q iv^v])
    A. Tempo: *Lento*. Reduction: 2:1 (m. 1–12 [m. 1–7]); 4:1 (m. 13–19 [m. 8–11]);
          2:1 (m. 20–end [m. 12–end]).
    B. Fol. [Q iv^v]: ¢3 (m. 13 [m. 8]).
    C. Errors: *a*) m. 12, Ba.: a [m. 7].
            b) In line 4 of the lyrics, a superfluous "*yo*" is printed between "*teñyo*" and "*color.*"

---

19. Juan Vásquez set the text of this villancico (*Juan Vásquez: Recopilación de Sonetos y Villancicos a quatro y a cinco, 1560*, ed. H. Anglés [series *Monumentos de la Música Española*, IV, 1946], 202–04) and of the next (No. 12 in his *Villancicos y Canciones . . . de Juan Vásquez*, Osuna, 1551). Refer to J. B. Trend, "Catalogue of the Music in the Biblioteca Medinaceli, Madrid," in *Revue Hispanique*, LXXI (1927), 485; Ward, "Vihuela de Mano," 449; Brown, *Instrumental Music*, 49.

Critical Notes

Fol. [Q iv^v]:
The following villancico is the same one; the singer is to sing [in an] unadorned [fashion] and the vihuela moves somewhat quickly; the *buelta* serves both [settings].

(67.) *Second Setting (B)*–(fol. [Q iv^v])
    A. Tempo: *Allegro Moderato*. Reduction: 2:1.

Fol. [Q iv^v]:
Here begin the *romances*. What consists of consonances is to be played slowly. The *redobles* that are at the cadences [*finales*], when the voice finishes, [are to be played] very quickly. Play the first part twice and the second part similarly. And, playing through these places on the vihuela, you are to raise the fourth fret a little toward the pegs of the vihuela.

68. Romance No. 3, "*Con pavor recordo el moro*" (fol. [Q iv^v])

    Lyrics: "With fear, I remember the Moor and I
        begin to shriek.
        My trappings are my arms, my rest is fighting.
        My bed hard rocks, my sleep is to
          keep watch always;[20]
        My clothing is annoying, for [I]
          cannot scratch.
        Not foregoing [any] customary thing
          for slaying as many [as] I can;
        Until I find death, which Love does
          not wish to give me."

    A. Tempo: *Moderato e Rubato*. Reduction: 2:1.
    B. Errors: *a*) m. 73, T., third and fifth n.: c′ [m. 33, be. 3].

Fol. R ii^r [refers initially to Romance No. 3]:
Return to the beginning and finish the *romance* where the first part finishes, singing this text that follows [i.e., lines 5 and 6 of the above]. And govern yourself as I tell you now and not as I told you at the beginning of the *romance*, in its explanation.

    The *romance* that follows [No. 69] is to be played very slowly. And at the *compás mayor*, [in] which a breve is comprehended per *compás*, as you see and in the way [in] which [the music] is arranged, the singer is to add vocal ornamentation when the vihuela does not perform *redobles*. This *romance* is to be played three times, because its text is to be sung [*leer*] three times from beginning to end.

69. Romance No. 4, "*Triste estava, muy quexosa, la triste reyna troyana*" (fol. R ii^r)

    Lyrics: "The Trojan queen was sad, very distraught,
        at seeing her children dead and the city
          devastated;
        And the lovely Polixena, beheaded in the temple,
          sacrificed by Pyrrhus on Achilles' tomb.
        'O treacherous one, how could you
          vent your rage on a woman? Her
        beauty was not enough against
          your cruel sword.' "

20. *Don Quixote*, Part I, Book i, Chapter 2, etc.; also, Querol Gavaldá, *La Musica*, 45.

El Maestro

A. Tempo: *Molto Lento*. Reduction: 2:1.

Fol. R ii[v]:
From here on begin the sonnets in Italian. And this first one that follows is to be played somewhat slow; the singer may add ornamentation wherever he finds that there is place [for it].

70. Sonnet No. 4, *"O gelosia d'amanti"* (fol. R ii[v])

   Lyrics: "O lovers' jealousy, horrible restraint,
      which leads me in one direction and holds
         so firmly;
      O sister of impious and bitter death,
      who, with your glance, disturb the
         serene sky;
      O serpent born in sweet breast,
      so that the happy flowers of my hopes
         have died;
      Among fortunate experiences, adverse
         happenings,
      in delicious food, bitter poison;
      From what infernal fury of the world
         did you come?
      O cruel monster, o plague of mortals,
      who have made my days bitter and sad.
      Go away, do not multiply my ills!
      Unhappy fear, whence did you come?
      Does not Love suffice, with its arrows?"

   SANNAZARO[21]

   A. Tempo: *Andante*. Reduction: 2:1.
   B. Errors: *a*) m. 29, be. 1, T. and V.: b [m. 12, T. and V., fifth n.].
      b) m. 122, be. 4, S.: c″ [m. 50, S., fifth n.].
      c) Line 12 of lyrics (m. 106 [m. 42]): *"gui"* (instead of *"giu"*).

Fol. R iii[v]:
The following sonnet is to be played very slowly. The singer may add vocal ornamentation. And you may play it, if you wish, without the *redobles*—that diminution in *corcheas* [i.e., fusae]—not written in colored ciphers. And if you play it without the *redobles*, you are to hold each final colored cipher that is before the *redoble* [for] two *compases*, in order to proceed without playing the *redoble*.

71. Sonnet No. 5, *"Madonna per voi ardo"* (fol. R iii[v])

   Lyrics: "Milady, I burn for you,
         and you do not believe it.
      Why aren't you as sweet as you are
         beautiful?
      Every hour, I look and gaze [to see]
         if you intend to change such cruelty.

21. For the original text, from which Milán's occasionally differs, see J. Sannazaro, *Opere Volgari*, ed. A. Mauro (series *Scittori d'Italia*, CXX, 1961), 155. Sannazaro's poem was also set by Alonso Mudarra in his *Tres Libros de Música en Cifra para Vihuela* (Seville, 1546); cf. edition by E. Pujol, forming *Monumentos de la Música Española*, VII (1949), 116.

Critical Notes

      Lady, don't you realize that I am
         dying and burning for you,
      and to look at your infinite beauty,
      and to serve only you, do I long for life;
      and to serve only you, do I long for life."[22]

    A. Tempo: *Molto Lento*. Reduction: 2:1.

Fol. [R iv^v]:
In the way [in] which the following sonnet is arranged, the singer is to sing very much [in an] unadorned [fashion], and the vihuela is to move somewhat fast.

72. Sonnet No. 6, "*Gentil mia donna*" (fol. [R iv^v])

    Lyrics: "My gentle Lady, I see in the motion
         of your eyes
      a gentle light that shows me the path
         that leads to Heaven;
      And through long habit, within which
         only my love has its place,
      almost visibly your heart shines forth,
         your heart shines forth, your heart
         shines forth."
                              PETRARCH[23]

    A. Tempo: *Allegro Moderato*. Reduction: 2:1.
    Errors: *a*) m. 23, be. 4, Ba.: b [m. 13, Ba., fourth n.].

---

22. For another setting of this text, see Miguel de Fuenllana, *Orphénica Lyra* (Seville, 1554), fol. 116^r.
23. There is a single slight difference between Petrarch's text and the reading of it in *El Maestro*: the original poem reads "dolce lume," rather than "gentil lume" (cf. line 2 above); in any event, only a fragment of the original poem is given in *El Maestro*. For the original, see Petrarca, *Rime*, 105; *Parnaso*, III, 101. Rhyming translations may be found in: Campbell, *Sonnets, Triumphs*, 74; Foulke, *Some Love Songs*, 142.